Lecture Notes in Computer Science   10007

Commenced Publication in 1973
Founding and Former Series Editors:
Gerhard Goos, Juris Hartmanis, and Jan van Leeuwen

More information about this series at http://www.springer.com/series/7408

Manjunath Gorentla Venkata · Neena Imam
Swaroop Pophale · Tiffany M. Mintz (Eds.)

OpenSHMEM and Related Technologies

Enhancing OpenSHMEM for Hybrid Environments

Third Workshop, OpenSHMEM 2016
Baltimore, MD, USA, August 2–4, 2016
Revised Selected Papers

 Springer

Editors
Manjunath Gorentla Venkata
Oak Ridge National Laboratory
Oak Ridge, TN
USA

Swaroop Pophale
Oak Ridge National Laboratory
Oak Ridge, TN
USA

Neena Imam
Oak Ridge National Laboratory
Oak Ridge, TN
USA

Tiffany M. Mintz
Oak Ridge National Laboratory
Oak Ridge, TN
USA

ISSN 0302-9743   ISSN 1611-3349 (electronic)
Lecture Notes in Computer Science
ISBN 978-3-319-50994-5   ISBN 978-3-319-50995-2   (eBook)
DOI 10.1007/978-3-319-50995-2

Library of Congress Control Number: 2016960195

LNCS Sublibrary: SL2 – Programming and Software Engineering

Printed on acid-free paper

This Springer imprint is published by Springer Nature
The registered company is Springer International Publishing AG
The registered company address is: Gewerbestrasse 11, 6330 Cham, Switzerland

Preface

The OpenSHMEM Workshop is the premier venue for presenting Partitioned Global Address Space (PGAS) research, particularly as it relates to OpenSHMEM. Open-SHMEM 2016 was the third event in the OpenSHMEM and Related Technologies workshop series. The workshop was organized by Oak Ridge National Laboratory and was held in Baltimore, Maryland, USA, and it was sponsored by ORNL, DoD, Intel, Mellanox, Cray, and SGI. The workshop was attended by participants from across academia, industry, and private and federal research organizations.

This year, the workshop focused on the role of OpenSHMEM in heterogeneous and hybrid environments. The two keynotes of the workshop included Steve Oberlin's (NVIDIA CTO) talk on the role of OpenSHMEM in future GPU-based extreme scale systems, and James Sexton's (IBM Fellow) talk on the usability of OpenSHMEM in data-centric architectures. Besides the keynote, the workshop included paper and vendor sessions as well as the OpenSHMEM committee meeting. The vendor session included talks from Intel, Cray, Mellanox, Allinea, and Paratools.

The paper session discussed a variety of concepts, including extending the OpenSHMEM API for future architectures, optimizing OpenSHMEM for current architectures, and enhancements to OpenSHMEM for the heterogeneous environments. All papers submitted to the workshop were peer-reviewed by the Technical Program Committee, which included members from universities, industry, and research labs. The Technical Program Committee members reviewed the papers with a very short turnaround time. Despite the short turnaround, each paper was reviewed by more than three reviewers, and in the end 14 full papers and 3 short papers were selected to be presented at the workshop.

This proceedings volume is a collection of papers presented at the workshop. The technical papers provided a variety of ideas for extending the OpenSHMEM specification and making it efficient for current and next-generation systems. This included active messages, non-blocking APIs, fault-tolerance capabilities, exploring implementation of OpenSHMEM using communication layers such as OFI and UCX, and implementing OpenSHMEM for heterogeneous architectures. The OpenSHMEM library is being explored as a high-performing communication layer for PGAS languages and Big Data frameworks, and those experiences from the developers were discussed at the OpenSHMEM workshop this year.

The third day of the OpenSHMEM workshop was focused on developing the OpenSHMEM specification. This year, like the year before, has been a very exciting year for the OpenSHMEM committee. The committee released OpenSHMEM version 1.3 in February 2016, and also a built a very active community that participates in the development of the specification. The OpenSHMEM meeting at the workshop is an annual and only face-to-face OpenSHMEM committee meeting. This was one of the most important meetings, as a set of rules and procedures were defined to be adopted by the OpenSHMEM committee. This included operation procedures for the

OpenSHMEM committee and participants, and the formalization of the process of development and ratification of the specification.

The general and program chairs would like to thank everyone who contributed to the organization of the workshop. In particular, we would like to thank the authors, Program Committee members, reviewers, session chairs, participants, and sponsors. We are grateful for the excellent support we received from our ORNL administrative staff and Daniel Pack, who maintained our workshop website.

November 2016

Neena Imam
Manjunath Gorentla Venkata
Swaroop Pophale
Tiffany Mintz

Organization

General Co-chairs

Neena Imam — Oak Ridge National Laboratory, USA
Manjunath Gorentla Venkata — Oak Ridge National Laboratory, USA
Nick Park — Department of Defense, USA

Technical Program Co-chairs

Tiffany M. Mintz — Oak Ridge National Laboratory, USA
Swaroop Pophale — Oak Ridge National Laboratory, USA

Technical Program Committee

Ferrol Aderholdt — Oak Ridge National Laboratory, USA
Aurelien Bouteiller — University of Tennessee - Knoxville, USA
Tony Curtis — Stony Brook University, USA
James Dinan — Intel Corporation, USA
Richard Graham — Mellanox Technologies, USA
Khaled Hamidouche — Ohio State University, USA
Jeff Hammond — Intel Labs, USA
Dounia Khaldi — Stony Brook University, USA
David Knaak — Cray Inc., USA
Andreas Knuepfer — ZIH, TU Dresden, Germany
Gregory Koenig — KPMG, USA
Bryant Lam — Department of Defense, USA
Arthur Maccabe — Oak Ridge National Laboratory, USA
Dhabaleswar (DK) Panda — Ohio State University, USA
Stephen Poole — OSSS, USA
Sreeram Potluri — NVIDIA, USA
Sarah Powers — Oak Ridge National Laboratory, USA
Michael Raymond — SGI, USA
Gilad Shainer — Mellanox Technologies, USA
Pavel Shamis — ARM, USA
Sameer Shende — University of Oregon, USA
Tom St. John — Intel Corporation, USA
Weikuan Yu — Florida State University, USA

Sponsors

Diamond Sponsors

Gold Sponsors

Silver Sponsors

Contents

OpenSHMEM Extensions

Integrating Asynchronous Task Parallelism with OpenSHMEM

Max Grossman$^{(\boxtimes)}$, Vivek Kumar, Zoran Budimlić, and Vivek Sarkar

Rice University, Houston, USA
jmg3@rice.edu

Abstract. Partitioned Global Address Space (PGAS) programming models combine shared and distributed memory features, and provide a foundation for high-productivity parallel programming using lightweight one-sided communications. The *OpenSHMEM* programming interface has recently begun gaining popularity as a lightweight library-based approach for developing PGAS applications, in part through its use of a *symmetric heap* to realize more efficient implementations of global pointers than in other PGAS systems. However, current approaches to *hybrid* inter-node and intra-node parallel programming in OpenSHMEM rely on the use of multithreaded programming models (e.g., pthreads, OpenMP) that harness intra-node parallelism but are opaque to the OpenSHMEM runtime. This OpenSHMEM+X approach can encounter performance challenges such as bottlenecks on shared resources, long pause times due to load imbalances, and poor data locality. Furthermore, OpenSH-MEM+X requires the expertise of hero-level programmers, compared to the use of just OpenSHMEM. All of these are hard challenges to mitigate with incremental changes. This situation will worsen as computing nodes increase their use of accelerators and heterogeneous memories.

In this paper, we introduce the *AsyncSHMEM* PGAS library which supports a tighter integration of shared and distributed memory parallelism than past OpenSHMEM implementations. AsyncSHMEM integrates the existing OpenSHMEM reference implementation with a thread-pool-based, intra-node, work-stealing runtime. It aims to prepare OpenSHMEM for future generations of HPC systems by enabling the use of asynchronous computation to hide data transfer latencies, supporting tight interoperability of OpenSHMEM with task parallel programming, improving load balance (both of communication and computation), and enhancing locality. In this paper we present the design of AsyncSH-MEM, and demonstrate the performance of our initial AsyncSHMEM implementation by performing a scalability analysis of two benchmarks on the Titan supercomputer. These early results are promising, and demonstrate that AsyncSHMEM is more programmable than the Open-SHMEM+OpenMP model, while delivering comparable performance for a regular benchmark (ISx) and superior performance for an irregular benchmark (UTS).

M. Gorentla Venkata et al. (Eds.): OpenSHMEM 2016, LNCS 10007, pp. 3–17, 2016.
DOI: 10.1007/978-3-319-50995-2_1

1   Introduction

Computing systems are rapidly moving toward exascale, requiring highly programmable means of specifying the communication and computation to be carried out by the machine. Because of the complexity of these systems, existing communication models for High Performance Computing (HPC) often run into performance and programmability limitations, as they can make it difficult to identify and exploit opportunities for computation-communication overlap. Existing communication models also lack tight integration with multi-threaded programming models, often requiring overly coarse or error-prone synchronization between the communication and multi-threaded components of applications.

Distributed memory systems with large amounts of parallelism available per node are notoriously difficult to program. Prevailing distributed memory approaches, such as MPI [23], UPC [11], or OpenSHMEM [7], are designed for scalability and communication. For certain applications they may not be well suited as a programming model for exploiting intra-node parallelism. On the other hand, prevailing programming models for exploiting intra-node parallelism, such as OpenMP [9], Cilk [12], and TBB [21] are not well suited for use in a distributed memory environment as the parallel programming paradigms used (tasks or groups of tasks, parallel loops, task synchronization) do not translate well or easily to a distributed memory environment.

The dominant solution to this problem so far has been to combine the distributed-memory and shared-memory programming models into "X+Y", e.g., MPI+OpenMP or OpenSHMEM+OpenMP. While such approaches to *hybrid* inter-node and intra-node parallel programming are attractive as they require no changes to either programming model, they also come with several challenges. First, the programming concepts for inter- and intra-node parallelism are often incompatible. For example, MPI communication and synchronization within OpenMP parallel regions may have undefined behavior. This forces some restrictions on how constructs can be used (for example, forcing all MPI communication to be done outside of the OpenMP parallel regions). Second, the fact that each runtime is unaware of the other can lead to performance or correctness problems (e.g. overly coarse-grain synchronization or deadlock) when using them together. Third, in-depth expertise in either distributed memory programming models or shared-memory programming models is rare, and expertise in both even more so. Fewer and fewer application developers are able to effectively program these hybrid software systems as they become more complex.

In this paper we propose AsyncSHMEM, a unified programming model that integrates Habanero tasking concepts [8] with the OpenSHMEM PGAS model. The Habanero tasking model is especially suited for this kind of implementation, since its asynchronous nature allows OpenSHMEM communication to be treated as tasks in a unified runtime system. AsyncSHMEM allows programmers to write code that exploits intra-node parallelism using Habanero tasks and distributed execution/communication using OpenSHMEM. AsyncSHMEM includes extensions to the OpenSHMEM specification for asynchronous task creation, extensions for tying together OpenSHMEM communication and Habanero tasking, and a runtime implementation that performs unified computation and communication scheduling of AsyncSHMEM programs.

We have implemented and evaluated two different implementations of the AsyncSHMEM interface. The first is referred to as the *Fork-Join approach* and is a lightweight integration of our task-based, multi-threaded runtime with the Open-SHMEM runtime with constraints on the programmer similar to those imposed by an OpenSHMEM+OpenMP approach. The second is referred to as the *Offload approach* and offers a tighter integration of the OpenSHMEM and tasking runtimes that permits OpenSHMEM calls to be performed from within parallel tasks. The runtime ensures that all OpenSHMEM operations are offloaded to a single runtime thread before calling in to the OpenSHMEM runtime. The Fork-Join approach offers small overheads but a more complicated programming model and is more restrictive in the use of the OpenSHMEM tasking API extensions. The Offload approach ensures that all OpenSHMEM operations are issued from a single thread, removing the need for a thread-safe OpenSHMEM implementation. We note that this *communication thread* is not dedicated exclusively to OpenSH-MEM operations, and is also used to execute user-created computational tasks if needed. The advantage of the Offload approach is that it supports a more flexible and intuitive programming model than the Fork-Join approach, and can also support higher degrees of communication-computation overlap.

The main contributions of this paper are as follows:

– The definition of the AsyncSHMEM programming interface, with extensions to OpenSHMEM to support asynchronous tasking.
– Two runtime implementations for AsyncSHMEM that perform unified computation and communication scheduling of AsyncSHMEM programs.
– A preliminary performance evaluation and comparison of these two implementations with flat OpenSHMEM and OpenSHMEM+OpenMP models, using two different applications and scaling them up to 16K cores on the Titan supercomputer.

The rest of the paper is organized as follows. Section 2 provides background on the Habanero tasking model that we use as inspiration for the proposed Open-SHMEM tasking extensions, as well as the OpenSHMEM PGAS programming model. Section 3 describes our extensions to the OpenSHMEM API specification and our two implementations of the AsyncSHMEM runtime in detail. Section 4 explains our experimental methodology. Section 5 presents and discusses experimental results comparing the performance of our two AsyncSHMEM implementations against OpenSHMEM and OpenSHMEM+OpenMP implementations of two benchmarks, UTS and ISx. This is followed by a discussion of related work in Sect. 6. Finally, Sect. 7 concludes the paper.

2   Background

In this section we describe the programming concepts and existing implementations that serve as the foundation for the hybrid AsyncSHMEM model: Habanero Tasking and OpenSHMEM.

2.1   Habanero Tasking

The Habanero task-parallel programming model [5] offers an `async-finish` API for exploiting intra-node parallelism. The Habanero-C Library (HClib) is a native library-based implementation of the Habanero programming model that offers C and C++ APIs. Here we briefly describe relevant features of both the abstract Habanero programming model and its HClib implementation. More details can be found in [22].

The Habanero `async` construct is used to create an asynchronous child task of the current task executing some user-defined computation. The `finish` construct is used to join all child `async` tasks (including any transitively spawned tasks) created inside of a logical scope. The `forasync` construct offers a parallel loop implementation which can be used to efficiently create many parallel tasks.

The Habanero model also supports defining dependencies between tasks using standard parallel programming constructs: promises and futures. A *promise* is a write-only value container which is initially empty. In the Habanero model, a promise can be satisfied once by having some value placed inside of it by any task. Every promise has a *future* associated with it, which can be used to read the value stored in the promise. At creation time tasks can be declared to be dependent on the satisfaction of a promise by registering on its future. This ensures that a task will not execute until that promise has been satisfied. In Habanero, the `asyncAwait` construct launches a task whose execution is predicated on a user-defined set of futures. User-created tasks can also explicitly block on futures while executing.

In the Habanero model, a `place` can be used to specify a hardware node within a hierarchical, intra-node place tree [24]. The `asyncAt` construct accepts a `place` argument, and creates a task that must be executed at that `place`.

HClib is a C/C++ library implementation that implements the abstract Habanero programming model. HClib sits on top of a multi-threaded, work-stealing, task-based runtime. HClib uses lightweight, runtime-managed stacks from the Boost Fibers [16] library to support blocking tasks without blocking the underlying runtime worker threads. Past work has shown HClib to be competitive in performance with industry-standard multi-threaded runtimes for a variety of workloads [13].

HClib serves as the foundation for the intra-node tasking implementation of AsyncSHMEM described in this paper.

2.2   OpenSHMEM

SHMEM is a communication library used for Partitioned Global Address Space (PGAS) [20] style programming. The SHMEM communications library was originally developed as a proprietary application interface by Cray for their T3D systems [15]. Since then different vendors have come up with variations of the SHMEM library implementation to match their individual requirements. These implementations have over the years diverged because of the lack of a standard specification. OpenSHMEM [7] is an open source community effort to unify all SHMEM library development effort.

3   AsyncSHMEM

In this section we present proposed API extensions to the OpenSHMEM specification, as well as two runtime implementations of those extensions.

3.1   API Extensions

The existing OpenSHMEM specification focuses on performing communication to and from processing elements (PEs) in a PGAS communication model. This work extends the OpenSHMEM specification with APIs for both creating asynchronously executing tasks as well as declaring dependencies between communication and computation. In this section, we briefly cover the major API extensions. Due to space limitations, these descriptions are not intended to be a comprehensive specification of these new APIs.

In general, the semantics of OpenSHMEM APIs in AsyncSHMEM are the same as any specification-compliant OpenSHMEM runtime. For collective routines, we expect that only a single call is made from each PE. The ordering of OpenSHMEM operations coming from independent tasks must be ensured using task-level synchronization constructs. For example, if a programmer requires that a **shmem_fence** call is made between two OpenSHMEM operations occurring in other tasks, it is their responsibility to ensure that the inter-task dependencies between those tasks ensure that ordering. The atomicity of atomic OpenSHMEM operations is guaranteed relative to other PEs as well as relative to all threads.

```
void shmem_task_nbi(void (*body)(void *), void *user_data);
```

shmem_task_nbi creates an asynchronously executing task defined by the user function **body** which is passed **user_data** when launched by the runtime.

```
void shmem_parallel_for_nbi(void (*body)(int, void *),
        void *user_data, int lower_bound, int upper_bound);
```

shmem_parallel_for_nbi provides a one-dimensional parallel loop construct for AsyncSHMEM programs, where the bounds of the parallel loop are defined by **lower_bound** and **upper_bound**. Each iteration of the parallel loop executes **body** and is passed both its iteration index and **user_data**.

```
void shmem_task_scope_begin();
void shmem_task_scope_end();
```

A pair of **shmem_task_scope_begin** and **shmem_task_scope_end** calls are analogous to a **finish** scope in the Habanero task parallel programming model. **shmem_task_scope_end** blocks until all transitively spawned child tasks since the last **shmem_task_scope_begin** have completed.

```
void shmem_task_nbi_when(void (*body)(void *), void *user_data,
        TYPE *ivar, int cmp, TYPE cmp_value);
```

The existing OpenSHMEM Wait APIs allow an OpenSHMEM PE to block and wait for a value in the symmetric heap to meet some condition.

The `shmem_task_nbi_when` API is similar, but rather than blocking makes the execution of an asynchronous task predicated on a condition. This is similar to the concept of promises and futures introduced in Sect. 2. This API also allows remote communication to create local work on a PE.

3.2   Fork-Join Implementation

The Fork-Join approach is an implementation of AsyncSHMEM that supports most of the proposed extensions from Sect. 3.1. It is open source and available at https://github.com/openshmem-org/openshmem-async.

This particular implementation of AsyncSHMEM integrates asynchronous task parallelism without making any changes to the core OpenSHMEM runtime. Changes are limited to the user-level API's in OpenSHMEM. The goal of the Fork-Join implementation was to study the impact of supporting basic asynchronous tasking in OpenSHMEM. In this approach, only the main thread (or process) is allowed to perform OpenSHMEM communication operations (blocking puts and gets, collectives). The asynchronous child tasks are not allowed to perform communication. The main thread can create child tasks by calling `shmem_task_nbi` or `shmem_parallel_for_nbi`. These child tasks can further create arbitrarily nested tasks. Synchronization over these tasks can be achieved either by explicitly creating task synchronization scopes by using `shmem_task_scope_begin` and `shmem_task_scope_end`, or implicitly by calling `shmem_barrier_all`. The `shmem_init` call starts a top-level synchronization scope by calling `shmem_task_scope_begin` internally. Each `shmem_barrier_all` call includes an implicit sequence of `shmem_task_scope_end` and `shmem_task_scope_begin` calls, i.e., it first closes the current synchronization scope and then starts a new scope. The call to `shmem_finalize` internally calls `shmem_task_scope_end` to close the top-level synchronization scope. The programmer is allowed to create arbitrarily nested task synchronization scopes using `shmem_task_scope_begin` and `shmem_task_scope_end`. We call this implementation of AsyncSHMEM a *Fork-Join approach* because of the implicit task synchronization scopes integrated inside the call to `shmem_barrier_all`, causing a join at each barrier but allowing the forking of asynchronous tasks between barriers. A typical usage of this implementation is shown in Fig. 1, which closely mirrors an OpenSHMEM+OpenMP based hybrid programming model.

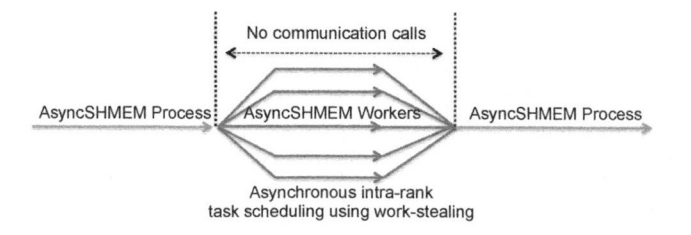

Fig. 1. Fork-Join asynchronous task programming model in OpenSHMEM. The intra-rank asynchronous child tasks cannot make any communication calls.

3.3 Offload Implementation

Similarly to the Fork-Join approach, the Offload approach does not require modifications to any existing OpenSHMEM implementations but does support a tighter integration of PGAS and task parallel programming with more flexible APIs. The Offload implementation is open source and available at https://github.com/habanero-rice/hclib/tree/resource_workers/modules/openshmem.

Similar to [8, 17], the Offload implementation ensures all OpenSHMEM operations are issued by a single worker thread in the multi-threaded, work-stealing runtime. However, the Offload approach differs in that no worker thread is dedicated exclusively to performing communication. Instead, the communication worker thread is free to execute user-written computation tasks if no communication work can be found.

To better illustrate the Offload approach, we will walk through the execution of a `shmem_int_put` operation in the Offload approach's runtime:

1. An arbitrary task in a given PE calls the OpenSHMEM `shmem_int_put` API as usual, but using the AsyncSHMEM library. Under the covers, this call results in the creation of a task that wraps a call to the `shmem_int_put` API of an OpenSHMEM implementation. That task is placed on the work-stealing deque of the communication worker. No threads are allowed to steal communication tasks from the communication worker.
2. Because `shmem_int_put` is a blocking operation, the stack of the currently executing task is saved as a continuation and its execution is predicated on the completion of the created `shmem_int_put` task. The worker thread that performed this OpenSHMEM operation is then able to continue executing useful work even while the `shmem_int_put` operation is incomplete.
3. At some point in the future, the communication worker thread discovers an OpenSHMEM operation has been placed in its work-stealing deque, picks it up, and performs the actual `shmem_int_put` operation using an available OpenSHMEM implementation. If the communication worker thread has no communication to perform, it behaves just as any other worker thread in the runtime system by executing user-written computation tasks.
4. Once this communication task has completed on the communication worker thread, the continuation task's dependency is satisfied and it is made eligible for execution again.

Unlike the Fork-Join approach, this approach places no limitations on where OpenSHMEM calls can be made. This flexibility comes at the cost of increased runtime complexity. For example, OpenSHMEM locks must be handled carefully. If two independent tasks on the same node are locking the same OpenSHMEM lock, naive offload of lock operations can easily lead to deadlock scenarios. Instead, lock operations targeting the same lock object are chained using futures to ensure only a single task in each node tries to enter the lock at a time.

4   Experimental Methodology

Before detailing our experimental results with AsyncSHMEM, we first explain our experimental methodology in this section.

4.1   Benchmarks

We have used the following two benchmarks for evaluation of AsyncSHMEM: (a) Integer Sorting (ISx) [14], and (b) Unbalanced Tree Search (UTS) [19].

ISx: ISx is a scalable integer sorting benchmark that was inspired by the NAS Parallel Benchmark integer sort. It uses a parallel bucket sorting algorithm. The reference implementation of ISx uses OpenSHMEM only. To ensure a fair comparison, we also implement an OpenSHMEM+OpenMP version of ISx as part of this work. The OpenSHMEM+OpenMP and AsyncSHMEM versions of ISx are identical and simply replace OpenMP loop parallelism with `shmem_parallel_for_nbi`. Our experiments use the weak scaling version of ISx. In the OpenSHMEM version, the total number of sorting keys per rank is 2^{25}, whereas in both multi-threaded versions it is $N \times 2^{25}$, where N is the total number of threads per rank. Hence, across all versions of ISx, the total number of keys per node is 2^{29}.

UTS: The UTS benchmark performs the parallel traversal of a randomly generated unbalanced tree. The reference UTS implementation only includes OpenSHMEM parallelism, so as part of this work we implement an AsyncSHMEM version, an OpenSHMEM+OpenMP version, and an OpenSHMEM+OpenMP Tasks version. The OpenSHMEM+OpenMP Tasks and AsyncSHMEM versions are nearly identical in structure, using tasking APIs to cleanly express the recursive, irregular parallelism of UTS. The OpenSHMEM+OpenMP implementation is a heavily hand-optimized SPMD implementation, for which the development time was much greater than any other version.

4.2   Experimental Infrastructure and Measurements

We performed all experiments on the Titan supercomputer at the Oak Ridge National Laboratory. This is a Cray XK7 system with each node containing an AMD Opteron 6274 CPU. There are two sockets per node (8 cores per socket) and an NVIDIA Tesla K20X GPU. For ISx, we use the OpenSHMEM-only version of ISx as our baseline, with one PE per core. For UTS, we use the OpenSHMEM+OpenMP version of UTS as our baseline, with one PE per node and 16 threads per PE. In both AsyncSHMEM and OpenMP versions we allocate one rank per socket with 8 threads per rank for ISx and one rank per node with 16 threads for UTS. We do not make use of the GPUs in these experiments, though our proposed changes do not affect the ability of OpenSHMEM to use GPU accelerators. Prior studies have found that on Cray supercomputers a communication heavy job can vary in performance across different job launches due to node allocation policies and other communication intensive jobs running in the neighborhood [4]. To ensure fair comparison across different versions of benchmark, we run each version as a part of a single job launch on a given set of nodes.

5 Results

5.1 ISx

In this section we perform weak scaling experiments (details in Sect. 4) of all four versions of ISx. The results of this experiment are shown in Fig. 2. Figure 2(a) shows the total execution time (computation and communication) at each node count. Figure 2(b) shows the time spent in ISx's single all-to-all key exchange communication call.

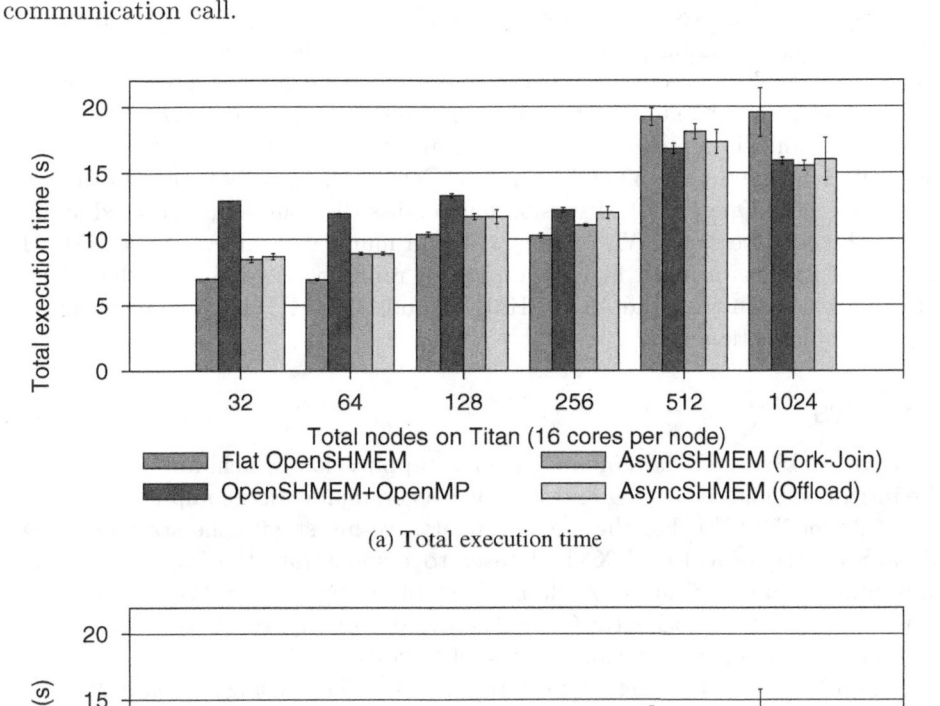

(a) Total execution time

(b) Time spent in all-to-all key exchange

Fig. 2. Weak scaling of ISx with total number of keys per node remaining constant in each version

From Fig. 2, we can see that at large node counts (512 and 1024), the multi-threaded versions of ISx (AsyncSHMEM and OpenMP) are relatively faster than the reference flat OpenSHMEM version. However, at smaller node counts (32 and 64 nodes in particular), the reference OpenSHMEM version shows better performance than the threaded versions. These variations are due to NUMA effects as well as the time spend in all-to-all communication. ISx is a memory intensive application. Both threaded versions running with 8 threads per rank (one rank per socket) use 8× more memory per rank than the single threaded reference version that uses 8 ranks per socket. Titan nodes have NUMA architecture. We used local allocation policy that favors memory allocations on the NUMA domain the rank is executing. This is more beneficial for the single threaded reference version, while in the threaded version the threads running on different NUMA domain will contend for the same memory locations. Due to the relatively fast key exchange time at 32 and 64 nodes (Fig. 2(b)), memory access advantage of the reference OpenSHMEM version outweights the communication reduction of the threaded versions. With the increase in number of nodes, OpenSHMEM version of ISx has a much higher number of ranks participating in the all-to-all communication than the AsyncSHMEM and OpenMP versions, resulting in large communication cost.

5.2 UTS

Relative to ISx, UTS is a more irregular application which further stresses the intra-node load balancing and inter-node communication-computation overlap of AsyncSHMEM. For these experiments, we investigate the strong scaling of UTS on the provided T1XXL dataset to demonstrate the improvement in computation-communication overlap achievable using AsyncSHMEM. We only run these experiments using the Offload runtime as our approach to UTS requires communication occurring inside of parallel regions.

Figure 3 plots the overall performance of UTS using OpenSHMEM+OpenMP, OpenSHMEM+OpenMP Tasks, and AsyncSHMEM.

Our optimized OpenSHMEM+OpenMP implementation performs similarly to AsyncSHMEM, though shows worse scalability beyond 128 nodes. We also note that it took significantly more development effort to build an efficient version of UTS using SPMD-style OpenSHMEM+OpenMP.

Because of the lack of integration between OpenSHMEM and OpenMP, the OpenSHMEM+OpenMP Tasks implementation also performs slowly as coarse-grain synchronization is required to join all tasks before performing distributed load balancing using OpenSHMEM.

As part of our UTS implementation, we explored using more complex techniques for distributed load balancing, as this is one of the primary bottlenecks for UTS performance. In particular, we experimented with using the proposed `shmem_task_nbi_when` extension to allow PEs to alert other PEs when work was available to be stolen in the hope that load balancing could occur in the background rather than in bulk-synchronous fashion. The challenge with this approach appears to lie in designing a `shmem_task_nbi_when` implementation

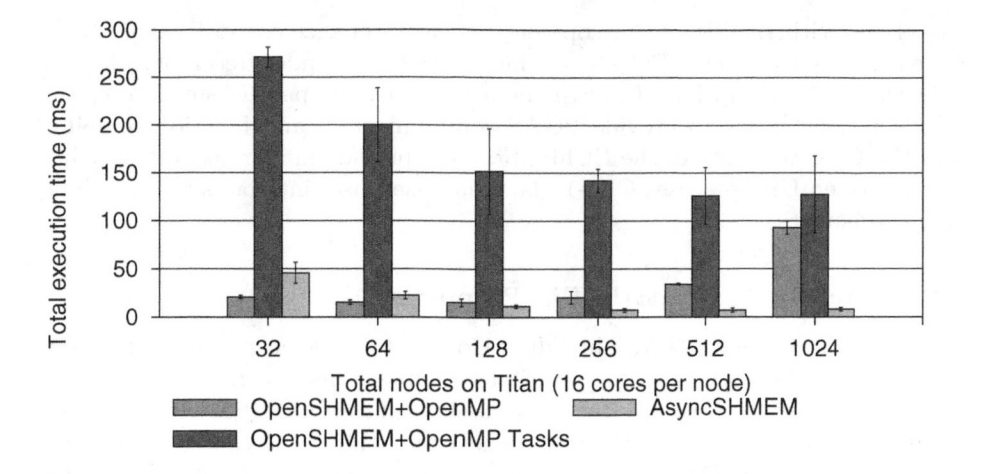

Fig. 3. Strong scaling of UTS on the T1XXL dataset.

that balances low latency between a symmetric variable being modified and the dependent task being launched with overheads from checking symmetric variable values. In our initial implementation of this API, we were unable to find an appropriate balance between these two and so UTS implementations that took advantage of more novel APIs were not able to out-perform or out-scale more conventional implementations.

6 Related Work

6.1 Combining Distributed Programming Models with Task-Parallel Programming

The *Partitioned Global Address Space* (PGAS) programming model [25] strikes a balance between shared and distributed memory models. It combines the ease of programming with a global address space with performance improvements from locality awareness. PGAS languages include Co-Array Fortran [18], Titanium [26], UPC [11], X10 [10] and Chapel [6]. These languages rely on compiler transformations to convert user code to native code. Some of these languages, such as Titanium, X10 and Chapel, use code transformations to provide dynamic tasking capabilities using a work-stealing scheduler for load balancing of the dynamically spawned asynchronous tasks.

Another related piece of work is HCMPI [8], a language-based implementation which combines MPI communication with Habanero tasking using a dedicated communication worker (similar to the Offload approach).

Language-based approaches to hybrid multi-node, multi-threaded programming have some inherent disadvantages relative to library-based techniques. Users have to first learn a new language, which often does not have mature debugging or performance analysis tools. Language-based approaches are also associated with significant development and maintenance costs. To avoid these shortcomings HabaneroUPC++ [17] introduced a compiler-free PGAS library that supports integration of intra-node and inter-node parallelism. It uses the UPC++ [27] library to provide PGAS communication and function shipping, and the C++ interface of the HClib library to provide intra-rank task scheduling. HabaneroUPC++ uses C++11 lambda-based user interfaces for launching asynchronous tasks.

6.2   Thread-Safe OpenSHMEM Proposals

Recently, the OpenSHMEM Threading Committee has been exploring extensions to the OpenSHMEM specification to support its use in multi-threaded environments on multi-core systems. Discussions in the OpenSHMEM Threading Committee have focused on three approaches to adding the concept of thread-safety to the OpenSHMEM specification. While AsyncSHMEM is not a thread-safe extension to OpenSHMEM per se, it has the same high-level goal as these thread-safety proposals: improving the usability and performance of OpenSH-MEM programs on multi-core platforms.

One proposal would make the entire OpenSHMEM runtime thread-safe by ensuring any code blocks that share resources are mutually exclusive. While this proposal is powerful in its simplicity and would have minimal impact on the existing OpenSHMEM APIs, the overheads from full thread-safety could quickly become a performance bottleneck for future multi-threaded OpenSHMEM applications. This proposal is summarized in Issue #218 on the OpenSHMEM Redmine [2]. Today, this proposal is orthogonal to the work on AsyncSHMEM. Because AsyncSHMEM serializes all OpenSHMEM communication through a single thread, any concurrent data structures within the OpenSHMEM implementation itself would only add unnecessary overhead. However, if in the future we were to explore multiple communication worker threads in the Offload approach then this thread-safety proposal would be one way to enable that work.

The second proposal would introduce the concept of thread registration to OpenSHMEM, in which any thread that wishes to make OpenSHMEM calls would have to register itself with the OpenSHMEM runtime. The runtime would be responsible for managing any thread-private or shared resources among registered threads. This proposal would also have minimal impact on the existing OpenSHMEM APIs, simply requiring that programmers remember to register threads before making any OpenSHMEM calls. Explicit thread registration would enable better handling of multi-threaded programs by the OpenSHMEM runtime, likely leading to improved performance than the simple thread-safety proposal. This proposal was put forward by Cray, and is summarized in [3]. Similar to the first simple thread safety proposal, this thread registration proposal is orthogonal to AsyncSHMEM until we consider multiple communication worker threads in the Offload approach.

The third proposal focuses on adding the idea of an OpenSHMEM context to the OpenSHMEM specification. A context would encapsulate all of the resources necessary to issue OpenSHMEM operations, and it would be the programmer's responsibility to ensure only a single thread operates on a context at a time. However, different threads could use different contexts to issue OpenSHMEM operations in parallel. This proposal would be the most disruptive to the existing OpenSHMEM specification and requires the most programmer effort, but could also benefit both multi- and single-threaded OpenSHMEM applications by enabling the creation of multiple independent communication streams. This proposal was made by Intel, and is summarized in [1]. Unlike the previous two proposals, OpenSHMEM contexts could be useful in conjuction with Async-SHMEM. Contexts would enable AsyncSHMEM to keep multiple streams of communication in-flight at once as long as no ordering constraints (e.g. via shmem_fence) prevented that.

The main way in which AsyncSHMEM differentiates itself is by being a complete extension to the OpenSHMEM specification, adding the concept of intra-node parallelism to OpenSHMEM's existing inter-node parallelism. This integration enables a better performing runtime implementation as well as the exploration of other novel APIs, such as shmem_task_nbi_when. However, the three thread-safety proposals above are more general in that they enable combining OpenSHMEM with any multi-threading programming model (e.g. OpenMP, pthreads, Cilk).

7   Conclusion

In this paper we present work on integrating task-parallel, multi-threaded programming models with the OpenSHMEM PGAS communication model. We present extensions to the OpenSHMEM specification to enable the creation of asynchronous, intra-node tasks and to allow local computation to be dependent on remote communication. We describe and implement two different approaches to implementing these extensions: the Fork-Join and Offload approaches. The Fork-Join approach is simple, but is similar to existing OpenSHMEM+X approaches in its limitations on the use of computation and communication APIs together. The Offload approach requires more complex runtime support, but offers more flexibility in how tasks and communication can be used together.

Our experimental evaluation shows that AsyncSHMEM performs similarly to existing OpenSHMEM+X approaches for regular applications and outperforms them for more irregular workloads. In our experience, the flexibility of the Offload approach also dramatically improves application programmability and maintainability.

There are many future directions for this work. We plan to focus development efforts on the Offload implementation, as the programmability and flexibility benefits it offers make it a better candidate for exploring more novel task-based extensions to the OpenSHMEM specification. We will perform more in-depth analysis of the performance characteristics of the ISx, UTS, and other benchmarks running on the Offload implementation. This investigation will focus on both quantifying overheads introduced by our implementation as well as pinpointing benefits.

Acknowledgments. This research was funded in part by the United States Department of Defense, and was supported by resources at Los Alamos National Laboratory.

References

1. OpenSHMEM context extension proposal draft. https://github.com/jdinan/openshmem-contexts
2. OpenSHMEM Redmine Issue #218 - Thread Safety Proposal. http://www.openshmem.org/redmine/issues/218
3. Thread-safe SHMEM Extensions. http://www.csm.ornl.gov/workshops/openshmem2014/documents/Thred-safeSHMEM_Extensions.pdf
4. Bhatele, A., Mohror, K., Langer, S.H., Isaacs, K.E.: There goes the neighborhood: performance degradation due to nearby jobs. In: SC, pp. 41:1–41:12. ACM (2013)
5. Cavé, V., Zhao, J., Shirako, J., Sarkar, V.: Habanero-Java: the new adventures of old X10. In: PPPJ 2011: Proceedings of the 9th International Conference on the Principles and Practice of Programming in Java (2011)
6. Chamberlain, B., Callahan, D., Zima, H.: Parallel programmability and the Chapel language. Int. J. High Perform. Comput. Appl. **21**(3), 291–312 (2007)
7. Chapman, B., Curtis, T., Pophale, S., Poole, S., Kuehn, J., Koelbel, C., Smith, L.: Introducing OpenSHMEM: SHMEM for the PGAS community. In: Proceedings of the Fourth Conference on Partitioned Global Address Space Programming Model, p. 2. ACM (2010)
8. Chatterjee, S.: Integrating asynchronous task parallelism with MPI. In: IPDPS 2013: Proceedings of the 2013 IEEE International Symposium on Parallel & Distributed Processing. IEEE Computer Society (2013)
9. Dagum, L., Menon, R.: OpenMP: an industry-standard API for shared-memory programming. IEEE Comput. Sci. Eng. **5**(1), 46–55 (1998)
10. Ebcioglu, K., Saraswat, V., Sarkar, V.: X10: an experimental language for high productivity programming of scalable systems. In: Proceedings of the Second Workshop on Productivity and Performance in High-End Computing, pp. 45–52. Citeseer (2005)
11. El-Ghazawi, T., Smith, L.: UPC: unified parallel C. In: SC (2006)
12. Frigo, M.: Multithreaded programming in Cilk. In: PASCO 2007, pp. 13–14 (2007)
13. Grossman, M., Shirako, J., Sarkar, V.: OpenMP as a high-level specification language for parallelism. In: IWOMP 2016 (2016)
14. Hanebutte, U., Hemstad, J.: ISx: a scalable integer sort for co-design in the exascale era. In: 2015 9th International Conference on Partitioned Global Address Space Programming Models (PGAS), pp. 102–104, September 2015
15. Kessler, R.E., Schwarzmeier, J.L.: Cray T3D: a new dimension for Cray research. In: COMPCON Spring 1993, Digest of Papers, pp. 176–182. IEEE (1993)
16. Kowalke, O.: Boost C++ Libraries. https://olk.github.io/libs/fiber/doc/html/
17. Kumar, V., Zheng, Y., Cavé, V., Budimlić, Z., Sarkar, V.: HabaneroUPC++: a compiler-free PGAS library. In: Proceedings of the 8th International Conference on Partitioned Global Address Space Programming Models, PGAS 2014, pp. 5:1–5:10. ACM, New York (2014). http://doi.acm.org/10.1145/2676870.2676879
18. Numrich, R.W., Reid, J.: Co-array Fortran for parallel programming. SIGPLAN Fortran Forum **17**(2), 1–31 (1998)

19. Olivier, S., Huan, J., Liu, J., Prins, J., Dinan, J., Sadayappan, P., Tseng, C.-W.:
    UTS: an unbalanced tree search benchmark. In: Almási, G., Caşcaval, C., Wu,
    P. (eds.) LCPC 2006. LNCS, vol. 4382, pp. 235–250. Springer, Heidelberg (2007).
    doi:10.1007/978-3-540-72521-3_18
20. PGAS: Partitioned Global Address Space (2011). http://www.pgas.org/
21. Reinders, J.: Intel Threading Building Blocks: Outfitting C++ for Multi-Core
    Processor Parallelism. O'Reilly Media, Inc., Sebastopol (2010)
22. Habanero-C Overview. Rice University (2013) https://wiki.rice.edu/confluence/
    display/HABANERO/Habanero-C
23. Snir, M., Otto, S.W., Walker, D.W., Dongarra, J., Huss-Lederman, S.: MPI: The
    Complete Reference. MIT Press, Cambridge (1995)
24. Yan, Y., Zhao, J., Guo, Y., Sarkar, V.: Hierarchical place trees: a portable abstrac-
    tion for task parallelism and data movement. In: Gao, G.R., Pollock, L.L., Cavazos,
    J., Li, X. (eds.) LCPC 2009. LNCS, vol. 5898, pp. 172–187. Springer, Heidelberg
    (2010). doi:10.1007/978-3-642-13374-9_12
25. Yelick, K. et al.: Productivity and performance using partitioned global address
    space languages. In: Proceedings of the 2007 International Workshop on Parallel
    Symbolic Computation, PASCO 2007, pp. 24–32. ACM (2007)
26. Yelick, K., Semenzato, L., Pike, G., Miyamoto, C., Liblit, B., Krishnamurthy,
    A., Hilfinger, P., Graham, S., Gay, D., Colella, P., Aiken, A.: Titanium: a high-
    performance Java dialect. In: ACM, pp. 10–11 (1998)
27. Zheng, Y., Kamil, A., Driscoll, M.B., Shan, H., Yelick, K.: UPC++: a PGAS
    extension for C++. In: 2014 IEEE 28th International Conference on Parallel and
    Distributed Processing Symposium, pp. 1105–1114. IEEE (2014)

Evaluating OpenSHMEM Explicit Remote Memory Access Operations and Merged Requests

Swen Boehm$^{(\boxtimes)}$, Swaroop Pophale, and Manjunath Gorentla Venkata

Oak Ridge National Laboratory, Oak Ridge, TN 37831, USA
{bohms,pophaless,manjugv}@ornl.gov

Abstract. The OpenSHMEM Library Specification has evolved considerably since version 1.0. Recently, non-blocking implicit Remote Memory Access (RMA) operations were introduced in OpenSHMEM 1.3. These provide a way to achieve better overlap between communication and computation. However, the implicit non-blocking operations do not provide a separate handle to track and complete the individual RMA operations. They are guaranteed to be completed after either a shmem_quiet(), shmem_barrier() or a shmem_barrier_all() is called. These are global completion and synchronization operations. Though this semantic is expected to achieve a higher message rate for the applications, the drawback is that it does not allow fine-grained control over the completion of RMA operations.

In this paper, first, we introduce non-blocking RMA operations with requests, where each operation has an explicit request to track and complete the operation. Second, we introduce interfaces to merge multiple requests into a single request handle. The merged request tracks multiple user-selected RMA operations, which provides the flexibility of tracking related communication operations with one request handle. Lastly, we explore the implications in terms of performance, productivity, usability and the possibility of defining different patterns of communication via merging of requests. Our experimental results show that a well designed and implemented OpenSHMEM stack can hide the overhead of allocating and managing the requests. The latency of RMA operations with requests is similar to blocking and implicit non-blocking RMA operations. We test our implementation with the Scalable Synthetic Compact Applications (SSCA #1) benchmark and observe that using RMA operations with requests and merging of these requests outperform the implementation using blocking RMA operations and implicit non-blocking operations by 49% and 74% respectively.

This manuscript has been authored by UT-Battelle, LLC under Contract No. DE-AC05-00OR22725 with the U.S. Department of Energy. The United States Government retains and the publisher, by accepting the article for publication, acknowledges that the United States Government retains a non-exclusive, paid-up, irrevocable, worldwide license to publish or reproduce the published form of this manuscript, or allow others to do so, for United States Government purposes. The Department of Energy will provide public access to these results of federally sponsored research in accordance with the DOE Public Access Plan (http://energy.gov/downloads/doe-public-access-plan).

© Springer International Publishing AG 2016
M. Gorentla Venkata et al. (Eds.): OpenSHMEM 2016, LNCS 10007, pp. 18–34, 2016.
DOI: 10.1007/978-3-319-50995-2_2

1 Introduction

OpenSHMEM 1.3 [1] introduced implicit non-blocking *puts* and *gets* to the existing library *Application Programming Interface* (API). The semantics of these operations allow to post the operation, and later wait for its completion. This has advantages over previous blocking semantics as overlap between the communication and other operations can be achieved. These operations are considered complete only after a remote memory update is guaranteed through the use of a *shmem_quiet*, *shmem_barrier* or a *shmem_barrier_all*. Since *shmem_quiet*, *shmem_barrier*, and *shmem_barrier_all* are global completion operations i.e., *shmem_quiet* completes all outstanding memory update operations by a particular Processing Element (PE) and *shmem_barrier* completes all outstanding memory update operations on all PEs (and synchronizes them), it can have a significant performance impact on applications that only require finer grained completion.

This paper proposes the introduction of non-blocking data transfer calls with explicit requests, the ability to use single request for multiple operations, and interfaces to merge multiple requests. Explicit requests provide the capability of tracking individual data transfer operations. The option to group related RMA operations together into a single request handle provides flexibility to the programmer and can improve the application performance.

As we often see in scientific code, a series of updates are made during the computation phase and are written during the communication phase. Most updates need to happen together to enable the next set of computations. Such updates can be merged together to enable easy checking for the user. This has many performance as well as productivity implications. This approach may greatly simplify how users write their code, replacing multiple request handles by a single request handle. The performance advantage comes from the fact that testing completion of a single handle is much more cost efficient than either checking individual handles or executing mass memory updates via *quiet* or *barrier* that will only return after **all** pending local and remote memory updates are processed.

In Sect. 2, we first motivate the scenarios where these interfaces are useful. In Sect. 3, we provide details of the interfaces introduced. In Sect. 4, we discuss the details of our implementation. In Sect. 5 we modify the application kernels and benchmarks to demonstrate the usability, productivity, and performance advantages of the interfaces. We discuss the results of Sect. 5 in depth in Sect. 6. Related work in this context is covered in Sect. 7 and our next steps are discussed in Sect. 8.

2 Motivation

The traditional OpenSHMEM programming model is based on the foundation of maximum computation-communication overlap through fast one-sided RMA operations that do not require the involvement of the destination PE. Implicit non-blocking calls were introduced in OpenSHMEM 1.3 [1]. These calls provide many advantages of non-blocking calls except the ability to track their completion. Even for 1.3 semantics, completion is guaranteed by either using a *quiet* or a *barrier*. Explicit non-blocking calls overcome this pitfall by providing fine grained control through individual request handles. The following are the scenarios where having merged handles for explicit RMA operations can be both advantageous and performant.

2.1   Use Case 1: OpenSHMEM Threads

As the OpenSHMEM Specification evolves to incorporate thread safety and a threading model, it becomes critical to define a synchronization mechanism within threads of a single PE. Many operations distributed within the threads may require sequential consistency. Merging handles for communication by a single thread allows for easy ordering of operations when compared to managing individual communication calls with explicit handles.

The Cray Threads proposal [4] offers a thread safe threading model that requires registering of threads after initializing threading support via *shmem_thread_register* at the start of a multithreaded OpenSHMEM program. Similarly, a *shmem_thread_unregister* is required to be called by threads that have registered via the *shmem_thread_register* call when threading support is no longer required within the OpenSHMEM program. Registering a thread that may make OpenSHMEM library calls during the lifetime of the program provides a means to track communication originating from that thread. This threading model also defines a *shmem_thread_quiet* as a means to coordinate activities between different threads of a single PE. Through our approach, a single handle can represent a collection of RMA operations made by a thread, thus allowing concurrency between non-related RMA operations issued by the same or different thread belonging to the same PE. We also eliminate the need for introducing, implementing, and maintaining three library calls which is an added bonus.

Dinan et al. [5] introduce *contexts* as a way to eliminate interference between threads by generating independent streams of communication operations that enable the OpenSHMEM library to map operations generated by threads to private communication resource sets. *Contexts* are intended to provide thread isolation and a greater control over ordering of operations. This can improve communication and computation overlap. The very same effect can be achieved with greater overlap opportunity by introducing non-blocking explicit RMA operations and providing the facility of merging related updates to a single request. The advantage of our approach is that many of the concepts already exist in other programming models and libraries, thus leading to better acceptance and use by the OpenSHMEM user community.

2.2   Use Case 2: Defining Patterns

The merging of the requests are particularly useful for communication and computation patterns where it is required to track a group of operations, and also require opportunity to overlap the operations with computation. For example in a stencil computation operation, each phase of communication within a *sweep* can be merged into a single request. Since the results are not required till the next time-step, the communication can progress asynchronously with other communication or computation operations. Also, the user does not need to test for the completion of all the individual communications.

2.3 Use Case 3: Defining New Collectives

The RMA operations with explicit requests along with merging can provide a way to define customized one-sided collectives with ability to asynchronously progress the collectives. For example, currently *broadcast* in OpenSHMEM is restricted to updates from a *root* PE to other PEs defined by a regular (power-of-two stride) *active-set*. If a program frequently needs to update an irregular set of PEs, this might be encapsulated in a single merged-handle. Following the same logic, other customized non-blocking collectives are also possible. Moreover, this approach provides a means of providing overlap between collectives that are not using/updating the same *symmetric objects*.

3 API and Semantics for RMA Operations with Requests

In this section, first, we introduce the interfaces required for non-blocking RMA operations with requests. We then look at two possible ways to merge the requests. One way is to create a single merged request handle (which is a collection of requests), and the other approach is to merge existing requests into a single request.

3.1 Explicit Non-blocking RMA Operations

The interfaces for the *Put* operations are in Box 1, and the *Get* operations are in Box 2. They are used for transferring data from the origin PE to the target PE (*pe*) and form the destination PE to the origin PE respectively. The source of the data is passed as the *source* and the target buffer is passed as the *target*. The handle to track the *Put* operation is created by the library and returned with *handle*.

```
shmem_TYPE_put_nbe (TYPE *target, const TYPE *source, size_t nelems, int pe,
shmem_request_handle_t **handle);
shmem_putSIZE_nbe (TYPE *target, const TYPE *source, size_t nelems, int pe,
shmem_request_handle_t **handle);
```

Box 1. *Put* operations with requests

These operations return after initiating the *Put* (or *Get*) operation, but not necessarily before copying data out of the source variable/array. These semantics are similar to implicit RMA operations introduced in OpenSHMEM 1.3 [1].

shmem_TYPE_get_nbe (TYPE *target, const TYPE *source, size_t nelems, int pe,
shmem_request_handle_t **handle);
shmem_getSIZE_nbe (TYPE *target, const TYPE *source, size_t nelems, int pe,
shmem_request_handle_t **handle);

Box 2. *Get* operations with requests

However, the difference is in the completion of operations. The RMA operations with requests are required to call the *Wait* (Box 3) function to guarantee completion, or they can use the *Test* (Box 3) function to query the status of the operations.

void shmem_wait_req(shmem_request_handle_t *handle);
void shmem_test_req(shmem_request_handle_t *handle);

Box 3. Wait and Test operations for completing and testing the status of requests, respectively.

3.2 Merging RMA Request Handles

The RMA interfaces that take in requests that represent more than one operation is shown in Box 4. Using this interface, the user provides a hint to the library about usage of the data from the operations. It indicates that the user expects to group a set of RMA operations, which can be synchronized and completed simultaneously. The library can optimize by allocating independent network resources that can be independently synchronized and flushed for completion.

shmem_TYPE_RMA_nbe_multiple(TYPE *target, const TYPE *source, size_t
nelems, int pe, shmem_request_handle_t **handle);

Box 4. RMA Operation with Merged Request Handles

The interface for merging already existing requests is shown in Box 5. This interface is useful for tracking and completing already existing groups of RMA operations. The user has the flexibility to cherry-pick RMA requests that may be grouped together for maximum overlap. Similar to RMA operations with requests, these operations are completed using the *Wait* operation.

shmem_merge_requests(int   num_req,   shmem_request_handle_t   **ReqArray,
shmem_request_handle_t **request);

Box 5. Interface for Merging the Requests

As merged handles are just a medium to provide a single request for multiple related RMA operations, they themselves do not impose any restrictions on the programmer when used alongside other OpenSHMEM API. All explicit non-blocking calls will complete after a *shmem_quiet*, *shmem_barrier*, or *shmem _barrier_all* is called but the user must call *shmem_wait_req* to release the request handle. This provides for a cleaner usage and better code readability as the user can easily match RMA operations to their corresponding *waits*. The use of *shmem_fence* has no effect on the ordering of explicit non-blocking RMA.

4   Implementation Using UCX

The implementation of explicit and merged non-blocking RMA operations is done in the OpenSHMEM reference implementation. The reference implementation can use two different networking libraries. Figure 1 shows an overview of the dependencies. One is GASNet and the other is Unified Communication X (UCX) [14].

UCX is a middleware that provides a portable API that targets different underlying networking components. By providing a highly performant API framework, UCX exposes the constructs for implementing various programming models such as Message Passing Interface (MPI) and Partioned Global Address Space (PGAS).

UCX is comprised of three major API frameworks. These frameworks can be used independently of each other. They include UC-Services (UCS) - provides services and common utilities, UC-Transports (UCT) - provides low level API for hardware transports, and UC-Protocols (UCP) - provides high level API that implement different protocols.

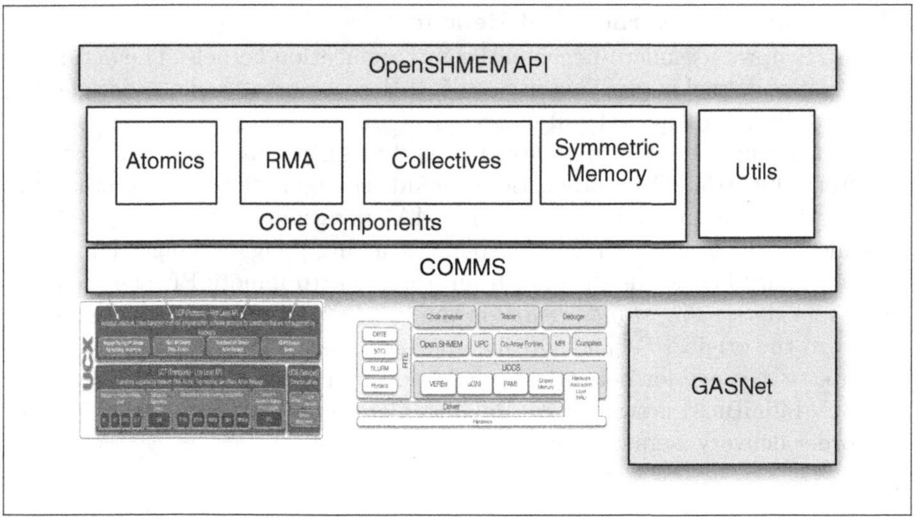

Fig. 1. Various components in the *OpenSHMEM* reference implementation

UCT abstracts the arduous details of the underlying hardware, thus providing a low-level API for implementing higher-level protocols. The API provides the necessary functionality for communication context management, device specific memory allocation and management, interfaces for various types of messages, remote memory access (RMA), *Atomic Memory Operations* (AMO), active messages, and collectives. The API is driven by the interconnect manufacturers.

UCP is layered over UCT and provides an abstraction of higher-level protocols. These can be used by programming models such as MPI and PGAS. UCP initializes the UCX library, allows for message fragmentation, and provides multi-rail communication.

To implement explicit RMA operations and merged requests, the UCX networking layer is used. While the OpenSHMEM reference implementation is setting up the symmetric heap and manages PEs, the RMA operations map directly to UCP functions. Therefore the explicit non-blocking operations are implemented in UCP with a small wrapper in OpenSHMEM.

5　Evaluation

5.1　Experimental TestBed

5.1.1　System

We run our experiments on a 16 node SGI cluster with Mellanox ConnectX-4 VPI adapter card, EDR IB (100 Gb/s) and 100 GbE, a single-port QSFP, and PCIe3.0 × 16. Each node comprises of two NUMA nodes with two sockets each and 10 cores per socket. Each of 40 CPUs is an Intel Xeon E5-2660 v3 operating at 2.6 GHz.

5.1.2　Application Kernels and Benchmarks

For evaluation, we use micro-benchmarks and application kernels. The details of the application kernel is provided in Sect. 5.3. Here we present the experimental results and discuss them in detail in Sect. 6.

For evaluating the latency, bandwidth, and message rate, we modify benchmarks from OSU [15]. The modifications include changing the *shmem* interfaces to use non-blocking implicit and explicit RMA operations.

We modify the latency benchmark to mimic a ping-pong exchange. The ping-pong benchmark first sends the data from origin PE to remote PE. The remote PE waits for data using *shmem_wait* on the last byte of the data, then sends a response to the origin PE. Though this approach may not reflect the arrival of the complete message for networks that do not guarantee in-order delivery, for Mellanox's InfiniBand network with Reliable Connection (RC) transport protocol, in-order delivery is guaranteed.

5.2 Performance Evaluation of RMA Operations with Requests and Merged Requests Using Micro-Benchmarks

5.2.1 Latency of Get Operations

In this experiment, the performance of *shmem_getmem*, *shmem_getmem_nbi*, and *shmem_getmem_nbe* operations is compared. The origin PE issues the *Get* operation, and waits for completion. In case of *shmem_getmem*, the data is updated when the call returns. In the case of *shmem_getmem_nbi*, and *shmem_getmem_nbe*, it waits for *shmem_quiet* and *shmem_wait_req* to complete respectively. Figure 2 shows that the latency of all *Get* operations are similar.

To understand the performance impact of global completion (*shmem_quiet* and *shmem_barrier*) used for completing implicit operations, we modify the *Get* benchmark to issue multiple *Get* operations. The origin PE issues *Get* operations to multiple PEs, and waits for completion only on one PE. From Fig. 3 we observe that the performance of RMA operations with requests outperform (as expected) both implicit non-blocking RMA operations and blocking RMA operations.

5.2.2 Ping-Pong Latency

Figures 4 and 5 compare the round trip time for *shmem_put, shmem_put_nbi, and shmem_put_nbe* for small and large messages respectively. The origin PE sends a *ping* using *shmem_put, shmem_put_nbi, or shmem_put_nbe*, and the destination

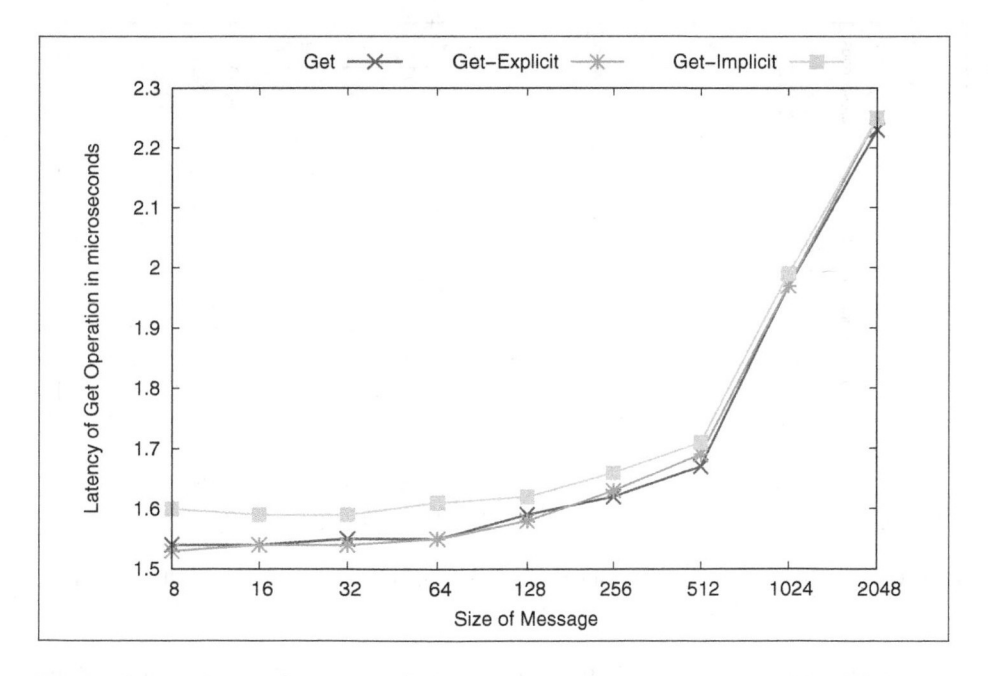

Fig. 2. Comparing performance of *shmem_getmem*, *shmem_getmem_nbi*, and *shmem_getmem_nbe*

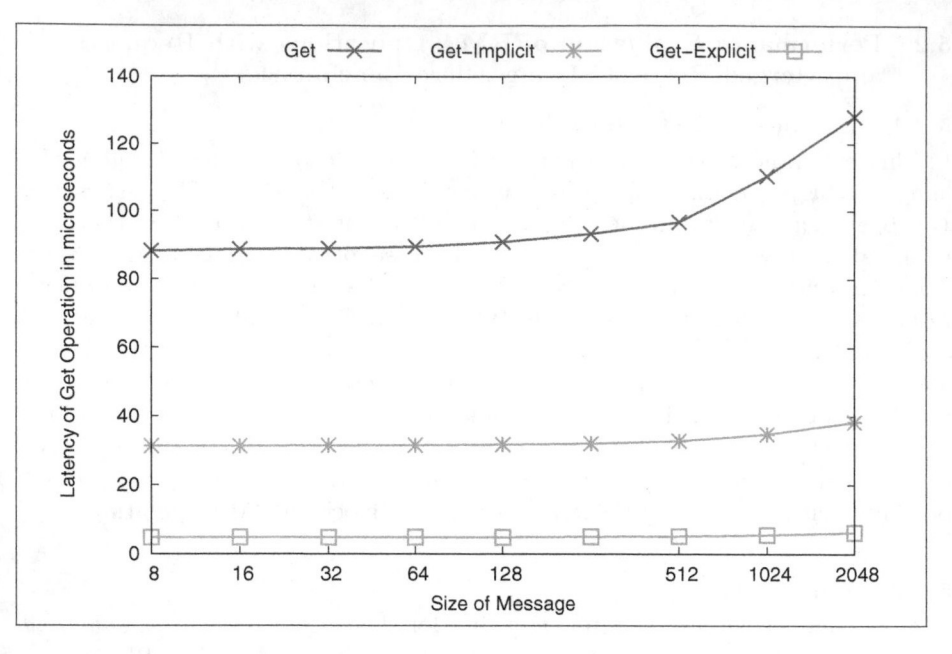

Fig. 3. Comparing performance of OpenSHMEM OSU *shmem get many* benchmark using 64 PEs

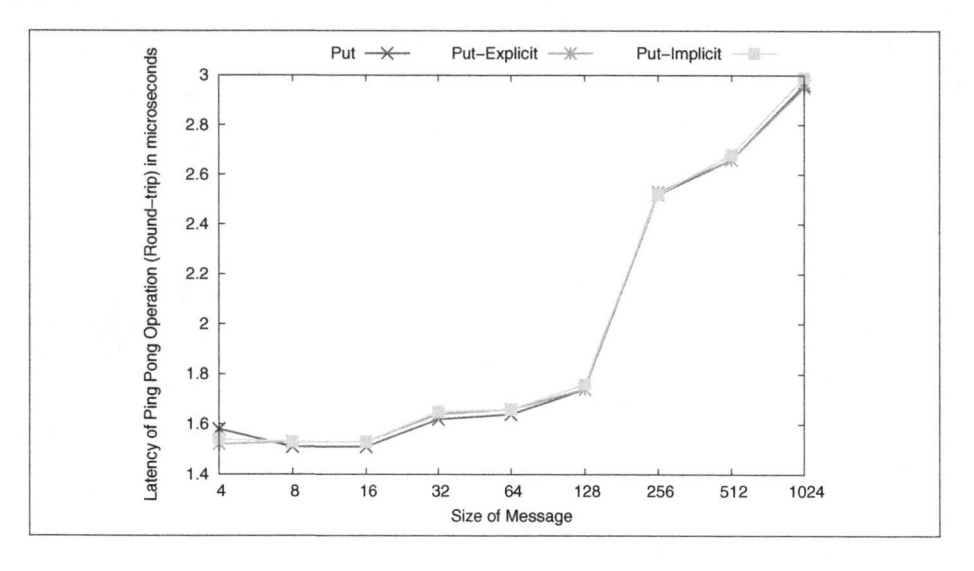

Fig. 4. Roundtrip latency using put-based ping-pong benchmark for small messages

PE and then waits on a corresponding *pong* using *shmem_int_wait_until*. On receiving the *ping*, the destination PE responds with a *pong* through a *Put*. The target PE waits on the last byte of the message.

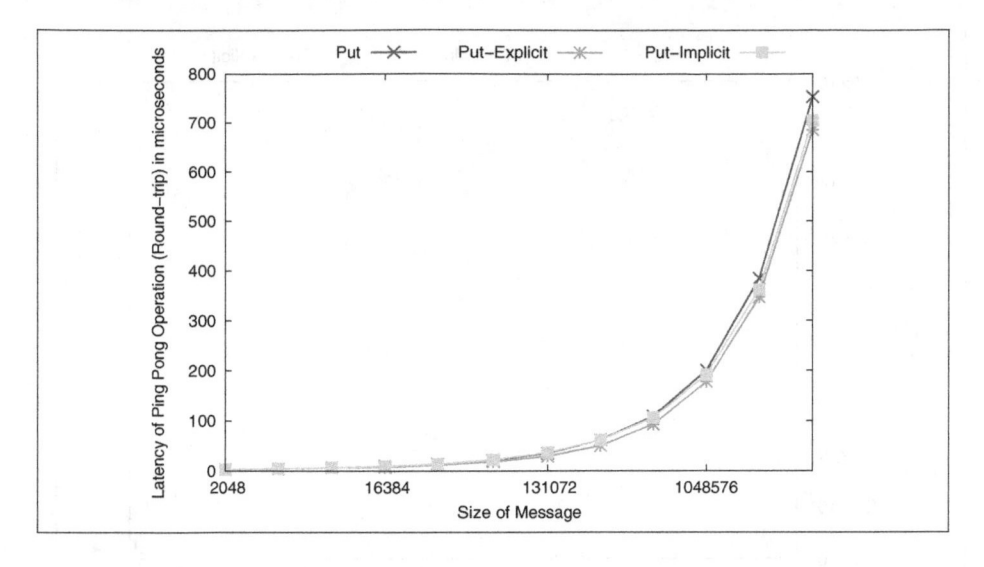

Fig. 5. Roundtrip latency using put-based ping-pong benchmark for large messages

For our experiments we use Mellanox's InfiniBand HCA as network and use RC protocol for data transfer, which guarantees in-order delivery of messages. For this setup, polling on the last byte of data to learn the completion is a reasonable approach, although it might be inaccurate for networks and memory architectures that do not guarantee in-order delivery of messages. For completion, the *shmem_put* and *shmem_put_nbi* calls require a *shmem_quiet*, while *shmem_put_nbe* requires a *shmem_wait_req* on the request.

From the graphs, one can observe that there are some performance differences. For a one byte message, the round trip latencies of *shmem_put, shmem_put_nbi, and shmem_put_nbe* are 1.58 μsec, 1.54 μsec, and 1.52 μsec respectively. For 4 MB message, the latencies are 753.29 μsec, 704.54 μsec, and 685.65 μsec respectively. The performance difference in case of small message is negligible.

5.2.3 Message Rate Evaluation

To understand the impact on message rate, we measure the message rate achievable using various *Put* interfaces. Figure 6 shows the message rate of *shmem_put_nbe, shmem_put_nbi* and *shmem_put*. For this experiment, we modify and use the message rate benchmark in OSU benchmark suite [15]. To measure the message rate of *shmem_put*, the benchmark issues a series of *Put* operations in a loop and single quite operation at the end of the loop. Similarly, the modified benchmark for implicit *Put* issues a series of *shmem_put_nbi* operations and single quite operation to measure the message rate of implicit non-blocking operations. For the non-blocking *Put* with requests, the benchmark issues a *shmem_put_nbe* and complete it with *shmem_wait_nb* (Box 3) operation. So, it

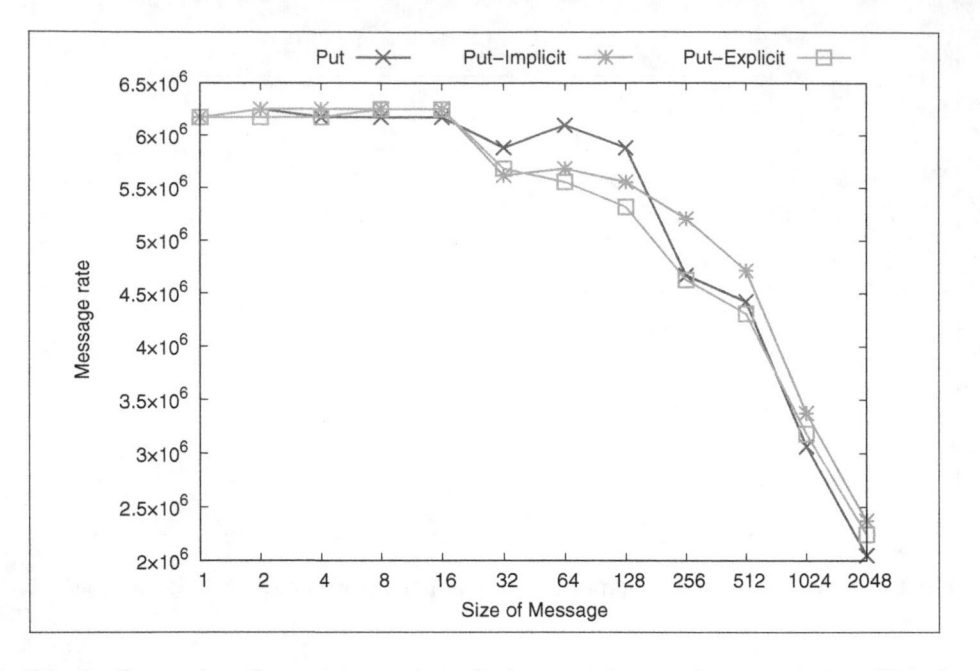

Fig. 6. Comparing the message rates of *shmem_putmem*, *shmem_putmem_nbi* and *shmem_putmem_nbe*

issues one *shmem_wait_nbe* operation per *shmem_put_nbe*. In the Fig. 6, we can observe that the message rate of RMA operations with requests is similar to blocking and implicit non-blocking *Put* operations.

5.3   Performance Evaluation with Scalable Synthetic Compact Applications (SSCA) #1 Kernel

SSCA #1 Description: The benchmark is an implementation of the Smith-Waterman local sequence alignment algorithm [2]. For our experiments, we use the OpenSHMEM version ported by Baker et al. [3]. This benchmark focuses on sequence alignment algorithms in computational biology. It stresses integer and character operations, and requires no floating point operations.

Listing 1.1. SSCA#1 Kernal 1 original source-code

```
1   get_data() {
2           previous_match = get(A, i-1, j-1);
3           main_codon = get(main_codon_seq ,i);
4           match_codon = get(match_codon_seq ,j);
5           gap_main = get(E,i-1,j);
6           gap_match = get(F,i,j-1);
7   }

9   put_data() {
10          put(A,i,j,new_score);
11          put(E,i,j,max(new_gap_score ,extend_main_gap));
12          put(F,i,j,max(new_gap_score ,extend_match_gap));
```

```
13   }

15   local_align(main_codon_seq , match_codon_seq){
16     /* A is the score Matrix */
17     A[len(main_codon)][len(match_codon)];
18     /* E is the main gap matrix */
19     E[len(main_codon)][len(match_codon)];
20     /* F is the match gap matrix */
21     F[len(main_codon)][len(match_codon)];
22     /* outer loop */
23     for(outer=0; outer < 2 * length(main_codon_seq)){
24       barrier_all();
25       start = compute_local_start_index(outer);
26       end = compute_local_end_index(outer);
27       /* inner loop */
28       for(inner = start; inner < end){
29         i = compute_main_index(outer, inner);
30         j = compute_match_index(outer, inner);

32         /* blocking gets */
33         get_data();

35         new_match = sim(main,codon);
36         new_score = max(new_match , gap_main , gap_match , 0);
37         if(is_score_good(new_score)){
38           add_new_pair(new_score , i, j);
39         }
40         new_gap_score = new_match - new_gap_penalty;
41         extend_main_gap = gap_main - extend_gap_penalty;
42         extend_match_gap = gap_match - extend_gap_penalty;

44         put_data();
45       }
46     }
47   }
```

Our work focuses on improving kernel 1 of the SSCA1 benchmark using the proposed semantics for explicit requests in OpenSHMEM as described in Sect. 3. Listing 1.1 shows the source code for Kernel 1. The main kernel is comprised of two loops. The outer loop computes the bounds for the inner loop, and the inner loop computes the scores and gaps for the current iteration. At the end of each iteration the score and gap values are updated. These values are not needed until the algorithm enters the next iteration of the outer loop.

From the message characteristics perspective, the inner loop issues *Get* and *Put* operations. The *Get* operations are completed before the start of next iteration, and the *Put* operations can be completed to after all iterations of the inner loop are completed.

The first experiment looks at improving the performance by replacing the *Put* operations to update the score and gap values at the end of the inner loop with non-blocking operations. Since the algorithm employs a barrier at the beginning of the outer loop, and the barrier completes all outstanding operations, implicit non-blocking operations are used (see Listing 1.3).

For the second set of experiments, we improve the benchmark by using explicit non-blocking operations for the prefetch operations in the inner loop. This removes the requirement to issue a *shmem_quiet* call, but uses a *shmem_wait_req* call on outstanding operation instead (see Listing 1.4).

Listing 1.2. SSCA1 with prefetching (ssca1-prefetch)

```
 1   get_data() {
 2          nb_previous_match = get_nb(A, nb_i-1, nb_j-1);
 3          nb_main_codon = get_nb(main_codon_seq, nb_i);
 4          nb_match_codon = get_nb(match_codon_seq, nb_j);
 5          nb_gap_main = get_nb(E, nb_i-1, nb_j);
 6          nb_gap_match = get_nb(F, nb_i, nb_j-1);
 7   }


14   wait_for_previous_gets() {
15          shmem_quiet();
16   }

18   local_align(main_codon_seq , match_codon_seq){

        ...

32          /* prestage non-blocking operations */
33          get_data()

35          /* inner loop */
36          for(inner = start; inner < end){
37            i = compute_main_index(outer, inner);
38            j = compute_match_index(outer, inner);

40            nb_i = compute_next_main_index(outer , inner);
41            nb_j = compute_next_match_index(outer , inner);

43            wait_for_previous_gets();
44            previous_match = nb_previous_match;
45            main_codon = nb_main_codon;
46            match_codon = nb_match_codon;
47            gap_main = nb_gap_main;
48            gap_match = nb_gap_match;

        ...
64   }
```

The last experiment uses the interfaces in Box 5 to merge the requests. Instead of keeping track of multiple outstanding operations, operations that are dependent use a merged request (see Listing 1.5). Thus improving the usability and simplifying the program. Furthermore, there are fewer calls into the OpenSHMEM library, since there are fewer requests to wait for. Additionally an OpenSHMEM library implementation could employ optimizations to improve the performance by completing the requests in batches.

Performance: Figure 7 shows the results of running the benchmark on 16 nodes and with an increasing number of processes per node. The various implementations used in the experiment are as follows: *SSCA1* is the original implementation [3]. The *prefetch* is the original implementation with prefetch enabled, and with implicit *Get* operations. The *prefetch-nbi* is a modification to implementation to use implicit non-blocking RMA operations. The *prefetch-explicit* is a modified version using RMA operations with requests, and *prefetch-merged* is a modified version using RMA operations with one request for multiple *Put* operations.

Listing 1.3. SSCA1 with non-blocking puts (ssca1-nbi)

```
 9   put_data() {
10         put_nbi(A,i,j,new_score);
11         put_nbi(E,i,j,max(new_gap_score, extend_main_gap));
12         put_nbi(F,i,j,max(new_gap_score, extend_match_gap));
13   }
```

Listing 1.4. SSCA1 with explicit non-blocking operations (ssca1-explicit)

```
 1   get_data() {
 2         nb_previous_match = get_nbe(A, nb_i-1, nb_j-1, req1);
 3         nb_main_codon = get_nbe(main_codon_seq, nb_i, req2);
 4         nb_match_codon = get_nbe(match_codon_seq, nb_j, req3);
 5         nb_gap_main = get_nbe(E, nb_i-1, nb_j, req4);
 6         nb_gap_match = get_nbe(F, nb_i, nb_j-1, req5);
 7   }

     wait_for_previous_gets() {
14         shmem_wait_req(req1);
15         shmem_wait_req(req2);
16         shmem_wait_req(req3);
17         shmem_wait_req(req4);
18         shmem_wait_req(req5);
19   }
```

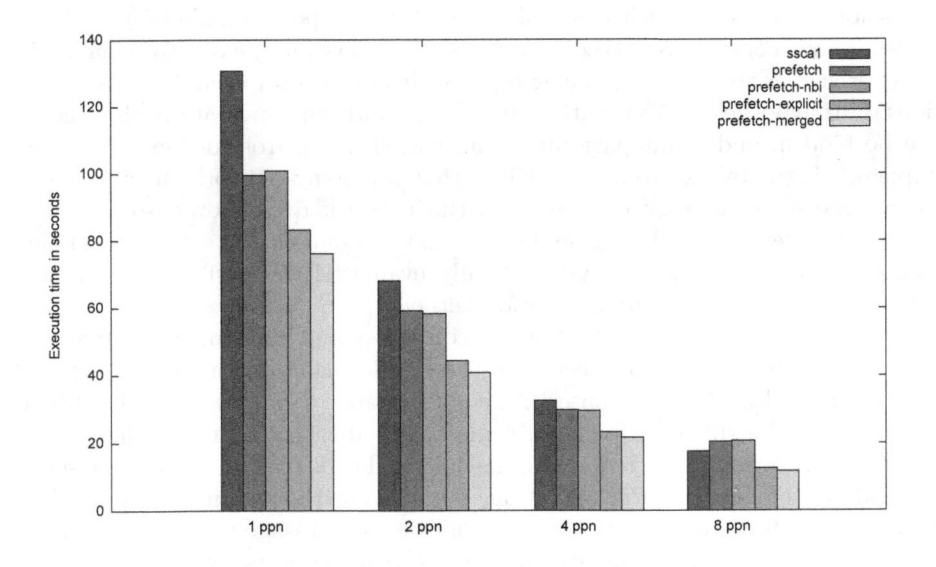

Fig. 7. Comparing performance of *ssca1* on 16 nodes

From Fig. 7, we observe the performance of the implementation using RMA operations with requests and merging of requests outperforms the original implementation and implementation with implicit RMA operations. For 16 nodes with one PE per node, the RMA operations with explicit requests outperforms the original implementation by 72% and the version with prefetch enabled by 31%. Similarly, for 128 PEs (16 nodes with 8ppn) it outperforms the original

Listing 1.5. SSCA1 with explicit non-blocking operations and merged requests (ssca1-merged)

```
 1   get_data() {
 2          nb_previous_match = get_nbe(A, nb_i-1, nb_j-1, req);
 3          nb_main_codon = get_nbe(main_codon_seq, nb_i, req);
 4          nb_match_codon = get_nbe(match_codon_seq, nb_j, req);
 5          nb_gap_main = get_nbe(E, nb_i-1, nb_j, req);
 6          nb_gap_match = get_nbe(F, nb_i, nb_j-1, req);
 7   }

        wait_for_previous_gets() {
14          shmem_wait_req(req);
15   }
```

implementation by 49% and the prefetching version 74% (Note, that for 128 PEs the original version is outperforming the prefetching version).

6   Discussion

In this paper we introduce RMA operations with explicit requests. Since each operation can be tracked with an explicit request, an OpenSHMEM user can have a fine grained control over these operations. The consequence of this semantic is the overhead of creating and managing explicit requests for each of these operations. Our hypothesis is that with sound design and implementation, these costs can be hidden, and the impact can be mitigated. Also, from our experience in implementing network layers, we believe that for many networks it is required to manage some network descriptor at the network driver level, so exposing this to the user adds only negligible overhead. To demonstrate this, we implemented these interfaces and systematically evaluated the performance impact with micro-benchmarks and application kernels.

Our results demonstrate that a well designed and implemented OpenSH-MEM stack can hide performance overhead of allocating and managing explicit handles. From Fig. 3, we can observe the performance advantages of using RMA operations with explicit requests for some communication patterns where completion of operation is not required immediately. From Figs. 4 and 5, we observe that latency of *Get* and *Put* operations with and without handles are similar. From the Fig. 6, we observe that the impact on the message rate is minimal.

In addition to RMA operations with explicit requests, we introduce the semantics of merging these requests. This can enhance the productivity and simplify some of OpenSHMEM programs as seen in modifying the SSCA #1 benchmark kernel in Sect. 5.3. Further, we see that rewriting the kernel using RMA operations with explicit requests and merging of requests can have performance benefits as seen in Fig. 7. From our investigation, we can attribute the performance advantages to the local completions used by RMA operations with explicit requests. In this case, we only flush the endpoints which exchange the messages. Further, in the case where we merge our requests, we complete the requests in a batch. On the contrary, in the case of RMA operations with no handles, all endpoints have to be flushed resulting in a higher overhead.

7 Related Work

Non-blocking communication is not a new concept. MPI [6] implementations of non-blocking message passing have been discussed since 2003. In the MPI-1 programming model non-booking operations were realized through *MPI_Isend, MPI_Irecv, MPI_Wait,* and *MPI_Test.* The non-blocking communication is accomplished by the sending process issuing a *MPI_Isend* and immediately returning to continue executing unrelated work, the receiving process would simultaneously issue an *MPI_Irecv* and overlap this with other computations till the requested data was actually required. Completion of a data transfer can be tested through *MPI_Test* and waited on till completion through *MPI_Wait.*

A number of studies have compared the different non-blocking implementations of the MPI Standard [11,13,16]. The implementations are largely dependent on the underlying implementation and hardware support. Non-blocking collectives have also been discussed and implemented in MPI-2 [8–10]. Many large scale scientific applications like simulation of seismic wave propagation [12] and parallel FDTD algorithm [7] have benefited from non-blocking communication operations.

8 Future Work

In the near future, we plan to implement an OpenSHMEM library that can safely invoke OpenSHMEM interfaces from multiple user threads using RMA operations with explicit requests. Then, we plan to implement and mimic implementation of the Context proposal [5] using RMA operations with merged requests. Also, we plan to explore and characterize the application communication characteristics that can take advantage of fine grained control and completion of RMA operations.

Acknowledgments. This work is supported by the United States Department of Defense and used resources of the Extreme Scale Systems Center located at the Oak Ridge National Laboratory.

References

1. OpenSHMEM specification 1.3. http://openshmem.org/site/sites/default/site_files/OpenSHMEM-1.3.pdf
2. Bader, D., Madduri, K., Gilbert, J., Shah, V., Kepner, J., Meuse, T., Krishnamurthy, A.: Designing scalable synthetic compact applications for benchmarking high productivity computing systems (2006)
3. Baker, M., Welch, A., Gorentla Venkata, M.: Parallelizing the Smith-Waterman algorithm using OpenSHMEM and MPI-3 one-sided interfaces. In: Gorentla Venkata, M., Shamis, P., Imam, N., Lopez, M.G. (eds.) OpenSHMEM 2014. LNCS, vol. 9397, pp. 178–191. Springer, Heidelberg (2015). doi:10.1007/978-3-319-26428-8_12

4. ten Bruggencate, M., Roweth, D., Oyanagi, S.: Thread-safe SHMEM extensions. In: Poole, S., Hernandez, O., Shamis, P. (eds.) OpenSHMEM 2014. LNCS, vol. 8356, pp. 178–185. Springer, Heidelberg (2014). doi:10.1007/978-3-319-05215-1_13

5. Dinan, J., Flajslik, M.: Contexts: a mechanism for high throughput communication in OpenSHMEM. In: Proceedings of the 8th International Conference on Partitioned Global Address Space Programming Models, PGAS 2014, NY, USA, pp. 10:1–10:9. ACM, New York (2014). http://doi.acm.org/10.1145/2676870.2676872

6. Dongarra, J.J., Otto, S.W., Snir, M., Walker, D.: An Introduction to the MPI Standard, University of Tennessee, Knoxville, TN, USA (1995). http://www.ncstrl. org:8900/ncstrl/servlet/search?formname=detail&id=oai%3Ancstrlh%3Autk_ cs%3Ancstrl.utk_cs%2F%2FUT-CS-95-274

7. Guiffaut, C., Mahdjoubi, K.: A parallel FDTD algorithm using the MPI library. IEEE Antennas Propag. Mag. **43**(2), 94–103 (2001)

8. Hoefler, T., Kambadur, P., Graham, R.L., Shipman, G., Lumsdaine, A.: A case for standard non-blocking collective operations. In: Cappello, F., Herault, T., Dongarra, J. (eds.) EuroPVM/MPI 2007. LNCS, vol. 4757, pp. 125–134. Springer, Heidelberg (2007). doi:10.1007/978-3-540-75416-9_22

9. Hoefler, T., Lumsdaine, A., Rehm, W.: Implementation and performance analysis of non-blocking collective operations for MPI. In: Proceedings of the 2007 ACM/IEEE Conference on Supercomputing, SC 2007, pp. 1–10. IEEE (2007)

10. Hoefler, T., Squyres, J., Bosilca, G., Fagg, G., Lumsdaine, A., Rehm, W.: Nonblocking collective operations for MPI-2. Open Systems Lab, Indiana University, Technical report 8 (2006)

11. Liu, J., Chandrasekaran, B., Wu, J., Jiang, W., Kini, S., Yu, W., Buntinas, D., Wyckoff, P., Panda, D.K.: Performance comparison of MPI implementations over InfiniBand, Myrinet and Quadrics. In: Supercomputing, 2003 ACM/IEEE Conference, pp. 58–58. IEEE (2003)

12. Martin, R., Komatitsch, D., Blitz, C., Goff, N.: Simulation of seismic wave propagation in an asteroid based upon an unstructured MPI spectral-element method: blocking and non-blocking communication strategies. In: Palma, J.M.L.M., Amestoy, P.R., Daydé, M., Mattoso, M., Lopes, J.C. (eds.) VECPAR 2008. LNCS, vol. 5336, pp. 350–363. Springer, Heidelberg (2008). doi:10.1007/ 978-3-540-92859-1_32

13. Saif, T., Parashar, M.: Understanding the behavior and performance of nonblocking communications in MPI. In: Danelutto, M., Vanneschi, M., Laforenza, D. (eds.) Euro-Par 2004. LNCS, vol. 3149, pp. 173–182. Springer, Heidelberg (2004). doi:10.1007/978-3-540-27866-5_22

14. Shamis, P., Venkata, M.G., Lopez, M.G., Baker, M.B., Hernandez, O., Itigin, Y., Dubman, M., Shainer, G., Graham, R.L., Liss, L., Shahar, Y., Potluri, S., Rossetti, D., Becker, D., Poole, D., Lamb, C., Kumar, S., Stunkel, C., Bosilca, G., Bouteiller, A.: UCX: an open source framework for HPC network APIs and beyond. In: 2015 IEEE 23rd Annual Symposium on High-Performance Interconnects, pp. 40–43, August 2015

15. The Ohio State University: OSU micro-benchmarks (2016). http://mvapich.cse. ohio-state.edu/benchmarks/

16. Tipparaju, V., Krishnan, M., Nieplocha, J., Santhanaraman, G., Panda, D.: Exploiting non-blocking remote memory access communication in scientific benchmarks. In: Pinkston, T.M., Prasanna, V.K. (eds.) HiPC 2003. LNCS, vol. 2913, pp. 248–258. Springer, Heidelberg (2003). doi:10.1007/978-3-540-24596-4_27

Increasing Computational Asynchrony in OpenSHMEM with Active Messages

Siddhartha Jana[1][(✉)], Tony Curtis[2], Dounia Khaldi[2], and Barbara Chapman[1,2]

[1] Department of Computer Science, University of Houston, Houston, TX, USA
{sidjana,chapman}@cs.uh.edu
[2] Institute for Advanced Computational Science,
Stony Brook University, Stony Brook, NY, USA
{anthony.curtis,dounia.khaldi,barbara.chapman}@stonybrook.edu

Abstract. Recent reports on challenges of programming models at extreme scale suggest a shift from traditional block synchronous execution models to those that support more asynchronous behavior. The OpenSHMEM programming model enables HPC programmers to exploit underlying network capabilities while designing asynchronous communication patterns. The strength of its communication model is fully realized when these patterns are characterized with small low-latency data transfers. However, for cases with large data payloads coupled with insufficient computation overlap, OpenSHMEM programs suffer from underutilized CPU cycles.

In order to tackle the above challenges, this paper explores the feasibility of introducing Active Messages in the OpenSHMEM model. Active Messages is a well established programming paradigm that enables a process to trigger execution of computation units on remote processes. Using empirical analyses, we show that this approach of moving computation closer to data provides a mechanism for OpenSHMEM applications to avoid the latency costs associated with bulk data transfers. In addition, this programming pattern helps reduce the need for unwanted synchronization among processes, thereby exploiting more asynchrony within an algorithm. As part of this preliminary work, we propose an API that supports the use of Active Messages within the OpenSHMEM execution model. We present a microbenchmark-based performance evaluation of our prototype implementation. We also compare the execution of a Traveling-Salesman Problem designed with and without Active Messages. Our experiments indicate promising benefits at scale.

1 Introduction

In recent years, research surveys that highlight the challenges faced by current programming models at extreme scale, have indicated a shift from the de facto SPMD style message passing models. With regards to the need for asynchrony within programming models, the report on *ASCR Programming Challenges for Exascale Computing* [4] states that, "The increased variation on execution speed of various components, due to error recovery and power management, will require

© Springer International Publishing AG 2016
M. Gorentla Venkata et al. (Eds.): OpenSHMEM 2016, LNCS 10007, pp. 35–51, 2016.
DOI: 10.1007/978-3-319-50995-2_3

codes that are more tolerant to noise, hence, more asynchronous". In accordance with this, multiple research efforts are being directed towards adopting programming languages and libraries that support task-based algorithm design.

In this paper, we explore the feasibility of introducing support for Active Messages to OpenSHMEM[1], a one-sided SPMD-based PGAS programming model. Active messages (AM) provide a means of triggering a user-specified unit of computation at a different process (or Processing Element or PE). The main motivation is to enable asynchronous execution of small compute paths and overlap of communication, with very little synchronization overhead incurred at the source and the target PE. The user-specified function (called a 'handler') has access to the user address space at the target PE. Thus, Active Messages (or AM) let PEs inject computation on remote destinations that host memory objects that are either remotely inaccessible due to the memory model or too costly for data movement.

The contribution of this work and the paper layout is as follows: (i) Description of a point-to-point interaction between a pair of processes using Active Messages (Sect. 2) and comparison of the AM handler with a task. (ii) Proposal of an API that introduces Active Messages within the OpenSHMEM programming model (Sect. 3) (iii) A prototype implementation of AM within the OpenSHMEM reference implementation over GASNet (iv) Empirical study using synthetic microbenchmarks and a miniapp that evaluates the performance of the prototype (Sect. 4) (v) List of different research efforts in the field of task management in a distributed environment (Sect. 5). (vi) A summary of the lessons learned and potential future work (Sect. 6).

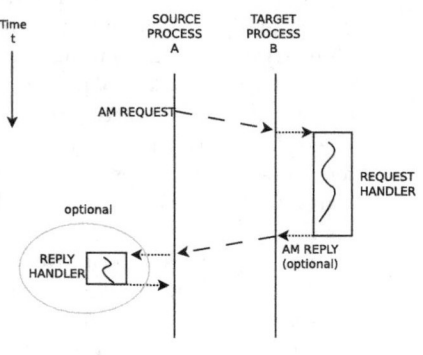

Fig. 1. Execution flow of an active message request

2   Overview of Active Messages

Figure 1 depicts the flow diagram of two processes communicating using Active Messages. The progress of the communication between the source process A and the target process B is described below:

1. Both A and B register the function handlers with the AM library.
2. Source process A sends an AM request to remote process B. This AM request mainly comprises (1) the identity of B, (2) the identity of the handler to be executed at B, and (3) optionally, contents of the data buffer to be passed as input to the handler.

---

[1] OpenSHMEM is a trademark of Silicon Graphics International Corp.

3. On receiving the AM request, process B chooses to asynchronously execute the requested function handler. At the start of the execution, it gains access to any data buffer that was transferred. This function that is executed at process B is called the *'request handler'*.
4. During the execution of the request handler, process B may optionally choose to post a reply AM back to A. Similar to the AM sent by A, this reply AM contains the identity of the handler to be executed at A along with an optional data payload.
5. At some point in time, on detecting the arrival of the above reply AM, A executes the handler corresponding to the identity listed in the incoming message. The handler which is executed as a response to this AM is called the *'reply handler'*.

2.1 Active Message v/s Tasking Models

Unlike a tasking model where one has to rely on a scheduler to assign resources for execution, the AM model allows the programmer to explicitly specifying the destination for the execution. While the computation associated with a task is expected to return a specific result to a 'parent' unit, computation of AM handlers are usually intended to update local data structures. Another notable difference is that while tasking models allow establishing dependence among multiple tasks, AM models focus on asynchronous execution of independent handlers.

3 Proposed Extension for Active Messages Support

This section describes the proposed interface of AM handlers and the related AM management functions[2] related to: (1) design of an AM handler, (2) registration of AM handlers, (3) initiating AMs, (4) the completion of AMs, and (5) handler safe locking. The set of the proposed interfaces for C is shown in Listing 1.1.

Design of an AM Handler. The actual body of an AM handler is enclosed within a user-defined function. The purpose of active messages is to enable injection of code paths that contain a small set of computation that remains independent of the progress of other PEs. The design of an AM handler should therefore adhere to the following set of constraints:

– The handler body should not call other function routines from the Open-SHMEM library, that have the potential to trigger an inter-PE communication. This includes point-to-point communication, synchronization constructs, atomic operations, and other AM related functions (excluding those related to mutual exclusion).

---

[2] Note: As a norm in the OpenSHMEM community, all the AM related functions in this paper have been prefixed with 'shmemx_' instead of 'shmem_' to indicate that they are *proposed extensions* to the standard and *not* part of the current specification.

– The execution of an AM handler can progress in an OS thread that runs concurrent to the one servicing the critical path of a PE. It becomes the responsibility of the programmer to ensure that no race conditions occur when a data object is made accessible to both an AM handler as well as the execution path of a PE. If one of the accesses is a write operation, handler-safe locks can be used to ensure mutual exclusion.
– If a data object is a target of a write operation during the execution of the handler routine, handler-safe locks should be used to avoid race conditions.

```
/** Function Handler Signature **/
void user_function_name (void* data_buffer, size_t
    buffer_size, int calling_peid, shmemx_am_token_t token)

/** (De)Registration of Active Message handlers **/
typedef void (*shmemx_am_handler) (void *buf, size_t nbytes,
    int req_pe, shmemx_am_token_t token)

void shmemx_am_attach (int handler_id, shmemx_am_handler
    handler_ptr)
void shmemx_am_detach (int handler_id)

/** Initiating Active Messages **/
void shmemx_am_request (int dest, int handler_id, void*
    source_addr, size_t nbytes)
void shmemx_am_reply (int handler_id, void* source_addr,
    size_t nbytes, shmemx_am_token_t temp_token)

/** Progress and Completion **/
void shmemx_am_quiet ()
void shmemx_am_poll ()

/** Handler Safe Locking **/
void shmemx_am_mutex_init (shmemx_am_mutex* t)
void shmemx_am_mutex_destroy (shmemx_am_mutex* t)
void shmemx_am_mutex_lock (shmemx_am_mutex* t)
void shmemx_am_mutex_unlock (shmemx_am_mutex* t)
int shmemx_am_mutex_trylock (shmemx_am_mutex* t)
```

Listing 1.1. Proposed API routines for Active Messages in OpenSHMEM

Registration of AM Handlers. This features the following two collective API routines:

– *shmemx_am_attach:* Enables the calling PE to register the function pointed to by the function pointer. The user passes a handler-id that is used to map the handler to the corresponding function. On return from this function, a PE can use the handler_id to launch an AM until its association to the handler function is removed using shmemx_am_detach. It must be noted that the remote PE itself need not register the handler if it does not intend to execute it during its lifetime. Since a function being registered can only be used as an AM handler after it has been registered, some type of synchronization between the two PEs may be necessary to ensure that the function registration is complete on the target PE. Different PEs can register the same function with different handler-ids.

- *shmemx_am_detach:* This removes the mapping between a handler-id and the function mapped to the id. Once detached, it is illegal for any other PE to reuse the same handler id to launch an AM unless it is explicitly remapped using shmemx_am_attach by the current PE.

Initiating Active Messages

- *shmemx_am_request:* This function is used to launch an AM on a remote PE destination. The contents of the user buffer is transferred to the target PE along with the id of the function. On receiving this request, the target PE executes the corresponding handler. On return from this request function, there is no guarantee of the completion of execution of the handler by the target PE. This asynchrony reduces the overhead at the source PE. To enable the source PE to reuse the data buffer, it is essential that this function copies the contents to a temporary buffer internally before returning to the user address space.

- *shmemx_am_reply:* In a two-sided request-reply communication model, this function is used by the request AM handler to launch a reply AM handler at the source PE that had issued the AM.

The Completion of Active Messages

- *shmemx_am_quiet:* This function enables the calling PE to ensure that the request handlers of all previously posted Active Messages and their corresponding response handlers (if any) have completed their execution.

- *shmemx_am_poll:* This polls the network for any outstanding AM requests. It must be noted that while this function can be used by a programmer to wait for a certain event to occur, it is not necessary for an OpenSHMEM implementation to rely on this function to make progress. An implementation should be free to exploit interrupt driven mechanisms or asynchronous notification capabilities of the underlying operating system or the hardware platform, respectively.

Handler Safe Locking. Since the critical path of the PE and the AM handler may run concurrently, it becomes necessary to ensure mutually exclusive accesses to shared data structures. For this, we propose a new data type called shmemx_am_mutex. It becomes the responsibility of the programmer to ensure that an object of this data type be visible to both the AM function handler as well as the main PE thread. An object of this type represents a mutex variable that can be passed to the following functions to avoid overlapping access of shared memory.

- *shmemx_am_mutex_init:* Initializes the mutex variable. Typically, the purpose is to ensure that the initial state of the variable becomes visible to both the critical path of the PE as well as the AM handler.
- *shmemx_am_mutex_destroy:* Ensures that the variable is no longer usable by the critical path of the PE or the calling thread. This provides an opportunity for an implementation to clean up memory associated with the variable.
- *shmemx_am_mutex_lock:* Attempts to acquire the mutex variable exclusively. If unsuccessful, the calling PE remains blocked until it gains access to the mutex.
- *shmemx_am_mutex_unlock:* Releases the ownership of the mutex variable.
- *shmemx_am_mutex_trylock:* Attempts to acquire the mutex variable exclusively. If unsuccessful, it returns 0 to the callee and its execution continues with blocking. If successful, it returns a non-zero number.

4   Prototype Evaluation

4.1   Implementation Design

The prototype implementation[3] was designed as part of the Open-SHMEM reference implementation [8] that in turn uses GASNet [5] for inter-process communication. Our prototype is built on top of the existing support of Active Messages that is offered by GASNet. The incorporation of the prototype within the OpenSHMEM reference implementation is illustrated in Fig. 2. It must be noted that fine-tuned implementations of Active Messages in OpenSHMEM should take advantage of network hardware capabilities (if any) and the exploration of different design approaches is out-of-scope of this paper.

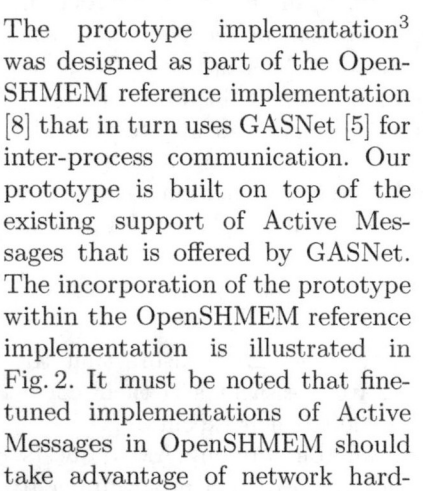

Fig. 2. Incorporation of the proposed active messages prototype into the OpenSHMEM reference implementation

4.2   Experimental Setup

The experimental results presented in the following sections were obtained using a cluster with AMD Opteron processors (model 6174) and Infiniband interconnect (Mellanox MT26418). Each compute node comprises of a total of 48 cores (4 sockets/node, 12 cores/socket) with approximately 5 MB shared L3 cache and 16 GB main memory. The OS distribution on each compute node is OpenSUSE Linux (ver. 3.11).

---

[3] The Active Message prototype implementation is available as a fork of the Open-SHMEM reference implementation and is available as a git repository at https://github.com/openshmem-org/openshmem-am.

Process Layout. The results from the bandwidth and message rate tests, microbenchmarks were obtained by binding each process (PE) to a specific core on different compute nodes. The results for the token-ring based tests and the miniapp (Traveling Salesman Problem) were obtained by launching multiple number of PEs - 2 through 512 and 256 respectively, each bound to a specific core across multiple nodes.

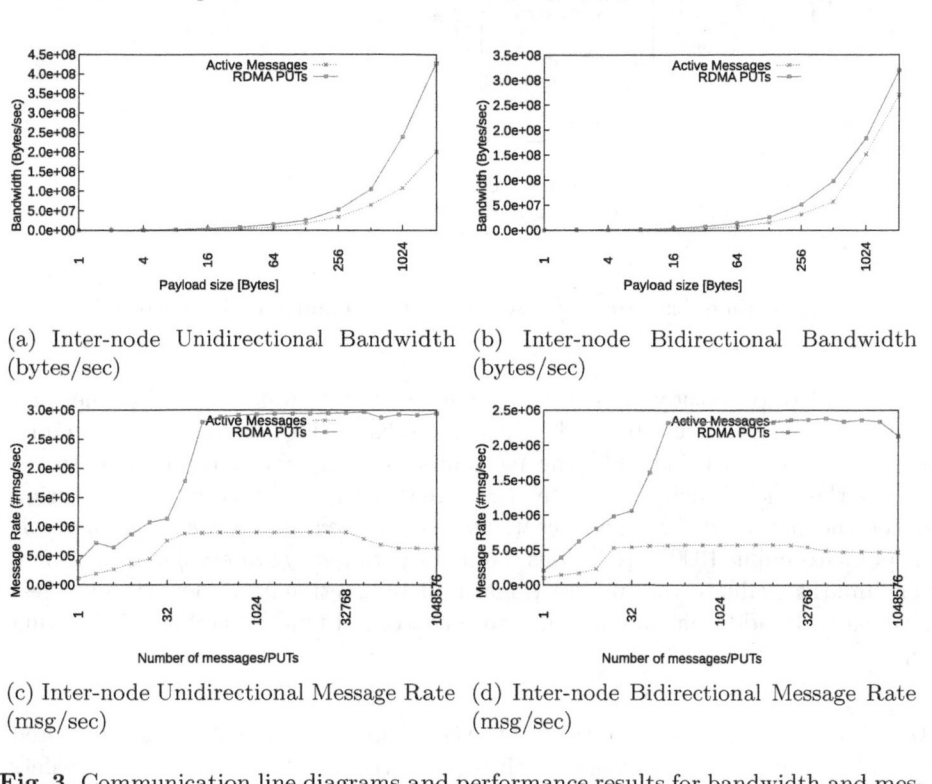

(a) Inter-node Unidirectional Bandwidth (bytes/sec)

(b) Inter-node Bidirectional Bandwidth (bytes/sec)

(c) Inter-node Unidirectional Message Rate (msg/sec)

(d) Inter-node Bidirectional Message Rate (msg/sec)

Fig. 3. Communication line diagrams and performance results for bandwidth and message rates

4.3   Performance Study

This section presents a performance analysis of the prototype implementation. As noted in previous sections, the proposed AM interface enables transfer of data buffers in addition to the invocation of remote handlers. This section investigates the feasibility of using Active Messages instead of OpenSHMEM point-to-point operations to transfer data among PEs. It must be noted that the results presented as part of this study correspond to the prototype implementation of Active Messages and is meant to highlight the difference in behavior between the prototype and one-sided operations. The reader must bear in mind that fine-tuned implementations of Active Messages can exploit additional features of the underlying hardware stack to achieve better performance.

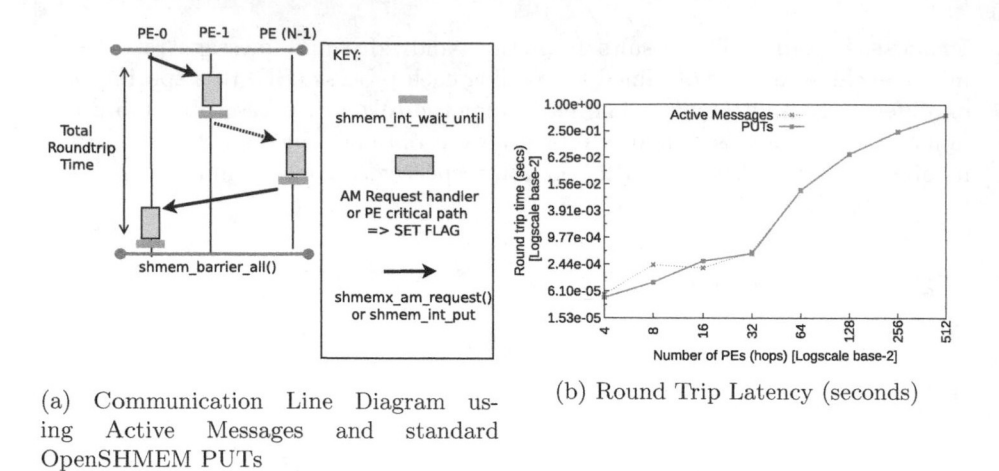

(a) Communication Line Diagram using Active Messages and standard OpenSHMEM PUTs

(b) Round Trip Latency (seconds)

Fig. 4. Empirical study of token ring based communication pattern

As part of this study, a microbenchmark test suite was designed to measure the achievable unidirectional and bidirectional bandwidth and message rate during data transfers using both the mechanisms[4]. The communication patterns within the microbenchmark suite use multiple PEs that communicate using either the proposed AM interface ($shmemx\_am\_request()$/$shmemx\_am\_quiet()$) or point-to-point PUT operations ($shmem\_putmem()$/$shmem\_quiet()$). These benchmarks evaluate the unidirectional and bidirectional bandwidth and message rates. In addition they also measure the round-trip latency of a token-ring topology.

Bandwidth:

Test Design: The execution time of the communication pattern was monitored for different payload sizes from 1B through 2 KB. We do not measure transfers beyond the 2 KB size because we learned that Active Messages are not a good data transport mechanism for bulk payloads.

Test Results: The unidirectional and bidirectional bandwidth using the proposed AM interface and the standard OpenSHMEM point-to-point PUT operations are depicted in Fig. 3a and b, respectively. The x-axis corresponds to the size of the data payload transferred (in log_2 scale) across the network. The value of the achievable bandwidth (in bytes/second) is plotted on the y-axis. From the figures, we observe that a higher bandwidth is achievable while using point-to-point PUT operations as compared to using the prototype implementation. This is not surprising since the AM request mechanism is associated with multiple cost factors. At the source, the PE is responsible for copying the contents of the data payload from the user's address space to a temporary buffer that gets packed along with additional information necessary for the target PE to respond.

---

[4] The microbenchmark test suite for OpenSHMEM AM is hosted as a git repository at https://github.com/sidjana/shmem_am_testsuite.

At the destination, the PE is responsible for detecting an incoming AM request, launching the corresponding AM handler and then notifying the source about the completion of the handler execution. It can be observed that the impact of these factors increases with the size of the data payload being transferred. This leads to an important conclusion that the purpose of using an AM is not to transfer data payloads, but rather to trigger computation at the same location as the transferred payload.

Message Rate:

Test Design: The execution time of the pattern was monitored for different number of messages initiated consecutively with minimal payload (4 bytes).

Test Results: The unidirectional and bidirectional message rate using the proposed AM interface and standard OpenSHMEM point-to-point PUT operations are depicted in Fig. 3c and d, respectively. The x-axis corresponds to the number of messages (PUT operations/AM requests) initiated before waiting for completion (in logscale, base 2)[5]. The value of the achievable message rate (in messages/second) is plotted on the y-axis. Similar to the bandwidth tests above, we observe that there is a negative impact on the message rate of the transfers. There is a significant impact when the number of consecutive AM requests increases beyond 32. The drop in message rate while using the AM interface is about 3X in case of unidirectional tests and 5X in case of bidirectional.

Token-Ring Communication Pattern:

Launching an AM is similar to triggering an event on a remote destination. Therefore, incorporating the support for AM into a programming model enables applications to be built using communication patterns that rely on sending and responding to asynchronous events. It enables the design of patterns wherein a single AM request can be used to propagate a signal across other remote PEs. In order to ensure high performance, it is essential that implementations invest as few CPU cycles as possible between detecting an AM request and executing the AM handler. In order to study the impact on latency of an AM request as it hops across multiple PEs, two synthetic microbenchmarks were designed to mimic a token-ring based communication topology. The benchmark was designed such that the token was propagated using either standard OpenSHMEM point-to-point synchronization or the proposed AM interface.

Test Design: The line diagrams of these patterns are depicted in Fig. 4a. As shown, the transfer of the token is achieved by transferring a single integer across consecutive pairs of PE in the ring topology. In an N-PE system, a PE k sends a signal (either via an AM or a PUT) to PE $((k+1)\%N)$ which then propagates the same to the PE $((k+2)\%N)$, and so on. PE $(N-1)$ sends the signal back to PE-0 thereby completing a single round-trip. The motivation for such a design is to measure the total round-trip latency for different ring sizes.

Test Results: As part of this study, we study the impact on the time taken to complete a single round trip as a function of the number of hops (PEs) within the

---

[5] Completion of a PUT operation/AM request is ensured by calling the functions - shmem_quiet()/shmemx_am_quiet(), respectively.

ring. In an implementation with minimal software overhead during AM handler management, the expectation is that the total round-trip time scales almost linearly with the number of hops. Figure 4b shows the empirical results for this test. The x-axis represents the number of hops (the number of PEs) in a single round-trip. The y-axis corresponds to the total time taken for the token initiated by PE-0 (in the form of an AM request or a PUT) to pass through all the PEs before returning to PE-0. From the graph we observe that the latency for the round-trip latency for both the approaches is almost the same. This can be attributed to the fact that the difference between the latencies of transferring data payloads using AM and standard PUT is more tangible for large data payloads. Since this pattern used a single 4-byte integer to represent the token, the performance is similar.

Summary:
From the bandwidth and message rate plots, we learn that the purpose of using Active Messages is *not* to transfer data payloads. To achieve *closer-to-metal* bandwidth and message rates for data transfers, the OpenSHMEM programmer is better off using traditional point-to-point operations that are currently provided by the standard. From the token-ring experiment, it can be seen that Active Messages are better suited for triggering specific events on remote PEs with the added benefit of providing a means for productivity (due to its coding style) and no significant loss in performance.

4.4   The Traveling Salesman Problem (TSP)

In order to study the impact of the proposed AM interface, the Traveling Salesman Problem (TSP) miniapp was chosen as the target benchmark because the algorithm can be divided into multiple independent tasks. This gives an opportunity to exploit asynchronous computation within the algorithm.

Miniapp Versions: The TSP miniapp uses a master-worker communication pattern. The master PE is responsible for reading an input cost matrix and for assigning different paths to the worker PEs. The worker PEs in turn are responsible for either breaking down a path into smaller subpaths, determining the shortest distance for a given path, or requesting a new path from the master PE. As part of the experiment, the performance of three different versions of the miniapp were evaluated. The difference between the three is in the deign of the master process. Active Messages provide a mechanism to map a function handler to an identifier. We noted that this is similar to the message-tagging mechanism provided by MPI. Not surprisingly, the logical flow of the algorithms that used MPI tag-matching algorithm and the OpenSHMEM with AM was similar. This is depicted in Fig. 5(a) and (b). The flow of the algorithm used to design the miniapp using standard OpenSHMEM without any AM interface is illustrated in Fig. 5(b) and (c). The design details are described below:

(i) With AM Interface/MPI Tag-Matching: In the OpenSHMEM version that uses the AM interface, the worker PE communicates with the master PE

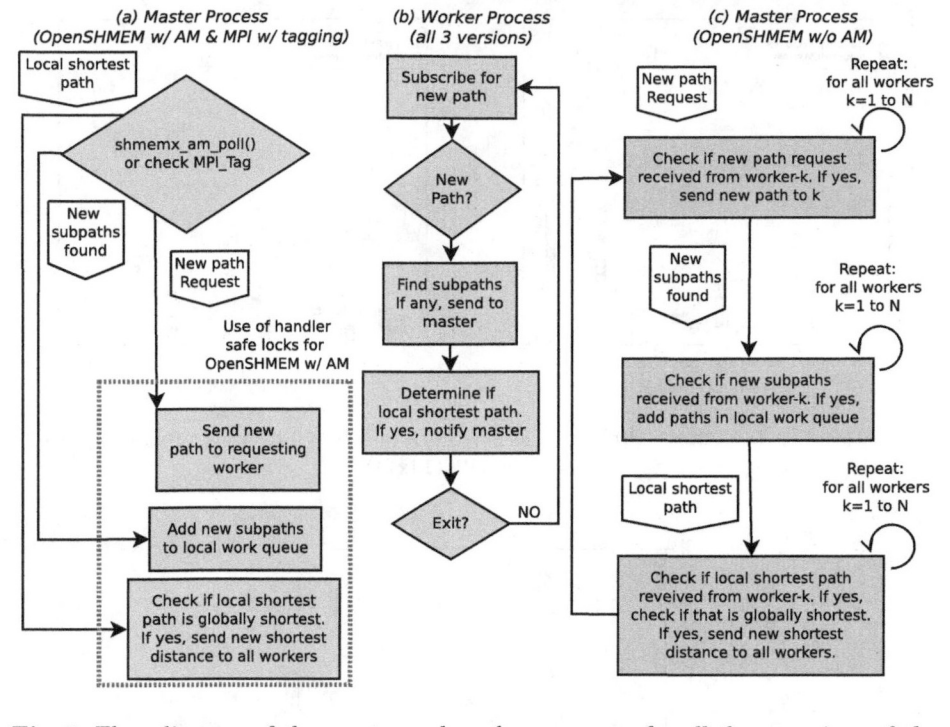

Fig. 5. Flow diagram of the master and worker processes for all three versions of the Traveling Salesman Problem (TSP): (a) Master for both OpenSHMEM with AM and MPI, (b) Worker for all three versions, (c) Master for OpenSHMEM without AM.

using Active Messages[6]. Each request contains the id of the function handler which on detection is triggered by the master PE. Since the handler function is presented with a pointer to the contents of the message, it is not responsible for costs associated with memory management. The MPI implementation[7] exploits the availability of message tags to differentiate between different messages sent by the worker ranks. In this case, the worker rank communicates with the master by appending MPI messages with tag-ids that correspond to different tasks. Because of this feature, the design of the master rank is similar to the master PE that uses the OpenSHMEM AM interface. One of the challenges in designing the OpenSHMEM version with AM is the need to share multiple data structures among different AM handlers. To ensure correctness and avoid race conditions, it becomes essential to use handler-safe locks to ensure exclusive access to these

---

[6] The version of the TSP miniapp using the proposed AM interface is hosted at https://github.com/sidjana/traveling_salesman_shmem_am/tree/master/shmem_MMPQ.

[7] The version of the TSP miniapp using MPI-tagging approach is hosted at http://www.eecg.toronto.edu/~amza/ece1747h/homeworks/examples/MPI.

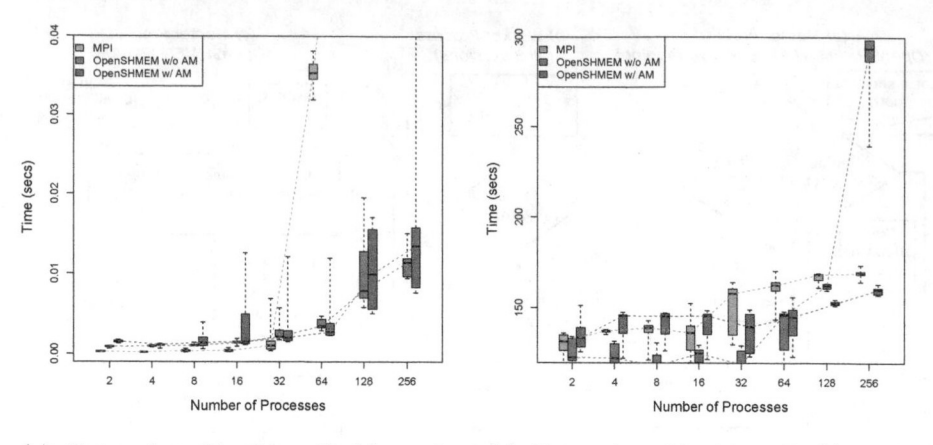

(a) Data size: 04 cities. Problem size: 16(4x4)

(b) Data size: 14 cities. Problem size: 196(14x14)

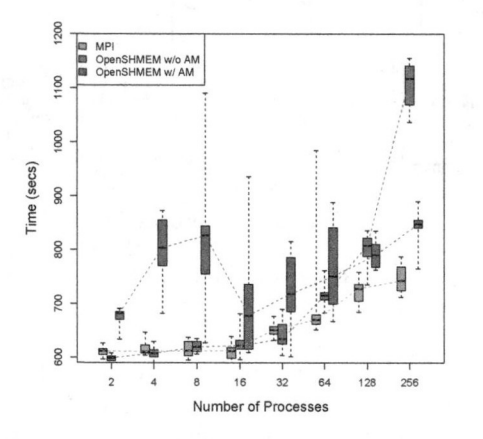

(c) Data size: 15 cities. Problem size: 255 (15x15)

Fig. 6. Performance results of a traveling salesman problem written - MPI (in GREEN) v/s standard OpenSHMEM (in RED) v/s OpenSHMEM with the proposed AM interface (in BLUE). The dashed line connects all the medians of the box-plots that correspond to each of the versions. (Color figure online)

data structures. This in turn leads to a potential rise in lock contention, and hence performance degradation for small data sets.

(ii) Without AM Interface: In this case, each worker PE remotely updates an assigned bucket stored on the master PE, using point-to-point communication operations[8]. The master PE is in charge of maintaining the remotely accessible

---

[8] The version of the TSP miniapp using standard OpenSHMEM interface is hosted at https://github.com/sidjana/traveling_salesman_shmem_am/tree/master/shmem_pure.

buckets. Since the communication pattern relies on a single master and multiple workers, there is a need to assign a different bucket for each worker PE. This helps avoid network congestion at the master PE due to repeated use of the distributed locking interfaces or atomic operations provided by OpenSHMEM. The disadvantage of this approach though is that the master PE has to repeatedly scan through all the buckets to check for any updates by the PEs. The cost of this access takes a toll on the performance for large count of buckets/worker PEs. Here the cost associated with accessing the buckets increases linearly with the number of worker PEs, this design has the potential for severe performance degradation at large PE count.

Experiment Methodology. Three different implementations of the TSP were chosen for the comparative study - two of which were designed using OpenSH-MEM (as explained above) and the third, using the MPI two-sided model. Three different problem sizes were chosen (number of cities = 4, 14, 15). The results are shown in Fig. 6(a), (b), and (c) respectively. Due to the highly irregular and dynamic nature of this miniapp, the execution time is prone to high variation. The results are therefore presented as a box plot distribution, where each plot for a given problem size and PE count corresponds to a distribution of 20 runs of the miniapp version. The X-axis plots the number of PEs used for execution. The Y-axis corresponds to the time taken (in seconds) to arrive at the solution (shortest path).

Empirical Results. The major observations are as follows:

– With a small input data set (Fig. 6a), we see a severe performance degradation with the MPI version. This can be attributed to the fact that the implementation heavily relies on the traditional two-sided blocking communication to transfer data among the master and multiple worker processes. The use of either the proposed AM interface or the standard non-blocking one-sided communication both alleviate this penalty.
– With large data sets (Fig. 6b and c), we see that the OpenSHMEM version that uses the standard interface suffers a significant performance loss when scaled beyond one node (number of PEs > 32). Since this version maintains a separate bucket for each worker, the master suffers a slowdown due to the cost associated with scanning multiple buckets iteratively. This cost is completely eliminated in case of the AM version where no CPU cycles are invested in determining the status of worker processes. Instead, the unordered incoming requests initiated by the worker processes are asynchronously executed at the master process.
– The plots also show that for large data sets and higher process count, the performance between the MPI and the OpenSHMEM with AM versions are close to each other. This is because the MPI implementation relies on tag matching to detect the task to be executed. Functionally, this is similar to the underlying AM implementation where the handler functions are invoked by matching the handler-id embedded within the incoming AM request.

– There is an interesting behavior by the OpenSHMEM version that uses AM
interfaces for the input data set with 15 cities (Fig. 6c). We see a very high
variation among execution time for small PE count. This high variation can
be attributed to use of handler safe locks among the AM request handlers,
thereby leading to heavy lock contention. This variation reduces for higher
PE count which can be explained by greater overlap of the computation at
the worker with that of the AM handler at the master. Since the MPI version
in synchronous, it does not rely on any locking mechanism thereby avoiding
the high variation in execution time for this data set. The lesson learned here
is that in order to exploit asynchronous execution of AM handlers, the use
of shared data structures, and hence the use of handler-safe locks should be
limited. Despite this, we observe that using Active Messages gives a high performance gain at scale over the version that uses the standard OpenSHMEM
interfaces.

5   Related Work

Active Messages were first introduced by Eicken et al. [11]. The original motivation was to enable communication/computation overlap and shift the responsibility of tolerating latency from the underlying hardware to the programmers/
compilers. The authors described a programming model called *Split-C* that
enables remote one-sided communication to be executed using Active Messages.

Multiple low-level communication libraries that support Active Messages
include GASNet [5], UCX [17], LAPI [20], and PAMI [15].

At a higher level in the software stack, the execution model of Active Messages can be compared to programming models that enable explicit launching of
tasks among processes in a distributed environment. These include ParalleX
[14] (*parcels*), UPC++ [24] (*function shipping*), Charm++ [2] (*entry methods*), Chapel [12] (*begin-at*), CAF 2.0 [19] (*spawn*), and GASPI [3] (*passive
communication*).

Research efforts have been made to also introduce Active Messages within
MPI [6,10,13,21,23]. Some of these approaches like AM++ [21] and AMMPI [6]
are designed on top of existing MPI libraries. Alternative approaches like Zhao
et al. [23] describe techniques for incorporating Active Messages directly within
the MPI runtime (e.g. by extension the semantics of *MPI_Accumulate* within
MPICH).

Unlike Active Messages that enable inter-process parallelism using explicitly
specified computation units, some programming models offer constructs that
help exploit dynamic parallelism within a process. Programming models like
X10 [9], Titanium [22], Chapel [12], and those based on the Habanero framework (which in turn is based on X10's *finish-async* constructs) - Habanero Java
[7], Habanero C [1], Habanero UPC [18], Habanero-C MPI [10], and Habanero-
UPC++ [16], all provide tasking mechanisms that incorporate dynamic load-
balancing strategies by scheduling work across a dedicated pool of workers.

6 Conclusion and Future Work

This paper explores the feasibility of introducing Active Messages (AM) within the OpenSHMEM programming model. As part of this work, an API was proposed along with an empirical study of a prototype implementation within the OpenSHMEM reference implementation.

Synthetic microbenchmarks were used to compare the performance of data movement using the proposed AM interface and the existing standard OpenSH-MEM remote write operations. The results show that the primary intent of using Active Messages should not be to transfer data to remote locations. Instead, the purpose is to facilitate the transfer of computation to a destination that hosts the data that needs to be computed upon. Nevertheless, a simple interface has been proposed that allows a process to attach a user buffer to the Active Message request. One potential approach to avoid the poor bandwidth costs of appending data payloads to an AM request maybe to instead perform a standard PUT operation followed by shmem_quiet and then the AM request with zero bytes of payload. This may help applications exploit the RDMA capabilities of underlying network.

Another noteworthy point in the proposed semantics is the lack of restriction on the size of the data payload that is appended to an AM request. One possible modification to this approach could be where the interface provides multiple variations for different sized data payloads while initiating Active Message. While this provides greater flexibility to the end user, there is also an increase of burden on the user to choose the right interface to achieve the expected performance. Examples of low-level communication libraries that do provide such interfaces include GASNet [5] (using *medium, long,* and *longasync* AM requests) and UCX [17] (using *short, buffered,* and *zero-copy* AM requests).

On comparing the performance of different implementations of a miniapp (the Traveling Salesman Problem), it was learned that while using Active Messages, sharing of data structures among different handlers of the same PE should be avoided, otherwise there is a potential for performance loss due to contention among *handler-safe locks*. However, it was observed that despite such a design of the algorithm, the miniapp was able to achieve significant performance improvement over the version that solely relied on using the standard OpenSHMEM interfaces.

Acknowledgments. Development at the University of Houston was supported in part by the US DOD under Subcontract No. 346023, the NSFs Computer Systems Research program under Award No. CRI-0958464, and the resources at LANL. Any opinions, findings, and conclusions or recommendations expressed in this material are those of the authors and do not necessarily reflect the views of the funding sources. Thanks are due to Deepak Eachempati and the anonymous reviewers for their feedback on the technical contents of this paper.

References

1. Habanero-C Overview (2013). https://wiki.rice.edu/confluence/display/HABANERO/Habanero-C
2. Acun, B., Gupta, A., Jain, N., Langer, A., Menon, H., Mikida, E., Ni, X., Robson, M., Sun, Y., Totoni, E., Wesolowski, L., Kale, L.: Parallel programming with migratable objects: charm++ in practice. In: Proceedings of the International Conference for High Performance Computing, Networking, Storage and Analysis, SC 2014, pp. 647–658. IEEE Press, Piscataway (2014)
3. Alrutz, T., et al.: GASPI – a partitioned global address space programming interface. In: Keller, R., Kramer, D., Weiss, J.-P. (eds.) Facing the Multicore-Challenge III. LNCS, vol. 7686, pp. 135–136. Springer, Heidelberg (2013). doi:10.1007/978-3-642-35893-7_18
4. Amarasinghe, S., Hall, M., Lathin, R., Pingarli, K., Quinlan, D., Sarkar, V., Shalf, J., Lucas, R., Yelick, K.: ASCR Programming Challenges for Exasacle Computing (2011)
5. Bonachea, D.: GASNet specification, v1.1, University of California, Berkely, Technical report CSD-0201207, October 2002
6. Bonachea, D.: AMMPI: Active Messages over MPI - Quick Overview. http://www.cs.berkeley.edu/~bonachea/ammpi/
7. Cavé, V., Zhao, J., Shirako, J., Sarkar, V.: Habanero-Java: the new adventures of old X10. In: Proceedings of the 9th International Conference on Principles and Practice of Programming in Java, PPPJ 2011, pp. 51–61. ACM, New York (2011). http://doi.acm.org/10.1145/2093157.2093165
8. Chapman, B., Curtis, T., Pophale, S., Poole, S., Kuehn, J., Koelbel, C., Smith, L.: Introducing OpenSHMEM: SHMEM for the PGAS community. In: Proceedings of the Fourth Conference on Partitioned Global Address Space Programming Model, PGAS 2010, pp. 2:1–2:3. ACM, New York (2010)
9. Charles, P., Grothoff, C., Saraswat, V., Donawa, C., Kielstra, A., Ebcioglu, K., von Praun, C., Sarkar, V.: X10: an object-oriented approach tononuniform cluster computing. SIGPLAN Not. **40**(10), 519–538 (2005). http://doi.acm.org/10.1145/1103845.1094852
10. Chatterjee, S., Tasirlar, S., Budimlic, Z., Cav, V., Chabbi, M., Grossman, M., Sarkar, V., Yan, Y.: Integrating asynchronous task parallelism with MPI. In: 2013 IEEE 27th International Symposium on Parallel Distributed Processing (IPDPS), pp. 712–725, May 2013
11. Eicken, T., Culler, D., Goldstein, S., Schauser, K.: Active messages: a mechanism for integrated communication and computation. In: Proceedings of the 19th Annual International Symposium on Computer Architecture, pp. 256–266, May 1992. http://ieeexplore.ieee.org/lpdocs/epic03/wrapper.htm?arnumber=753322
12. Gu, B., Yu, W., Kwak, Y.: Communication and computation overlap through task synchronization in multi-locale chapel environment. In: Park, J.J., Yang, L.T., Lee, C. (eds.) FutureTech 2011. CCIS, vol. 184, pp. 285–292. Springer, Heidelberg (2011). doi:10.1007/978-3-642-22333-4_37
13. Hoefler, T., Willcock, J.: Active Messages for MPI (2009)
14. Kaiser, H., Brodowicz, M., Sterling, T.: ParalleX an advanced parallel execution model for scaling-impaired applications. In: Proceedings of the 2009 International Conference on Parallel Processing Workshops, ICPPW 2009, pp. 394–401. IEEE Computer Society, Washington, DC (2009)

15. Kumar, S., Mamidala, A.R., Faraj, D.A., Smith, B., Blocksome, M., Cernohous, B., Miller, D., Parker, J., Ratterman, J., Heidelberger, P., Chen, D., Steinmacher-Burrow, B.: PAMI: a parallel active message interface for the Blue Gene/Q super-computer. In: 2012 IEEE 26th International Parallel Distributed Processing Symposium (IPDPS), pp. 763–773, May 2012

16. Kumar, V., Zheng, Y., Cavé, V., Budimlić, Z., Sarkar, V.: HabaneroUPC++: a compiler-free PGAS library. In: Proceedings of the 8th International Conference on Partitioned Global Address Space Programming Models, PGAS 2014, pp. 5:1–5:10. ACM, New York (2014). http://doi.acm.org/10.1145/2676870.2676879

17. OpenUCX: Unified Communication X (UCX) API Documentation. https://github.com/openucx/ucx/wiki/ucx.pdf

18. Rice, H.: Habanero UPC. https://github.com/habanero-rice/habanero-upc

19. Scherer III, W.N., Adhianto, L., Jin, G., Mellor-Crummey, J., Yang, C.: Hiding latency in coarray fortran 2.0. In: Proceedings of the Fourth Conference on Partitioned Global Address Space Programming Model, PGAS 2010, pp. 14:1–14:9. ACM, New York (2010)

20. Shah, G., Bender, C.: Performance and experience with LAPI - a new high-performance communication library for the IBM RS/6000 SP. In: Proceedings of the 12th International Parallel Processing Symposium on IPPS 1998, p. 260. IEEE Computer Society, Washington, DC (1998)

21. Willcock, J.J., Ave, S.W., Edmonds, N.G., Lumsdaine, A.: AM ++ : A Generalized Active Message Framework (2010)

22. Yelick, K., Semenzato, L., Pike, G., Miyamoto, C., Liblit, B., Krishnamurthy, A., Hilfinger, P., Graham, S., Gay, D., Colella, P., Aiken, A.: Titanium: a high-performance JAVA dialect. In: In ACM, pp. 10–11 (1998)

23. Zhao, X., Buntinas, D., Zounmevo, J., Dinan, J., Goodell, D., Balaji, P., Thakur, R., Afsahi, A., Gropp, W.: Toward asynchronous and MPI-interoperable active messages. In: Proceedings - 13th IEEE/ACM International Symposium on Cluster, Cloud, and Grid Computing, CCGrid 2013, pp. 87–94 (2013)

24. Zheng, Y., Kamil, A., Driscoll, M.B., Shan, H., Yelick, K.: UPC++: a PGAS extension for C++. In: 2014 IEEE 28th International Parallel and Distributed Processing Symposium, pp. 1105–1114, May 2014

System-Level Transparent Checkpointing for OpenSHMEM

Rohan Garg[1]([⊠]), Jérôme Vienne[2], and Gene Cooperman[1]

[1] Northeastern University, Boston, MA 02115, USA
{rohgarg,gene}@ccs.neu.edu
[2] Texas Advanced Computing Center,
The University of Texas at Austin, Austin, TX 78758, USA
viennej@tacc.utexas.edu

Abstract. Fault tolerance is an active area of research for OpenSHMEM programs. In this work, we present the first approach using system-level transparent checkpointing. This complements an existing approach based on application-level checkpointing. Application-level checkpointing has advantages for algorithm-based fault tolerance, while transparent checkpointing can be invoked by the system at an arbitrary time. Unlike the earlier application-level work of Hao et al., this system-level approach creates checkpoint images in stable storage, thus enabling restart at a later time or even process migration. An experimental evaluation is presented using NAS NPB benchmarks for OpenSHMEM. In order to support this work, The design of DMTCP (Distributed MultiThreaded CheckPointing) was extended to support shared memory regions in the absence of virtual memory.

Keywords: Checkpointing · Fault tolerance · OpenSHMEM · Process migration

1 Introduction

Checkpoint-restart is an area of research with a long history Work in this area has largely been split according to two approaches: *system-level* checkpointing and *application-level* checkpointing. System-level checkpointing typically is also *transparent*, in that it can be invoked by an external system service or by the operating system. Application-level checkpointing can also support transparent checkpointing by interposing on existing libraries.

This work presents the first system-level checkpointing solution for OpenSH-MEM [9,18]. The DMTCP (Distributed MultiThreaded CheckPointing) platform [2] is used in this approach. DMTCP directly supports checkpointing of distributed computations. This contrasts with a previous application-level approach to checkpointing by Hao et al. [15], which relies on interposing on the OpenSHMEM runtime library itself.

R. Garg and G. Cooperman—This work was partially supported by the National Science Foundation under Grant ACI-1440788.

© Springer International Publishing AG 2016
M. Gorentla Venkata et al. (Eds.): OpenSHMEM 2016, LNCS 10007, pp. 52–65, 2016.
DOI: 10.1007/978-3-319-50995-2_4

In principle, an alternative approach would be to use an implementation of OpenSHMEM on top of MPI, and then invoke system-level checkpointing of OpenSHMEM through checkpointing of the underlying MPI checkpoint-restart service. However, this is not feasible, since the current MPI implementations delegate to BLCR [10,17] for checkpointing of a single process, and BLCR does not support the POSIX SysV shared memory objects on which most OpenSHMEM implementations depend. See Sect. 4 for a fuller discussion.

The barriers to supporting system-level checkpointing for OpenSHEM can be understood by reviewing the primary features of OpenSHMEM [18]. The Open-SHMEM standard is motivated by at least three extensions from shared memory between processes on a single computer to shared memory between computers on distributed hardware. SysV system calls such as shmget() and semop() must be extended to distributed hardware. And an RDMA-like technology such as InfiniBand must be used to efficiently support one-sided communication.

Specifically, the difficulties of supporting OpenSHMEM with a traditional checkpoint-restart package are three-fold.

1. shared memory objects (e.g., shmget() in SysV) were generalized from POSIX system calls on one computer to distributed hardware.
2. InfiniBand or a related RDMA technology is required. The OpenSHMEM standard [18] insists on the importance of one-sided communication: "The key feature of OpenSHMEM is that data transfer operations are one-sided in nature." [18, Sect. 2]. InfiniBand provides this.
3. synchronization primitives are generalized from APIs for inter-thread and inter-process communication [18, Sects. 8.5 and 8.8].

As mentioned earlier, an MPI-based checkpoint-restart approach relies on BLCR. Unfortunately, BLCR does not support either of items 1 or 3 above. Case 2 is supported by the various checkpoint-restart services of different MPI implementations. But Case 2 is not directly supported by a checkpointing package itself.

A significant barrier to using the DMTCP checkpointing system was the inability of DMTCP to support large shared memory regions on systems that lack virtual memory. Typically, supercomputers do not support virtual memory. An important contribution of the current work is extending the design of DMTCP to support large shared memory regions in the absence of virtual memory (see Sect. 3). Typical OpenSHMEM implementations require this, due to their use of SysV shared memory objects.

One can also contrast the advantages and disadvantages of the current work with the prior checkpointing work of Hao et al. [15]. Hao et al. copy the shared memory region along with privately mapped memory to the RAM of a peer process during runtime. In doing so, they protect against a single computer node failure, an important failure mode to be considered in the future exascale generation. In contrast, the current work saves into stable storage (typically a Lustre filesystem, on a supercomputer) at checkpoint time. This has the advantage that the current work supports migration of an OpenSHMEM computation to a new cluster, as well as saving a computation for restart on the same cluster at a later time—for example, for long-running jobs on a batch system where the batch queue limits users to a maximum runtime slot of 24 h.

The current work is based on the reference implementation of OpenSHMEM, on top of the MVAPICH2 implementation of MPI. Thus, this work also relies on the ability of DMTCP to directly checkpoint MVAPICH2. (DMTCP treats MVAPICH2 like any other distributed application, and does not rely on any MPI-specific information.)

Finally, because DMTCP does not depend on any MPI implementation, the result of this work opens the way for future support for hybrid MPI+OpenSHMEM codes. For example, MVAPICH2-X [27] provides advanced MPI features and a unified high-performance runtime for both MPI and PGAS programming models on InfiniBand clusters. MVAPICH2-X used all optimized features for communications and memory resources on Infiniband Cluster provided by the MPI library MVAPICH2 [19,26] to improve the performance and scalability of communication on PGAS programming models [22,23]. MVAPICH2-X supports multiples PGAS models such as Unified Parallel C and UPC++ (based on Berkeley UPC 2.20.0), OpenSHMEM (based on the Open-SHMEM reference implementation 1.0h) and Coarray Fortran (CAF) (based on Houston CAF implementation 3.0.39).

The rest of this paper is organized as follows. Section 2 briefly reviews the internals of DMTCP. Section 3 describes the places in which DMTCP needed to be extended in order to support the features of OpenSHMEM in a user program. Section 4 presents the related work. Section 5 presents an experimental evaluation, which was executed on the Stampede supercomputer at the Texas Advanced Computing Center (TACC). Section 6 then offers a conclusion and the plans for future work.

2   Review of Checkpointing

The architecture of DMTCP is described in Fig. 1. A centralized DMTCP coordinator process accepts requests for checkpointing. Upon checkpoint, it sends a checkpoint message to a checkpoint thread within each user process. The checkponit thread "quiesces" the user threads, interrogates the kernel for state (e.g., open file descriptors and file offsets), and then copies the memory to a checkpoint image file. There is one checkpoint image file for each user process. See [2] for more details.

The original version of DMTCP supported only TCP-based sockets. Later, Cao et al. added support for checkpointing InfiniBand without the need to first disconnect an MPI computation from the network [8].

Two areas of novelty that are not reported elsewhere are the ability of DMTCP to checkpoint UNIX domain sockets and the ability to use leader election in order to checkpoint to correctly restore a single shared copy of a shared memory region, rather than restoring separate private memory regions on restart (one memory region for each process, or PE in the context of OpenSHMEM).

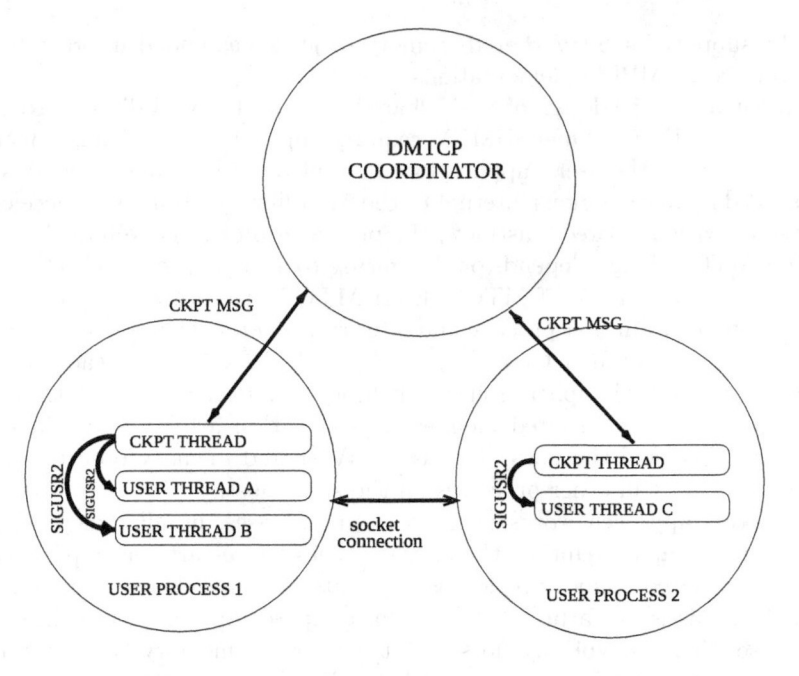

Fig. 1. The distributed architecture of DMTCP

3 Design Modification of DMTCP to Support OpenSHMEM

The design of DMTCP had to be extended in three areas in order to support both checkpointing of modern MPI implementations and checkpointing of Open-SHEM. The three areas are UNIX domain sockets, SysV shared memory objects, and InfiniBand. The addition of support for InfiniBand is reported elsewhere [8]. This work describes the design of the first two capabilities.

UNIX domain sockets. The original DMTCP design in 2009 [2] was sufficient to support the MPI implementations at that time. However, those earlier MPI implementations generally did not use UNIX domain sockets, and could be configured so as to avoid the use of shared memory regions for communication.

The design of support for UNIX domain sockets is similar to the TCP socket support reported in [2]. UNIX domain sockets allow one to pass a file descriptor from one process to another within the same Linux host. As with TCP sockets, one sends a "cookie" (a unique 64-bit value) through the UNIX domain socket. When the receiver reads it on the UNIX domain socket, it is known that there is no more data in the network.

SysV shared memory objects. Second, the DMTCP design was extended to support SysV shared memory objects. The original DMTCP design [2] supported only BSD-style shared memory regions (using mmap and "MAP_SHARED").

Recently, support for SysV shared memory objects was added in order to support more recent MPI implementations.

Unfortunately, the design of SysV shared memory for MPI did not extend to support OpenSHMEM. OpenSHMEM requires support for large shared memory regions created by the user's application. In contrast, MPI directly creates only small shared memory regions internal to the MPI library itself, as an accelerator for communication between distinct MPI processes on the same host.

The DMTCP design depends on delegating to a single-process checkpointing package, under the name of MTCP. Each MTCP instance saves *every* shared memory region within that process, and later restore *every* shared memory region on restart. It is only at a later stage that DMTCP employs a leader election strategy to: (i) discard duplicate shared memory regions not owned by the leader; (ii) embed the leader's shared memory region within a SysV shared memory object; and (iii) send the newly created SysV shared memory object from the leader's process to all other processes on the same host.

While this approach works in most common cases, it fails when for large shared-memory areas. During the initial stages of restart, each process has mapped the shared memory region as a private region. Where virtual memory is available, this is not a problem. But on a supercomputer such as Stampede in our case, there is typically no support for virtual memory. This is because virtual memory normally resides on a hard disk, and supercomputer compute nodes generally do not have any local disks. Paging to a remote storage node on a supercomputer would produce an unacceptable performance penalty.

In order to support checkpointing of SysV shared memory regions in the absence of virtual memory, an alternative strategy was created. *Every* shared memory region is created initially as a region of zero pages. In Linux, zero pages do not require significant resources, and are easily supported even in the absence of virtual memory.

At checkpoint time, the MTCP component continues to write individual copies of the shared memory region into the process-specific checkpoint image file. But at the time of restart, instead of reading back into RAM the data of the shared memory region, MTCP simply writes the filename of the checkpoint image file for that process, and the file offset and size of the shared memory region in question. This information is written only into the first page of shared memory, and the remaining region remains as zero pages.

Finally, the same leader election strategy can be used for restart as with the existing SysV shared memory support. But in this case, the leader does not have the shared memory data resident in RAM. Instead, the leader reads the shared memory data into RAM. Only at this late stage of restart, and after an appropriate host-wide barrier. All other processes wait while the leader reads the shared memory data. While this makes restart slower, this is generally acceptable, since checkpointing is the common operation, and restart is the rare operation.

OpenSHMEM and the hardware cache. One of the weaknesses of the current approach concerns the OpenSHMEM support for data cache control, i.e., "mechanisms to exploit the capabilities of hardware cache". This is *not* provided by

DMTCP since that requires operating system extensions either to POSIX or to common Linux systems mechanisms such as the proc filesystem. An alternative approach that directly supports the abstractions of the OpenSHMEM library, such as [15], has the potential to use the OpenSHMEM API to save and restore information about the capabilities of the hardware cache.

4   Related Work

The OpenSHMEM standard is described in [9,18]. Research in the area of Checkpoint-Restart for OpenSHMEM and other PGAS models is still sparse. In 2011, Ali et al. [1] proposed an application-specific fault tolerance mechanism. They achieved fault-tolerance using redundant communication and shadow copies. Hao et al. [15,16] have proposed a more generic approach based on User Level Fault Mitigation (ULFM) using shadow memory in which the shared memory regions of peers are backed up by peers. The user code is responsible for invoking a checkpoint and for restoring correct operation during a restart.

An important distinction between the approach of Hao et al. [15] and the current work is that Hao et al. copy the shared memory region along with privately mapped memory to a peer process during runtime. This places added pressure on the network fabric and on the RAM. (The latter is significant since supercomputers typically do not support virtual memory.) In the current work, the shared memory region and privately mapped memory are copied to stable storage (often a Lustre filesystem on a supercomputer). This places added pressure on the Lustre filesystem at the time of checkpoint. Thus, each strategy has its separate advantages and problems.

Of course, a second important distinction is that the approach of Hao et al. directly support User Level Fault Mitigation (ULFM), while the current work does not directly support such a strategy.

Multiple MPI libraries support SHMEM parallel programming model. Open MPI [12] supports OpenSHMEM since version 1.7.5. In [14], Hammond et al. introduced OSHMPI [13], another implementation of SHMEM over MPI taking advantages of MPI-3 one-sided communication. As DMTCP is doing a transparent checkpoint restart, all these MPI implementations can be checkpointed and restarted transparently.

Since some implementations of OpenSHMEM are built on top of MPI, it is important to also discuss approaches to checkpointing MPI. As described earlier, such approaches split into an application-specific and system-level approach. For application-level checkpointing of MPI one notes [6,7]. These packages provide hooks by which scientific applications on top of MPI can easily build their own checkpoint-restart routines. Such solutions add complexity at the petascale level, since they are not transparent to the end programmer.

For system-level checkpointing of OpenSHMEM, it would be tempting to employ an OpenSHMEM built on top of MPI, and then checkpoint the underlying MPI. Unfortunately, all of the checkpoint-restart services of current MPI implementations are built on top of BLCR [10,17]. BLCR does not support the SysV IPC objects. In particular, it does not support the POSIX-standard SysV shared memory (shm) objects [4].

Many MPI implementations provide a checkpoint-restart service based on BLCR. At the time of checkpoint, the MPI checkpoint-restart service detaches from the network, and then invokes BLCR as a single-process checkpointing utility for the individual processes. Among the MPI implementations using BLCR are OpenMPI [20], LAM/MPI [30], MPICH-V [5], and MVAPICH2 [11].

As stated above, BLCR does not support SysV shared memory objects. Hence, there is a problem if an OpenSHMEM implementation uses SysV shared memory objects (which is a common choice on a POSIX platform), and if the OpenSHMEM implementation is implemented on top of MPI. When a checkpoint is requested, the request will be passed to the checkpoint-restart service of the underlying MPI, which will delegate to BLCR. The BLCR FAQ states that "Such [SysV ipc] resources are silently ignored at checkpoint time and are not restored."

Finally, DMTCP (Distributed MultiThreaded CheckPointing) [2] provides checkpointing for general distributed computations, independently of MPI. There have also been at least three other checkpoint-restart systems that are independent of MPI and still able through Linux kernel modules to checkpoint distributed computations [21,24,25,31]. However, none of these latter three appear to be under active development, and so their details are not discussed here.

Even though DMTCP operates independently of MPI, the OpenSHMEM reference implementation being used does depend on MPI. For this reason, DMTCP is checkpointing both OpenSHMEM and the MVAPICH implementation of MPI in the experiments.

5   Experimental Evaluation

5.1   Experimental Setup

The experiments have been conducted on TACC's Stampede supercomputer. Stampede is currently the # 12 supercomputer on the top500 list [32] (as of June, 2016). Stampede contains 6400 dual-socket eight-core Sandy-Bridge E5-2680 server nodes with 32 GB of memory, called "compute nodes", and 16 quad-socket eight-core Sandy-Bridge E5-4650 server nodes at 2.7 GHz with 1 TB of memory, called "large memory nodes". The nodes are interconnected by Infini-Band HCAs in FDR mode [33] and the operating system used is CentOS 6.4 with Linux kernel 2.6.32-431.el6. Experiments use the Lustre parallel filesystem version 2.5.5 on Stampede.

To do this evaluation, we use the Intel compiler version 13.0.2.146 on Stampede with the OpenSHMEM library. See [23] for a comparison of different Open-SHMEM implementations on Stampede. For the evaluation, we use a port of the NAS Parallel Benchmarks (NPB) to OpenSHMEM [29]. The NAS Parallel Benchmarks for MPI are already well-documented and widely used as a benchmark [3,28,34]. It consists of a suite of parallel workloads designed to evaluate performance of various hardware and software components of a parallel computing system.

5.2 Scalability

For evaluating performance, we measure the runtime overhead, the checkpoint overhead, and the restart overhead as we scale up. The NAS BT and SP benchmarks were used to measure the scalability of DMTCP.

Table 1 shows the number of nodes used and the number of processes per node for a given number of processes (PE's). The same configuration was used for all the experiments.

Table 1. Distribution of processes among nodes

Num of PE's	Num of nodes	Processes per node
4	2	2
9	3	3
16	4	4
36	6	6
64	8	8
121	11	11
256	16	16

Figure 2 shows the runtime overhead imposed by DMTCP. The runtime overhead is less than 1% in all cases. DMTCP's wrapper functions impose a negligible runtime overhead and the cost is further amortized over the duration of the run.

For a given number of PE's, all the runs—with and without DMTCP—were conducted on the same set of nodes to reduce the variability due to network topology and traffic.

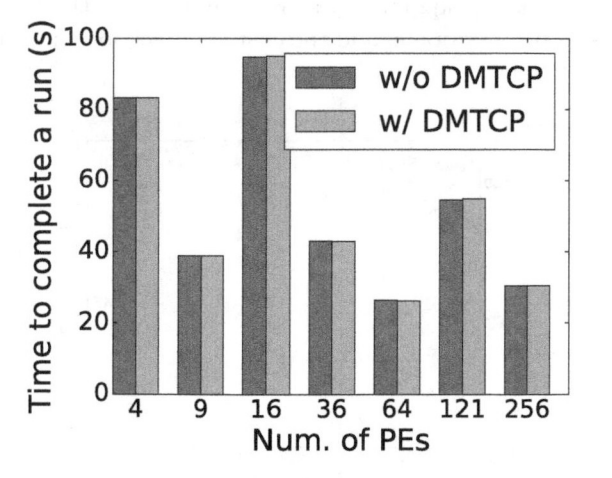

Fig. 2. Runtime overhead on OpenSHMEM NAS BT benchmark with DMTCP. BT class A was used for 4, and 9 PE's. BT class B was used for 16, 36, and 64 PE's. BT class C was used for the runs with 121 and higher PE's.

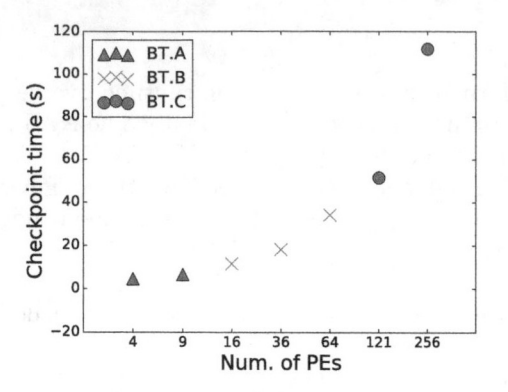

Fig. 3. Checkpoint times for OpenSHMEM NAS BT benchmark with DMTCP. BT class A was used for 4, and 9 PE's. BT class B was used for 16, 36, and 64 PE's. BT class C was used for the runs with 121 and higher PE's.

Average checkpoint times for the NAS BT benchmark are shown in Fig. 3. Five successive checkpoints were taken for a given number of processes on the same set of nodes.

Figure 4 shows the average checkpoint times for the NAS SP benchmark. Five successive checkpoints were taken for a given number of processes on the same set of nodes. The checkpoint times include the cost of synchronizing the state of distributed processes, including communications with the central checkpointing coordinator.

For both benchmarks, BT and SP, checkpoint times grow linearly with the total amount of checkpoint image data (see Figs. 5 and 6). At the largest scale, 256 processes, the total data written to the disk is 2.2 TB, with an effective bandwidth of 20 GB per second.

In all the cases, the checkpoint times are dominated by the time to write the checkpoint data to stable storage, and the cost for checkpointing the state of the application is negligible.

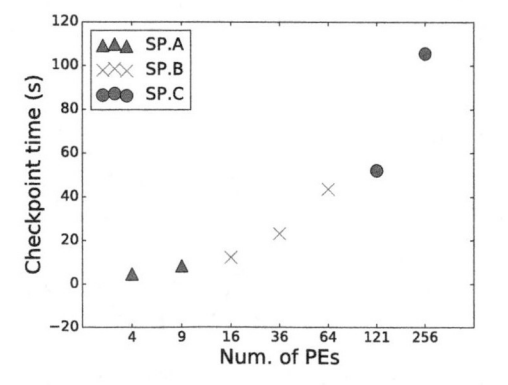

Fig. 4. Checkpoint times for OpenSHMEM NAS SP benchmark with DMTCP. SP class A was used for 4, and 9 PE's. SP class B was used for 16, 36, and 64 PE's. SP class C was used for the runs with 121 and higher PE's.

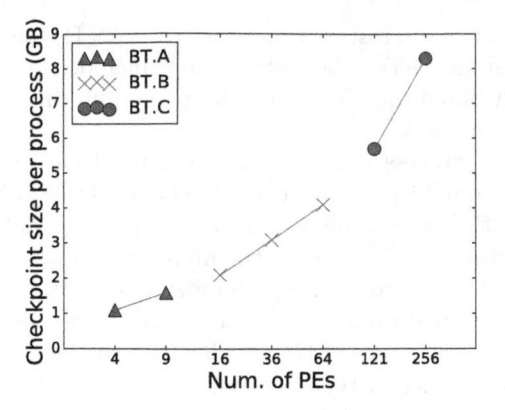

Fig. 5. Uncompressed checkpoint image sizes for OpenSHMEM NAS BT benchmark with DMTCP. BT class A was used for 4, and 9 PE's. BT class B was used for 16, 36, and 64 PE's. BT class C was used for the runs with 121 and higher PE's.

The checkpoint image sizes for a single process for NAS benchmarks BT and SP are shown in Figs. 5 and 6, respectively.

Note that the checkpoint image size is directly proportional to the number of processes sharing a computer node. For a given number of total processes, the number of processes sharing a node is shown in Table 1.

We observe that largest component, 90–97%, in a checkpoint image is an OpenSHMEM shared-memory region, which is used for intra-node communication. Each process on a node contributes roughly 0.5 GB to the shared-memory region. The rest of the checkpoint image contains process's private memory regions.

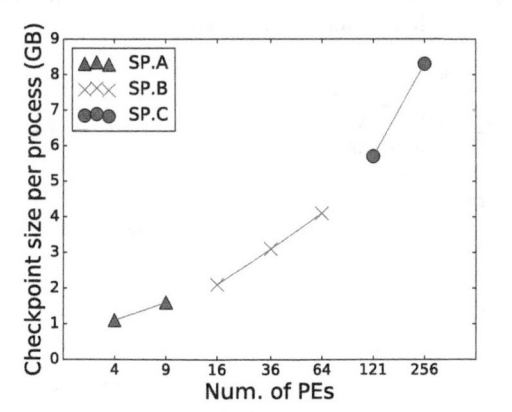

Fig. 6. Uncompressed checkpoint image sizes for OpenSHMEM NAS SP benchmark with DMTCP. SP class A was used for 4, and 9 PE's. SP class B was used for 16, 36, and 64 PE's. SP class C was used for the runs with 121 and higher PE's.

Figures 7 and 8 show the restart times for the NAS BT and SP benchmarks, respectively, at different scales. The restart times include the cost of synchronizing the state of distributed processes, including communications with the central checkpointing coordinator.

At the scale of 16 processes and beyond, the total memory footprint of the checkpoint images required per node exceeds the available RAM on each node, 32 GB, and hence, it's not possible to directly map in the data from the checkpoint image. On restart, while restoring the memory of a process, DMTCP identifies the OpenSHMEM shared-memory memory region in its checkpoint image, reads in rest of the private data in to the memory of the process, and finally maps in the shared-memory region as *MAP_SHARED* in to the process's memory.

The restart times are nearly twice as large compared to the checkpoint times. We speculate this is because while writing the checkpoint images, Lustre buffers

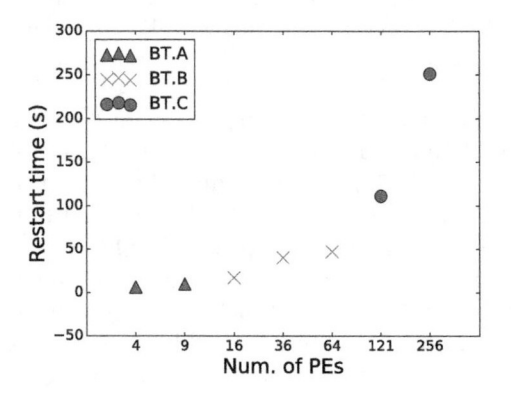

Fig. 7. Restart times for OpenSHMEM NAS BT benchmark with DMTCP. BT class A was used for 4, and 9 PE's. BT class B was used for 16, 36, and 64 PE's. BT class C was used for the runs with 121 and higher PE's.

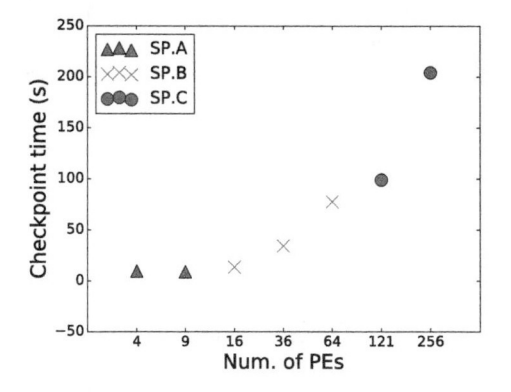

Fig. 8. Restart times for OpenSHMEM NAS SP benchmark with DMTCP. SP class A was used for 4, and 9 PE's. SP class B was used for 16, 36, and 64 PE's. SP class C was used for the runs with 121 and higher PE's.

the checkpoint data. On restart, any buffered data must first be synchronized to the disk, transferred to each node, and then read in to the memory of each process.

6   Conclusion and Future Work

A system-level approach to checkpointing OpenSHMEM was presented. This approach enables one to save the state of a computation to stable storage at checkpoint time. This contrasts with the previous approach of Hao et al., in which they save to the RAM of a remote peer computer. The latter approach supports fault tolerance in the case of a single host failing, and has the potential for a fast restart, since only one computer node must be restored. In contrast, the current approach has the capability of saving the state of an entire computation for restart at a later time on the same cluster, or else for migration to a new cluster.

The current work saves the state of the shared memory region of each process to stable storage. In this case (with 16 cores supporting 16 processes (16 PEs), this can potentially place a large burden on the Lustre filesytem by saving 16 identical copies of the shared memory regions on a single host, when executing at very large scale. While this was not observed to incur significant performance penalty at the medium scale of the current experiments, it is intended to employ a leader election strategy early (at checkpoint time) in a future implementation. In this way only one copy of each shared memory region will be saved on a single host. This will significantly reduce the time to write to back-end storage. (Note that current OpenSHMEM implementations do not appear to replicate shared memory regions across hots, and so deduplication on a single host is deemed to be sufficient for good performance.)

Acknowledgment. We would like to thank both Kapil Arya and Jiajun Cao for many useful discussions on the internals of DMTCP, and the design of those internal components. We also acknowledge the support of the Texas Advanced Computing Center (TACC) and the Extreme Science and Engineering Discovery Environment (XSEDE), which is supported by National Science Foundation grant number ACI-1053575.

References

1. Ali, N., Krishnamoorthy, S., Govind, N., Palmer, B.J.: A Redundant Communication Approach to Scalable Fault Tolerance in PGAS Programming Models. IEEE Computer Society, Los Alamitos (2011)
2. Ansel, J., Arya, K., Cooperman, G.: DMTCP: transparent checkpointing for cluster computations and the desktop. In: IEEE International Symposium on Parallel and Distributed Processing (IPDPS), pp. 1–12. IEEE Press (2009)
3. Bailey, D.H., Barszcz, E., Barton, J.T., Browning, D.S., Carter, R.L., Dagum, D., Fatoohi, R.A., Frederickson, P.O., Lasinski, T.A., Schreiber, R.S., Simon, H.D., Venkatakrishnan, V., Weeratunga, S.K.: The NAS parallel benchmarks. Intl. J. Supercomput. Appl. **5**(3), 63–73 (1991)

4. BLCR team: BLCR frequently asked questions (for version 0.8.5). https://upc-bugs.lbl.gov/blcr/doc/html/FAQ.html#limitations. Accessed June 2016

5. Bouteiler, A., Herault, T., Krawezik, G., Lemarinier, P., Cappello, F.: MPICH-V project: a multiprotocol automatic fault tolerant MPI. Int. J. High Perform. Comput. Appl. **20**, 319–333 (2006)

6. Bronevetsky, G., Marques, D., Pingali, K., Rugina, R., McKee, S.A.: Compiler-enhanced incremental checkpointing for OpenMP applications. In: Proceedings of IEEE International Parallel and Distributed Processing Symposium (IPDPS), May 2009

7. Bronevetsky, G., Marques, D., Pingali, K., Stodghill, P.: Automated application-level checkpointing of MPI programs. In: PPoPP 2003: Proceedings of the Ninth ACM SIGPLAN Symposium on Principles and Practice of Parallel Programming, NY, USA, pp. 84–94. ACM, New York (2003)

8. Cao, J., Kerr, G., Arya, K., Cooperman, G.: Transparent checkpoint-restart over InfiniBand. In: Proceedings of the 23rd International Symposium on High-performance Parallel and Distributed Computing, pp. 13–24. ACM Press (2014)

9. Chapman, B., Curtis, T., Pophale, S., Poole, S., Kuehn, J., Koelbel, C., Smith, L.: Introducing OpenSHMEM: SHMEM for the PGAS community. In: Proceedings of the Fourth Conference on Partitioned Global Address Space Programming Model, pp. 2:1–2:3, PGAS 2010, NY, USA. ACM, New York (2010)

10. Duell, J., Hargrove, P., Roman, E.: The design and implementation of Berkeley lab's Linux checkpoint/restart (BLCR). Technical report LBNL-54941, Lawrence Berkeley National Laboratory (2003)

11. Gao, Q., Yu, W., Huang, W., Panda, D.K.: Application-transparent checkpoint/restart for MPI programs over InfiniBand. In: ICPP 2006: Proceedings of the 2006 International Conference on Parallel Processing, pp. 471–478. IEEE Computer Society, Washington, DC (2006)

12. Graham, R.L., Woodall, T.S., Squyres, J.M.: Open MPI: a flexible high performance MPI. In: Proceedings of the 6th Annual International Conference on Parallel Processing and Applied Mathematics, Poznan, Poland, September 2005

13. Hammond, J.: OSHMPI (06 2016). https://github.com/jeffhammond/oshmpi

14. Hammond, J.R., Ghosh, S., Chapman, B.M.: Implementing OpenSHMEM using MPI-3 one-sided communication. In: Poole, S., Hernandez, O., Shamis, P. (eds.) OpenSHMEM 2014. LNCS, vol. 8356, pp. 44–58. Springer, Heidelberg (2014). doi:10.1007/978-3-319-05215-1_4

15. Hao, P., Pophale, S., Shamis, P., Curtis, T., Chapman, B.: Check-pointing approach for fault tolerance in OpenSHMEM. In: Gorentla Venkata, M., Shamis, P., Imam, N., Lopez, M.G. (eds.) OpenSHMEM 2014. LNCS, vol. 9397, pp. 36–52. Springer, Heidelberg (2015). doi:10.1007/978-3-319-26428-8_3

16. Hao, P., Shamis, P., Venkata, M.G., Pophale, S., Welch, A., Poole, S., Chapman, B.: Fault tolerance for OpenSHMEM. In: Proceedings of the 8th International Conference on Partitioned Global Address Space Programming Models, PGAS 2014, pp. 23:1–23:3 (2014)

17. Hargrove, P., Duell, J.: Berkeley lab checkpoint/restart (BLCR) for Linux clusters. J. Phys. Conf. Ser. **46**, 494–499 (2006)

18. High Performance Computing Tools Group at the University of Houston, Extreme Scale Systems Center, Oak Ridge National Laboratory: OpenSHMEM Application Programming interface (version 1.3). http://openshmem.org/site/sites/default/site_files/OpenSHMEM-1.3.pdf. Accessed June 2016

19. Huang, W., Santhanaraman, G., Jin, H., Gao, Q., Panda, D.: Design and Implementation of High Performance MVAPICH2: MPI2 Over InfiniBand, May 2007

20. Hursey, J., Squyres, J.M., Mattox, T.I., Lumsdain, A.: The design and implementation of checkpoint/restart process fault tolerance for open MPI. In: Proceedings of the 21st IEEE International Parallel and Distributed Processing Symposium (IPDPS)/12th IEEE Workshop on Dependable Parallel, Distributed and Network-Centric Systems. IEEE Computer Society, March 2007
21. Janakiraman, G., Santos, J., Subhraveti, D., Turner, Y.: Cruz: application-transparent distributed checkpoint-restart on standard operating systems. In: Dependable Systems and Networks (DSN 2005), pp. 260–269 (2005)
22. Jose, J., Hamidouche, K., Zhang, J., Venkatesh, A., Panda, D.: Optimizing collective communication in UPC, May 2014
23. Jose, J., Zhang, J., Venkatesh, A., Potluri, S., Panda, D.K.D.: A comprehensive performance evaluation of OpenSHMEM libraries on InfiniBand clusters. In: Poole, S., Hernandez, O., Shamis, P. (eds.) OpenSHMEM 2014. LNCS, vol. 8356, pp. 14–28. Springer, Heidelberg (2014). doi:10.1007/978-3-319-05215-1_2
24. Laadan, O., Nieh, J.: Transparent checkpoint-restart of multiple processes for commodity clusters. In: 2007 USENIX Annual Technical Conference, pp. 323–336 (2007)
25. Laadan, O., Phung, D., Nieh, J.: Transparent networked checkpoint-restart for commodity clusters. In: 2005 IEEE International Conference on Cluster Computing. IEEE Press (2005)
26. Laboratory, N.B.C.: MVAPICH2 (06 2016). http://mvapich.cse.ohio-state.edu/
27. Laboratory, N.B.C.: MVAPICH2-X (06 2016). http://mvapich.cse.ohio-state.edu/
28. NASA Advanced Supercomputing Division: NAS Parallel Benchmarks. http://www.nas.nasa.gov/publications/npb.html. Accessed Apr 2016
29. Pophale, S., Nanjegowda, R., Curtis, T., Chapman, B., Jin, H., Poole, S., Kuehn, J.: OpenSHMEM performance and potential: a NPB experimental study. In: The 6th Conference on Partitioned Global Address Space Programming Models (PGAS 2012). Citeseer (2012)
30. Sankaran, S., Squyres, J.M., Barrett, B., Sahay, V., Lumsdaine, A., Duell, J., Hargrove, P., Roman, E.: The LAM/MPI checkpoint/restart framework: system-initiated checkpointing. Int. J. High Perform. Comput. Appl. **19**(4), 479–493 (2005)
31. Sudakov, O.O., Meshcheriakov, I.S., Boyko, Y.V.: CHPOX: transparent checkpointing system for Linux clusters. In: IEEE International Workshop on Intelligent Data Acquisition and Advanced Computing Systems: Technology and Applications, pp. 159–164 (2007). software available at http://freshmeat.net/projects/chpox/
32. TOP500 supercomputer sites (Jun 2016). http://top500.org/list/2016/06/
33. Vienne, J., Chen, J., Wasi-Ur-Rahman, M., Islam, N.S., Subramoni, H., Panda, D.K.: Performance analysis and evaluation of InfiniBand FDR and 40GigE RoCE on HPC and cloud computing systems. In: Hot Interconnects, pp. 48–55 (2012)
34. Wong, F.C., Martin, R.P., Arpaci-Dusseau, R.H., Culler, D.E.: Architectural requirements and scalability of the NAS parallel benchmarks. In: Supercomputing (1999)

Surviving Errors with OpenSHMEM

Aurelien Bouteiller[1]([⊠]), George Bosilca[1], and Manjunath Gorentla Venkata[2]

[1] Innovative Computing Laboratory, University of Tennessee, Knoxville, USA
{bouteill,bosilca}@icl.utk.edu
[2] Oak Ridge National Laboratory, Oak Ridge, USA
manjugv@ornl.gov

Abstract. Unexpected error conditions stem from a variety of under-lying causes, including resource exhaustion, network failures, hardware failures, or program errors. As the scale of HPC systems continues to grow, so does the probability of encountering a condition that causes a failure; meanwhile, error recovery and run-through failure management are becoming mature, and interoperable HPC programming paradigms are beginning to feature advanced error management. As a result from these developments, it becomes increasingly desirable to gracefully handle error conditions in OpenSHMEM. In this paper, we present the design and rationale behind an extension of the OpenSHMEM API that can (1) notify user code of unexpected erroneous conditions, (2) permit customized user response to errors without incurring overhead on an error-free execution path, (3) propagate the occurence of an error condition to all Processing Elements, and (4) consistently close the erroneous epoch in order to resume the application.

1 Introduction

OpenSHMEM [21] is an emerging partitioned global address space (PGAS) specification that provides interfaces for one-sided and collective communication, synchronization, and atomic operations. The one-sided communication operations do not require the active participation of the target process when receiving or exposing data, freeing the target process to work on other tasks while the data transfer is ongoing. It also supports some collective communication patterns such as synchronizations, broadcast, collection, and reduction operations. In addition OpenSHMEM provides interfaces for a variety of atomic operations including

M.G. Venkata—This manuscript has been authored by UT-Battelle, LLC under Contract No. DE-AC05-00OR22725 with the U.S. Department of Energy. The United States Government retains and the publisher, by accepting the article for publication, acknowledges that the United States Government retains a non-exclusive, paid-up, irrevocable, world-wide license to publish or reproduce the published form of this manuscript, or allow others to do so, for United States Government purposes. The Department of Energy will provide public access to these results of federally sponsored research in accordance with the DOE Public Access Plan (http://energy.gov/downloads/doe-public-access-plan).

M. Gorentla Venkata et al. (Eds.): OpenSHMEM 2016, LNCS 10007, pp. 66–81, 2016.
DOI: 10.1007/978-3-319-50995-2_5

both 32-bit and 64-bit operations. Overall, it provides a rich set of interfaces for implementing parallel scientific applications, and OpenSHMEM implementations are expected to perform well on modern high performance computing (HPC) systems. This expectation stems from the design philosophy of OpenSH-MEM, which focus on providing a lightweight and high performing minimalistic set of operations, and a close match between the OpenSHMEM semantic and hardware-supported native operations. This tight integration between the hardware and the programming paradigm is expected to result in close to optimal latency and bandwidth in synthetic benchmarks, meanwhile preserving simple and powerful end-user semantics.

Despite this rich feature set, the OpenSHMEM specification has lacked error management and failure mitigation primitives. However, the complexity of High Perfomance Computing systems keeps increasing steadily along multiple axes. On one axis, heterogeneous computing, with accelerators, different instruction sets, and possibly multiple interoperable programming paradigms are becoming pervasive [13]. This proliferation of software levels within the same application increases the probability of hitting unforeseen interactions between the runtime libraries, leading, in the worse case, to more programming errors from the more numerous code paths, or to imperfect resource sharing between levels, hitherto more occurrences of runtime resource exhaustion errors. Along another axis, HPC is moving further toward massive parallelism, harnessing millions of processing cores, in commonly tens of thousand of nodes. As the number of components comprising HPC systems increases, probabilistic amplification entails that failures (*i.e.,* a system malfunction) are becoming common events in the lifecycle of an application. Currently deployed petascale machines experience approximately one crash failure every 10 h [22], a situation which is expected to worsen with the introduction of exascale systems in the near future [1,7,14]. Although some faillures may not be immediately visible (especially the so called *silent errors* that corrupt the application dataset without interrupting the computation), in many cases, failures (including a large number of memory corruptions) do manifest detectable behavior, either in the form of a process crash, a network disconnect, or as a memory corruption that can't be corrected by ECC.

As these failure vectors become more common, most HPC programming interfaces are being enriched to provide meaningful error reporting and mitigation strategies. For example, the Message Passing Interface (MPI) has long provided error reporting capabilities, and further semantics to tolerate process failures are under consideration [5]. In this paper we present a set of extensions to the OpenSHMEM specification that will enable capturing errors resulting from various unexpected runtime conditions, stabilize the state of the application—and thereby open the possibility for recovering from the condition, and possibly interoperate with another error managing middleware. Due to its one-sided nature, and the form in which synchronization are expressed, OpenSHMEM poses a specific set of constraints for resolving the global state generated by the occurence of unexpected errors at some PEs, which in turns calls for an original approach. The rest of this paper is organized as follows: Sect. 2 presents a succint view of the type of failures we address and the general benefits expected from their handling; Sect. 3 describes the limitations on error reporting scope and uniformity accross process to preserve latency sensitive operations' performance; Sect. 4 presents the OpenSHMEM API to capture errors; Sect. 5 discusses the need for, and the mean for, the error propagation mechanism; Sect. 6 presents the construct for stabilizing the post-error situation, and resuming communicating; Sect. 7 presents related work on fault tolerant communication libraries, and we conclude in Sect. 8.

2   Background

Error masking and automatic failure recovery are valuable properties in system designs. Indeed, they relieve end-users from the duress of managing erroneous cases, and abstract the system as a stable platform. Aside from component hardware technologies, like packet retransmission in network interfaces, and ECC memory, the main vessel for sustaining the abstraction of a stable platform has been Coordinated Checkpoint/Restart (CR), either at the application or at the system level. One of its strong features is that it can be implemented without the communication library providing a meaningful support for fault tolerance, or even error reporting. In exchange, the recovery strategy involves a coarse grain full restart of the application in the previously saved global state. However, models and analysis [7,14] indicate that the status-quo is not sustainable, and either CR must drastically improve (for example by deploying in-place checkpointing [3,19]), or alternative recovery strategies must be considered. The variety of prospective techniques is wide, and notably includes checkpoint-restart variations based on uncoordinated rollback recovery [9], replication [14], or algorithm based fault tolerance—where mathematical properties are leveraged to avoid checkpoints [12]. A common feature required by most of these advanced failure recovery strategies is that, unlike historical rollback recovery, the application continues to operate in-line and in-place, possibly only demanding the replacement of a limited number of processors. Furthermore, considering the general spectrum of causes that can trigger an error, not all errors are indicative of a catastrophic, or at least severe enough failure, as to justify a full, expensive restart of the platform. The first step to enable an alternative management of errors, or simply to enable scalable checkpointing, is to introduce a mean to report errors from the application's communication support environment.

Failures can be classified into four broad categories of increasing severity. Note that these failure classes do not necessarily map directly to a particular type of ailment; for example, both a memory corruption and an incorrect program can result in a crash failure, or, depending on runtime conditions, both may also produce a silent error, arguably a more severe outcome. In this section we discuss these failure classes' details, and how the OpenSHMEM error reporting system can help their management.

Resource Exhaustion: The first class, which generally is the easiest to circumvent, represents resource exhaustion errors, and other correctable conditions arising from temporary or maleable overload of capacities. In the general OpenSHMEM philosophy, these errors should generally be handled internally by the library itself, and never propagate to the end-user. However, in some cases, the automatic, internal circumvention of an error is not possible. A program that tries to allocate a large amount of symmetric memory is a simple example. On some architectures, the memory that can be exposed for direct one-sided operations is smaller than the general memory capacity. Should a program require more than the available capacity, a potential corrective action could be to move the least used dataset from a symmetric memory segment to some non-registered memory. However, the OpenSHMEM implementation does not hold enough information about the intent of the application to safely undergo such an action: other Processing Elements (PEs, which is the name for an OpenSHMEM process) may initiate one-sided operations targeting these segments, and it would be unsafe to displace them. As a consequence, an implementation may be forced to report that the symmetric memory is exhausted, and delegate remediation actions to the user's program. These actions could range from operating with a smaller dataset when the algorithm is amenable to such an outcome, or moving some least used symmetric memory to non-symmetric memory explicitly, or continuing with an alternative interoperable communication library to complete the program successfully, albeit with reduced performance.

Crash Failures: The second class captures simple crash failures. A crash failure is characterized by the fact that some PEs stop being responsive definitively, that is, they no longer emit messages. Aside from obvious power supply failures, multiple vectors (including failures of network cables, bit-flips that raise signals, etc.) can ultimately manifest as a PE exhibiting a crash failure. Crash failure detection in distributed systems is a well studied domain [10], with practical solutions [6], outside the scope of the present work. One may note, however, that in a distributed system, surveillance of every process by every process can generate a significant amount of noise, which in turn cause a significant performance degradation [20]. Meanwhile, performing periodic failure resilient consensus to agree upon a set of failed processes is expensive. As a consequence, in practice, failures are detected opportunistically, and a PE may know, at any instant, of only a subset of the full set of failed PEs (as could be observed from an omniscient observer). A desired property with respect to an OpenSHMEM implementation is that it should be free of deadlocks, even when some PE fails, which means that OpenSHMEM operations trigger an appropriate error when PE failures are detected.

Network Failures: The third class is network failures and intermittent failures. These failures manifest when network links and processors are slow, when link failures result in partial disconnection of the network (that is, a PE may appear nonresponsive to some neighbors, but responsive to others), or when network messages are lost. Traditionally, message losses and retransmission are easily managed internally by the HPC communication library, and are seldom reported to the end-user. Partial disconnect of the network is a very difficult condition to correct or even diagnose (for a particular PE, it may appear as if some other alive PE has been the victim of a crash failure). Possible resolutions involve routing around the problematic links, or promoting the link failure to a crash failure of the non-reachable processes. Even when the OpenSHMEM library resolves a link failure internally with rerouting, the potential for a severe reduction in performance motivates reporting an error to the application, to interrupt the normal execution flow and inform the user about the condition. Given supplementary introspection capabilities of the network topology, a maleable application may choose to adjust its communication pattern to match the new network capacity, or abort orderly if it is not maleable or when the performance loss is deemed too severe.

Corruption Failures: The last class of failures are referred to as byzantine failures. In this class of failures, affected processes may behave erratically, including malicious and intentionally disruptive behavior [18]. Although this class is generally intractable in asynchronous distributed systems, given reasonable assumptions about the type of erratic behavior, for example limited to dataset (not program) corruption [15], a variety of detection and mitigation strategies can be deployed. Beyond the protection provided by ECC memory, the detection of a silent error, and often the correction strategies are highly algorithm and/or dataset dependent [4, 11] and cannot be detected or managed by the OpenSHMEM library. However, it may be desirable for an application detecting such an erroneous condition to receive support from the OpenSHMEM library in order to trigger a "recovery action" with other PEs.

3   Scope and Locality of Error Reporting

3.1   Local Versus Global Error Reporting

First, as we have discussed above, many of the failure classes that are the root cause for reporting errors are local to a PE, or are detected locally by some PE. Meanwhile other PEs have no chance to even observe the erroneous behavior. In a limited number of cases, *e.g.,* for some resource exhaustion errors, the PE triggering the error may be able to correct the error independently. There is therefore no strong case for alerting other PEs of the condition, as it will soon be corrected without their involvement, or knowledge. In many cases, however, some failures have to be reported at multiple, potentially all, PEs. In the case of a collective synchronization operation, for example, when a crash failure happens at a PE before it enters the operation, other PEs cannot possibly synchronize, and will have to report an error. The one-sided nature of many OpenSHMEM operations can also force reporting a failure at multiple PEs, without a direct mapping between the failed PE and which PEs have to report the error. Consider the case described in the left of Fig. 1, where P_1 issues a `shmem_wait` operation. This operation blocks until the remote updates performed from remote PEs toggle a conditional statement on the value. The origin PE (or PEs) that perform the remote updates are not specified by the operation. Consequently, if a process crash failure happens, the communication library cannot infer if one

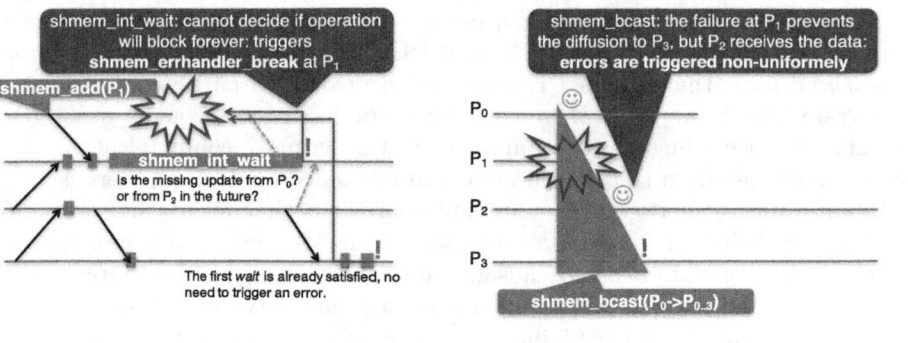

Fig. 1. Scope and uniformity semantics for error reporting. On the left, errors are reported locally, only for operations that are at risk of blocking indefinitely. On the right, a failure results in non-uniform errors: some PEs complete the broadcast, unaware that other PEs have triggered an error during the same collective communication.

of the failed PEs (here P_0) was supposed to perform the needed update, or if another PE (for example P_2) is soon going to post the update. In order to avoid leaving the target PE blocking in the posted shmem_wait operation indefinitely, the OpenSHMEM library has to report an error, ending that operation. However, other PEs may be able to satisfy all their blocking operations independently, and an error may be delayed until an operation would block. An advantage of this approach is that PEs that do not need to block (the second shmem_wait at P_3, for which the update has already happened) can spare the cost of checking for errors in the performance critical, non-erroneous execution path, unless an operation effectively blocks.

The general semantic is that error reporting is local, mandated to happen only at PEs whose completion of a blocking operation is rendered impossible by a failure (possibly multiple PEs, if they had issued a collective operations or shmem_wait operations), and is by default not propagated. However, we observe a dichotomy in use-cases. Some errors, for example resource exhaustion and some *soft* failures, can be easily corrected locally, and the local reporting permits maximal performance in that case. Some errors demand a collective correction action, and the proposed OpenSHMEM interface needs the capability to report errors both locally or globally. We will further discuss how global reporting can be triggered in Sect. 5.

3.2 Non-uniform Error Reporting

Conserving a strongly consistent global state, even after an error has been reported, is a very natural desire for application programmers. In a distributed system, providing such a strong semantic is unfortunately rife with multiple caveats. Even considering that some errors may trigger on a global scope, at all PEs, performance considerations still discourage providing uniform error reporting.

First, let's further define what it means for an error to be uniformly reported. An error is uniformly reported when all PEs get the notification of the error *at the same time*, that is, if a PE observes an error at a particular point in the program life, it can infer when a similar error has been triggered at target or origin PEs according to the Lamport causal ordering of communication operations in the program [17]. In collective and two-sided operations, there is a clear semantic linkage between the matching operations that form a line where one can easily define what uniform reporting means. In one-sided communication, such a clear operation based causality line is absent from the source code at the target, but one can still define a semantic line between the operation that failed at the origin, and the failure for the specified behavior to manifest at the target (*i.e.*, an origin performs an shmem_add, but the value is not updated at the target due to a failure of some sort).

Second, let's observe the performance implications of uniform reporting on OpenSHMEM operations. Consider, for example, the case of reporting errors during a shmem_bcast, as illustrated on the right of Fig. 1. When the operation completes at a non-root PE, the shmem_bcast specification states that the destination array contains the broadcast values. However, it does not give any information about the state of the completion of the broadcast at other PEs (it actually explicitly forewarns that reusing the Psync argument in another call may require a separate, explicit synchronization). In essence, the cost of the broadcast operation does not include the cost of synchronizing. In many implementations, a broadcast will leverage the relaxed semantic to optimize the operation with a tree topology. In such an implementation, the broadcast is complete at PEs high in the tree (that is, closest to the root) long before the broadcast completes at leaf PEs. Without further modification, this can result in potentially non-uniform triggering of errors, with some PEs reporting that the operation succeeded while other PEs report that it failed. With the added requirement that any error reported at a leaf PE must be consistently observed as an error reported at all other PEs, the overall cost of the broadcast then increases. The operation becomes semantically equivalent to an all-to-all operation (where each process contributes with the error code value), whose minimal cost is that of an AllReduce. That cost is present even when there is no error to report. Furthermore, if a PE fails *during* a synchronizing operation (that is, after it started contributing to the collective call), the failed PE could have passed its contribution to only a subset of its neighbors (in the topology used internally by the library). If the remaining PEs have to report uniformly that the operation has failed, the synchronization has to operate between non-failed PEs to agree, in a fault tolerant fashion, what the operation should report at all PEs. In practice, a fault tolerant synchronization (an agreement on a single value) can be twice as expensive as an AllReduce [16].

Similar to the case of collective operations, a strong mandate for reporting errors at the origin for any violation of the semantic at the target requires synchronizing all one-sided operations. The difference between the shmem_fadd and shmem_add operations is a prime exhibit of the cost of this implicit synchronization with the target. The former returns the result of the operation at the origin, while the later does not, henceforth sparing the semantic synchronization with the target. These two operations have been separated, because the addition of this synchronization semantic has a salient impact on injection rate and latency performance of one-sided operations.

For these reasons, uniform error reporting is not required from OpenSHMEM operations. Instead, users are provided with additional interface to resynchronize PEs after an error has been reported. We will see in Sect. 6 how additional OpenSHMEM interfaces can help users in creating error handling epochs that ensure a clear discrimination between errors arising before and after the epoch starts.

4   Error Reporting Interface

In this section, we present the interface that embraces the principles exposed above, with some discussion about alternative software engineering designs that have been considered but rejected.

Error Handlers. Most OpenSHMEM operations may report errors. Errors can originate from invalid arguments being passed to OpenSHMEM operations, or from unexpected runtime conditions such as a processor or a network link failure, resource exhaustion, etc. Errors are reported by the invocation of the *error handler* associated with the error code (Fig. 2 presents a list of error handler management functions). The default error handler is set to **shmem_errhandler_gexit**, a predefined error handler that calls *shmem_global_exit*, thereby ending the entire application. This behavior is consistent with expectations of non error-managing OpenSHMEM applications. A program that manages errors should set an appropriate error handler, using the **shmem_errhandler_set** function, for each error code it can handle (or for all errors when using the special error code **SHMEM_ERR_ALL**). The error handler can be set with a predefined error handler (see Table 1 for the full list), or with an user provided function that receives the error code as input. Setting an error handler is a local operation, and each PE may set a different error handler for the same error code.

```
1   typedef void (*shmem_errhandler_cb_fn)(int errcode, void* user_params);
2
3   void shmem_errhandler_set(
4     int errcode,                       /* IN: the managed error type */
5     shmem_errhandler_cb_fn errh,       /* IN: the error handling function */
6     void* user_params);                /* IN: an user parameter to the callback */
7
8   void shmem_errhandler_get(
9     int errcode,                       /* IN: the managed error type */
10    shmem_errhandler_cb_fn errh,       /* OUT: the currently set error handler */
11    void* user_params);                /* OUT: the currently set user parameter */
```

Fig. 2. C Interfaces to manage error handlers in OpenSHMEM.

Table 1. List of predefined error handlers in OpenSHMEM.

shmem_errhandler_gexit	The error handler calls *shmem_global_exit* with the error code as parameter, which effectively terminates the application. This is the default error handler
shmem_errhandler_break	The error handler breaks from blocking OpenSHMEM operations at the PE. It has no effect at other PEs
shmem_errhandler_gbreak	The error handler breaks from blocking OpenSHMEM operations at all PEs

Rationale: During the design phase of the interface, alternative approaches where considered. Using return codes from OpenSHMEM functions would require to add a non-void return from most of the API functions. However, some operations, like **shmem_fadd**, already return a semantically important value from the function (the value of the target variable at the remote PE), which would have rendered that API change non-backward compatible. Another alternative, the use of a global **shmem_errno** value, was also considered. But this approach would entail difficulties for thread-safe operations in multithreaded programs. In addition, a programming style where the user has to check errors after all OpenSHMEM library calls was deemed to impose a high productivity tax on users, and for all these reasons, a reactive approach based on error handling callbacks has been preferred.

When an Error Handler Triggers. Implementations are encouraged to report the occurence of failures by triggering the local error handler function, with an appropriate error code, and strive not to leave any PE blocking in an operation disrupted by a failure. However, depending on the severity of the failure, it may not always be possible to do so (for example, in the case of a byzantine failure). Passing invalid arguments to OpenSHMEM operations generally results in undefined behavior; however, a debugging version of an OpenSHMEM implementation may check for invalid arguments and report errors.

When a user-provided error handler function returns, it has the same effect as if it had called **shmem_errhandler_break** as its last statement, that is, it interrupts ongoing OpenSHMEM communication blocking calls at the local PE. After an error handler has been triggered, OpenSHMEM communication operations do not block, and possibly do not respect their specification. That is, a synchronizing operation may return before synchronizing, or the data objects could be partially or incorrectly updated. Implicit non-blocking operations originating at the PE are also interrupted. It should also be noted that, due to the one-sided nature of OpenSHMEM operations, when an error is reported at an origin PE, incorrect behavior may also be observed at the target PEs without that PE reporting an error. It is possible to force an error to be reported at all PEs by calling the predefined error handler **shmem_errhandler_gbreak**, described in Sect. 5.

After an error has been reported, communicating with the OpenSHMEM library may not be possible. However, the memory allocated for symmetric data objects remains available at the local PE, giving the application a chance to verify the correctness of the data, take checkpoints before exiting, or continue using a resilient communication library. Operations that restore the communication capability of the OpenSHMEM library are described in Sect. 6.

Stacking of Error Handlers. The user may call an error handler at any time, as a normal C function (including the predefined error handlers). In particular, a user defined error handler function can call another error handler function. In order to call the currently set error handler, a user can obtain the error handler and its parameter with **shmem_errhandler_get**, and can then call that error handler directly, or set the error handler with its own, and chain the call from within the replacement error handler. Similar interfaces are provided for Fortran, with the addition of an interface to call an error handler function.

Thread Safety. Although OpenSHMEM does not have complete definitions regarding thread safe operations at this point, we envision the following behavior with regard to error handler invocation in multithreaded programs. The error handler would be invoked once per PE. After the error handler would have been invoked, operation blocking at any thread of the PE would break. The apparent ordering of concurrent operations and error handler invocation would be implementation dependent.

5   Error Propagation

After an error has been reported to a particular PE, that PE may choose, or be constrained to stop performing operations and updates from the error free execution path. If the communication pattern is complex, the occurrence of failures can deeply disturb the application and, with only local error reporting, could prevent an effective recovery from being implemented. Consider the example in Fig. 3: as long as no failure occurs, the processes are following a communication pattern called *plan A*. PE P_0 does a **shmem_put** on a value at P_1. P_1 is blocking in a **shmem_wait** until that update from P_0 is made, then combines the result of the updated value with a local state, and broadcast that value to all other PEs, except for P_0.

Let's observe the effect of introducing a crash failure in *plan A*, and consider that P_0 has failed. As only P_1 blocks in an operation that could originate at P_0, other processes do not have to detect this condition, and only P_1 is guaranteed to have the failure of P_0 reported, as it issued a **shmem_wait** operation. The situation at P_1 now raises a dilemma: $P_{1..N}$ wait on the contribution of P_1 to the **shmem_bcast**. As all processes participating in the broadcast are alive (P_1 being a non-failed process), the operation may block until the matching **shmem_bcast** is posted at P_1. However, P_1 knows that P_0 has failed, and that the application

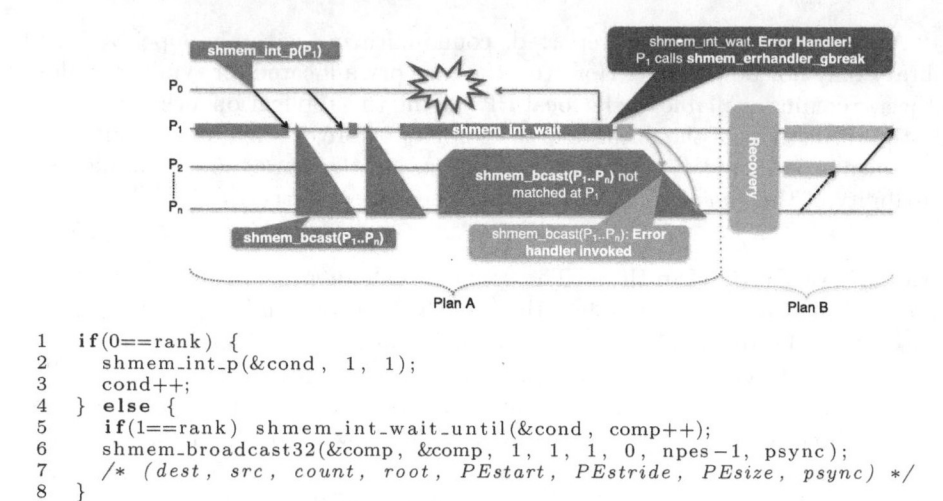

Plan A   Plan B

```
1    if (0==rank ) {
2       shmem_int_p(&cond ,  1,  1);
3       cond++;
4    } else {
5       if (1==rank )  shmem_int_wait_until (&cond ,  comp++);
6       shmem_broadcast32(&comp ,  &comp ,  1,  1,  1,  0,  npes −1,  psync );
7       /* (dest ,  src ,  count ,  root ,  PEstart ,  PEstride ,  PEsize ,  psync) */
8    }
```

Fig. 3. The transitive communication pattern *plan A*, from the source code, must be interrupted before the PEs can switch to the recovery communication pattern *plan B*. By calling the **shmem_errhandler_gbreak** error handler, P_1 ensures that all possibly unmatched operations in *plan A*, which could provoke deadlocks, are interrupted.

should branch into its recovery procedure *plan B*; if P_0 were to switch abruptly to *plan B*, it would cease matching the broadcast $P_{1..N}$ posted, following *plan A*. At this point, P_1 needs an effective way of interrupting operations that it does not intend to match anymore, otherwise, the application would reach a deadlock.

The proposed solution to resolve this scenario is that, before switching to *plan B*, the user code in P_1 sets the error handler to **shmem_errhandler_gbreak**, or explicitly calls **shmem_errhandler_gbreak** from within the user supplied error handler. The invocation of the predefined **shmem_errhandler_gbreak** error handler at any PE forces the invocation of the locally set error handler, with the same error code, at all PEs. As a consequence, communication operations do not block anymore and the OpenSHMEM library returns control to the user at all PEs, thereby solving potential transitive dependence deadlocks.

Implementation Challenges: An implementation has to be able to process the reception of a **shmem_errhandler_gbreak** notification. Some implementations use an asynchronous state machine to manage communication calls, and in these implementations, receiving the notification and interrupting ongoing operations is relatively simple. For implementation that employ blocking transport calls, different options are available. The implementation may employ a service thread to poll for **shmem_errhandler_gbreak** notifications and externally cancel blocking transport calls, or it may employ timeouts to interrupt blocking transport calls when their duration is excessive, and poll for notification only in this case. Ideally, polling for notification should be a low priority task, and the specification permits delaying error notification after any latency and injection rate critical operations have completed.

As this operation aims at managing error cases, it has to itself tolerate the failures it reports. As such, this operation is not interrupted by normal errors. In particular, in an OpenSHMEM implementation that can tolerate crash failures, it has to perform a reliable broadcast to all surviving PEs. Fortunately, efficient implementations of a similar operation in fault-tolerant MPI exist (`MPI_Comm_revoke`), and have been demonstrated to be scalable [8].

6 Post-error Stabilization

At this point, the proposed interfaces have permitted reporting errors for locally observed failures, propagating these errors to all PEs in order to interrupt the code flow and regroup in a recovery procedure, but these interfaces have not permitted resuming OpenSHMEM communication after an error handler has been invoked.

One of the difficult points in resuming communication is determining that all PEs are aware of the same set of erroneous conditions. As described in Sect. 3.2, some errors may have been reported only at some PEs. Even when these PEs have triggered a global propagation with `shmem_errhandler_gbreak`, the notification of these propagated errors have communication delays, and may be observed at different causal times at different PEs. In order to stabilize the state of the application, the user needs to have an operation that (1) drains pending error notifications and ensures that the propagation of `shmem_errhandler_gbreak` notifications have completed, and (2) restores the communication capabilities between a globally agreed upon set of PEs that report a good health state.

The `shmem_error_barrier_all` provides these two capabilities in OpenSHMEM. It is a collective operation that provides a fault tolerant barrier between all non-failed PEs, which quiets all communications, and enforces that `shmem_errhandler_gbreak` propagation have completed. If, at a PE, the invocation of the `shmem_errhandler_gbreak` error handler precedes the call to the `shmem_error_barrier_all`, then, the local error handler is invoked at all PEs before the call completes. The error handler may be invoked from within the `shmem_error_barrier_all` without interrupting the operation, and it is the users' responsibility to ensure that the error handler does not call recursively `shmem_error_barrier_all`. The `shmem_error_barrier_all` operation completes in the presence of the failure types the OpenSHMEM implementation can tolerate, that is, the operation will block until an agreement is made that all the necessary error handlers have been invoked, and that the status of failed PEs has been agreed upon.

When the `shmem_error_barrier_all` operation completes, the status of PEs can be queried with the new local operation `shmem_error_query`, which, for the same PE argument, returns the same error status at all querying PEs. If a PE continues to be in a failed state, a query of its status returns the error code representing the type of failure preventing the PE from continued participation in OpenSHMEM, or the special status 0 when the PE is capable of resuming communication with OpenSHMEM. Note that the status of a process changes only when `shmem_error_barrier_all` is called. A PE may query its own status, which may report that it cannot use OpenSHMEM anymore. In this case, the PE may initiate an orderly termination for itself, take checkpoints, or resort to an alternate communication library (such as MPI) to continue the parallel application.

Communications targeting a PE in error status trigger an error at the origin. Collective operations are collective over the subset of PEs that do not have an error status. PE ranks, the size of the pSync array, and offsets in data buffers remain unchanged. The content of the source and destination buffers that would have been sent or received from a PE in error status is unused.

7   Related Work

Fault tolerance and error reporting in communication middleware has a long history. The UNIX Socket interface is notably resilient to many failure types, and has the ability to report errors to endpoints on a socket. One of the main differences, which simplifies greatly the problem, is that sockets are bidirectional connected streams between two participants. In HPC communication libraries, managing an error not only means that the two endpoints of a failed stream are informed, but that mechanisms are in place to unblock all processes of the application that may risk blocking in multipartite communication operations, and globally establish a recoverable application state. Also, performance consideration are more stringent, as zero-copy and one-sided operations leave little opportunity to hide the cost of failure detection activities.

MPI faces many of the same distributed system challenges as OpenSHMEM, and has long provided the capacity of reporting errors. Efforts to define in the standard a recoverable state after MPI errors is however fairly recent, considering mostly crash-failures [5]. In two-sided MPI operations the participants to the operation are usually well specified (receives from named sources, etc.), which has permitted the fault tolerance specification to strictly scope which communication operations are interrupted when an error is reported. As a consequence, resilience extension in MPI are very operation centric and provide only explicit error reporting propagation. In contrast, the OpenSHMEM interface observes that many 1-sided operations do not specify clearly the origin, henceforth OpenSHMEM provides both explicit and implicit error propagation.

GASPI [23] is another PGAS communication library which features error management capabilities. Unlike in OpenSHMEM, all operations in GASPI have a timeout, after which they stop blocking (even when the operation has not completed). GASPI then provides explicit failure detection and observation routines to detect crash failures. In contrast, this fine grain handling is internal to the OpenSHMEM library, which returns from blocking operations only when the implementation has observed that a failure (not necessarily limited to a crash-failure) may result in the operation blocking indefinitely, therefore simplifying the error management code.

Global View Resilience (GVR) [24] is a PGAS programming model that provides resilience to failures (bit flips, crash, etc.) with a resilient storage of multiple versions of the dataset. Distributed array can be streamed concurrently, and independently to the resilient storage, which keeps an history of multiple versions. Callbacks permit reconstructing damaged dataset when applicable. The extensions proposed in OpenSHMEM are orthogonal to the advanced abstraction of checkpointing proposed in GVR, which may benefit from resilience capabilities in OpenSHMEM to accelerate its own communications.

8 Conclusions and Future Work

In this work, we explore the addition of error semantics to the OpenSHMEM specification, and how one can leverage these constructs to recover from unexpected runtime errors and resource failures. The proposed interface is carefully crafted to preserve performance, avoiding the pitfalls of uniform or global error reporting. Instead, end-users are provided with the means to express their preference regarding the scope of reporting (global or local), and can restore the consistency of the application's global state after an error has been reported, by employing an easy to understand error barrier construct.

Overall, the designs makes OpenSHMEM capable of managing many failure vectors and resource exhaustion conditions by deferring the ultimate recovery action to the end-user, which can then try to stabilize the application and resume OpenSHMEM operations, or may fallback to an alternative interoperable communication interface to complete the application in a degraded mode.

At this point, the interface does not support spawning replacement PEs in stead of PEs in an unrecoverable state (wether they have encountered a hardware or crash failure, or a non-crash failure has rendered the state of the software stack unsafe to recover from). Many applications are not malleable, and require a fixed number of PEs. Thus, future works should explore extensions to this interface that permit replacing the failed processes, or, as an alternative, cooperate with an external mechanism (such as PMIx [2], or a fault tolerant MPI [5], etc.) to spawn the needed replacement PEs.

References

1. Amarasinghe, S., et al.: Exascale programming challenges. In: Proceedings of the Workshop on Exascale Programming Challenges, Marina del Rey, CA, USA. U.S Department of Energy, Office of Science, Office of Advanced Scientific Computing Research (ASCR), July 2011. http://science.energy.gov/~/media/ascr/pdf/program-documents/docs/ProgrammingChallengesWorkshopReport.pdf

2. Balaji, P., Buntinas, D., Goodell, D., Gropp, W., Krishna, J., Lusk, E., Thakur, R.: PMI: a scalable parallel process-management interface for extreme-scale systems. In: Keller, R., Gabriel, E., Resch, M., Dongarra, J. (eds.) EuroMPI 2010. LNCS, vol. 6305, pp. 31–41. Springer, Heidelberg (2010). doi:10.1007/978-3-642-15646-5_4. http://dl.acm.org/citation.cfm?id=1894122.1894127

3. Bautista-Gomez, L., Tsuboi, S., Komatitsch, D., Cappello, F., Maruyama, N., Matsuoka, S.: FTI: high performance fault tolerance interface for hybrid systems. In: International Conference on High Performance Computing, Networking, Storage and Analysis, SC 2011 (2011)

4. Benoit, A., Cavelan, A., Robert, Y., Sun, H.: Assessing general-purpose algorithms to cope with fail-stop and silent errors. In: Jarvis, S.A., Wright, S.A., Hammond, S.D. (eds.) PMBS 2014. LNCS, vol. 8966, pp. 215–236. Springer, Heidelberg (2015). doi:10.1007/978-3-319-17248-4_11

5. Bland, W., Bouteiller, A., Herault, T., Bosilca, G., Dongarra, J.: Post-failure recovery of MPI communication capability: design and rationale. Int. J. High Perform. Comput. Appl. **27**(3), 244–254 (2013). http://hpc.sagepub.com/content/27/3/244.abstract

6. Bosilca, G., Bouteiller, A., Guermouche, A., Herault, T., Sens, P., Robert, Y., Dongarra, J.J.: Failure detection and propagation in HPC systems. In: Proceedings of the International Conference for High Performance Computing, Networking, Storage and Analysis, SC 2016. ACM, New York (2016, to appear)

7. Bosilca, G., Bouteiller, A., Brunet, E., Cappello, F., Dongarra, J., Guermouche, A., Herault, T., Robert, Y., Vivien, F., Zaidouni, D.: Unified model for assessing checkpointing protocols at extreme-scale. Concur. Comput. Pract. Exp. **26**(17), 2772–2791 (2014). doi:10.1002/cpe.3173

8. Bouteiller, A., Bosilca, G., Dongarra, J.J.: Plan B: Interruption of ongoing MPI operations to support failure recovery. In: Proceedings of the 22nd European MPI Users' Group Meeting, EuroMPI 2015, pp. 11:1–11:9 (2015). http://doi.acm.org/10.1145/2802658.2802668

9. Bouteiller, A., Herault, T., Bosilca, G., Dongarra, J.J.: Correlated set coordination in fault tolerant message logging protocols for many-core clusters. Concur. Comput. Pract. Exp. **25**(4), 572–585 (2013). doi:10.1002/cpe.2859

10. Chandra, T.D., Toueg, S.: Unreliable failure detectors for reliable distributed systems. J. ACM (JACM) **43**(2), 225–267 (1996)

11. Chen, Z.: Online-ABFT: an online algorithm based fault tolerance scheme for soft error detection in iterative methods. In: Proceedings of the PPoPP, pp. 167–176 (2013)

12. Davies, T., Karlsson, C., Liu, H., Ding, C., Chen, Z.: High performance linpack benchmark: a fault tolerant implementation without checkpointing. In: Proceedings of the 25th ACM International Conference on Supercomputing (ICS 2011). ACM (2011)

13. Dongarra, J., et al.: The international exascale software project roadmap. Int. J. High Perform. Comput. Appl. **25**(1), 3–60 (2011). doi:10.1177/1094342010391989

14. Ferreira, K., Stearley, J., Laros III, J.H., Oldfield, R., Pedretti, K., Brightwell, R., Riesen, R., Bridges, P.G., Arnold, D.: Evaluating the viability of process replication reliability for exascale systems. In: Proceedings of 2011 International Conference for High Performance Computing, Networking, Storage and Analysis, SC 2011, pp. 44:1–44:12. ACM, New York (2011). http://doi.acm.org/10.1145/2063384.2063443

15. Fiala, D., Mueller, F., Engelmann, C., Riesen, R., Ferreira, K., Brightwell, R.: Detection and correction of silent data corruption for large-scale high-performance computing. In: Proceedings of the SC 2012, p. 78 (2012)

16. Herault, T., Bouteiller, A., Bosilca, G., Gamell, M., Teranishi, K., Parashar, M., Dongarra, J.: Practical scalable consensus for pseudo-synchronous distributed systems. In: Proceedings of the International Conference for High Performance Computing, Networking, Storage and Analysis, SC 2015, pp. 31:1–31:12. ACM, New York (2015). http://doi.acm.org/10.1145/2807591.2807665
17. Lamport, L.: Time, clocks, and the ordering of events in a distributed system. Commun. ACM **21**(7), 558–565 (1978)
18. Lamport, L., Shostak, R., Pease, M.: The byzantine generals problem. ACM Trans. Program. Lang. Syst. **4**(3), 382–401 (1982). doi:10.1145/357172.357176
19. Moody, A., Bronevetsky, G., Mohror, K., de Supinski, B.R.: Design, modeling, and evaluation of a scalable multi-level checkpointing system. In: Proceedings of the 2010 ACM/IEEE International Conference for High Performance Computing, Networking, Storage and Analysis, pp. 1–11 (2010). http://dx.doi.org/10.1109/SC.2010.18
20. Petrini, F., Frachtenberg, E., Hoisie, A., Coll, S.: Performance evaluation of the quadrics interconnection network. Cluster Comput. **6**(2), 125–142 (2003). doi:10.1023/A:1022852505633
21. Poole, S.W., Hernandez, O.R., Kuehn, J.A., Shipman, G.M., Curtis, A., Feind, K.: OpenSHMEM - toward a unified RMA model. In: Padua, D.A. (ed.) Encyclopedia of Parallel Computing, pp. 1379–1391. Springer, Heidelberg (2011)
22. Schroeder, B., Gibson, G.: Understanding failures in petascale computers. J. Phys.: Conf. Ser. **78**, 12–22 (2007). IOP Publishing
23. Shahzad, F., Kreutzer, M., Zeiser, T., Machado, R., Pieper, A., Hager, G., Wellein, G.: Building a fault tolerant application using the GASPI communication layer. In: Proceedings of the 2015 IEEE International Conference on Cluster Computing, CLUSTER 2015, pp. 580–587. IEEE Computer Society, Washington (2015). http://dx.doi.org/10.1109/CLUSTER.2015.106
24. Zheng, Z., Chien, A.A., Teranishi, K.: Fault tolerance in an inner-outer solver: a GVR-enabled case study. In: Daydé, M., Marques, O., Nakajima, K. (eds.) VECPAR 2014. LNCS, vol. 8969, pp. 124–132. Springer, Heidelberg (2015). doi:10.1007/978-3-319-17353-5_11

On Synchronisation and Memory Reuse in OpenSHMEM

Aaron Welch$^{(\boxtimes)}$ and Manjunath Gorentla Venkata

Extreme Scale Systems Center, Oak Ridge National Laboratory, Oak Ridge, USA
{welchda,manjugv}@ornl.gov

Abstract. OpenSHMEM is an open standard for PGAS libraries that provides one-sided communication semantics. Since the standardisation process was completed in 2012, the OpenSHMEM API has seen a rapid succession of proposed extensions. Among these extensions is the addition of *teams* of processing element (PEs) for greater flexibility in defining PE subsets for problem decomposition. Adding further to this, *spaces* introduced the ability to manage memory exclusive to *teams* without the need for global synchronisation. However, one problem still remains that affects the usability of *teams*, and that is the need for the user to manage memory used internally by the implementation for synchronisation in collective operations. This paper explores the possibilities for moving this responsibility from the user to the implementation, as well as the consequences that may arise as a result. To this end, we describe three methods of implementation and discuss the implications of their use compared to traditional user management of synchronisation buffers.

1 Introduction

OpenSHMEM [1] is the de facto standard for SHMEM communication libraries, which implements the Partitioned Global Address Space (PGAS) model. Each PE manages a partition of a symmetric memory heap used for symmetric data object allocations. These allocations can be accessed through a rich set of remote memory access (RMA) operations including atomic memory operation (AMOs). In addition, OpenSHMEM defines a set of memory synchronisation and collective operations for sets of PEs. OpenSHMEM libraries expose an API for the C, C++, and Fortran programming languages, though the majority of open source OpenSHMEM applications are developed using C.

This manuscript has been authored by UT-Battelle, LLC under Contract No. DE-AC05-00OR22725 with the U.S. Department of Energy. The United States Government retains and the publisher, by accepting the article for publication, acknowledges that the United States Government retains a non-exclusive, paid-up, irrevocable, world-wide license to publish or reproduce the published form of this manuscript, or allow others to do so, for United States Government purposes. The Department of Energy will provide public access to these results of federally sponsored research in accordance with the DOE Public Access Plan (http://energy.gov/downloads/doe-public-access-plan).

© Springer International Publishing AG 2016
M. Gorentla Venkata et al. (Eds.): OpenSHMEM 2016, LNCS 10007, pp. 82–94, 2016.
DOI: 10.1007/978-3-319-50995-2_6

The OpenSHMEM library API follows the PGAS programming model to support communication, synchronisation and other operations between PEs executing C, C++, or Fortran SPMD programs. Other useful operations provided by the OpenSHMEM library include calls for collective operations (symmetric memory allocation, broadcast, reduction, collection and synchronisation), atomic memory operations, distributed locks and data transfer ordering primitives (fence and quiet). Most collective calls are collective over a subset of PEs that are defined by an *active set*, which is defined by a triplet of parameters within each collective call.

Historically, there have been two primary elements of a particular communication operation in OpenSHMEM - the target PE (or multiple PEs in the case of collectives) and where the memory of interest is located. While these have been separate components in past iterations of the specification, they have both suffered from the same kinds of constraints imposed by the emphasis on a global view. However, while the former issue is resolved by offering ways to work with well defined subsets of the same operating set, the latter issue demands instead widening the scope of the current OpenSHMEM memory model to include any number of additional and disparate memory regions.

Solutions to these problems have been proposed in the form of *teams*, which are explicitly defined and reusable objects representing subsets of PEs, and *spaces*, which provides the ability to perform memory allocation within particular *teams* [2]. However, one issue remains a concern - the memory used internally by OpenSHMEM in collective operations. This has traditionally been handled by the user, who is expected to allocate, initialise, and manage the needed memory in the form of pSync and pWrk arrays. Unfortunately, this can be quite a hassle, particularly if *teams* may allow for more complicated formations of PE subsets. The ability to allocate memory within *spaces* helps to prevent the headache of allocating this memory, but it doesn't eliminate the management burden altogether, and fails to be sufficient to facilitate reuse.

The goal of this paper is to determine ways in which the allocation and management of this memory may be moved into the implementation. We will not focus on how exactly to allocate memory only across particular *teams*, as that was already explored in [2]. We will also not focus on pWrk, since it is tuned to each particular collective operation that uses it and thus would need to be freshly allocated and deallocated each time. However, pSync buffers are generic enough that it should be unnecessary and excessive to create and destroy them upon every call, so the real problem we will focus on is how to determine when a previously created buffer may be reused. We will describe three such solutions and analyse the potential consequences of their use. Additionally, we will discuss how these may be impacted or enhanced to support other proposed extensions in the form of threading support and non-blocking collective operations.

The rest of the paper is organised as follows. Section 2 describes other areas of work that have similar goals or otherwise may be relevant. Section 3 addresses some of the concerns or issues encountered when developing solutions to the problem, and how they affected the ultimate design. Section 4 describes three different solutions that could be used to allow the implementation to be responsible for handling synchronisation buffers. Section 5 provides an analysis on expected performance of these solutions, and Sect. 6 briefly summarises our work and possible avenues for future work.

2   Related Work

As this paper is largely focused on the internal use of symmetric memory for synchronisation purposes and when this "shared" memory may be reused, there are a few notable problems with similar goals. In particular, this is very similar in nature to the problem of cache coherency. There are two main classes of cache coherency protocols - snoopy [3] and directory-based [4] protocols. Snoopy cache coherency strategies rely on sniffing the bus and monitoring memory accesses to cache lines of interest, while directory-based protocols manage central directories for storing the state of the cache, which must be remotely queried to determine the state of a particular cache line.

There are many ways in which this state is defined and managed, generally consisting of a set of states a cache line may be in, and actions/transitions for each of those states. A well-known protocol is MESI [5], which stands for the different states it uses - modified, exclusive, shared, and invalid. If a cache line is in the modified state, then it is contained in the current core's cache and is "dirty," or contains a different value than that of main memory. If the line is in exclusive state, then it is contained only in the current core's cache but is "clean," in that its value is the same as that of main memory. If the line is shared, then it is stored in the current cache and also other caches, but is clean. Finally, if the line is invalid, then it is unused/not in the current cache. This protocol is well suited for the snooping strategy.

Another related problem is that of dependence analysis [6]. Dependence analysis is most often used in compiler theory, where it is useful in determining when it is safe to reorder statements. There are two main categories of dependencies - *control dependencies*, which refer to statements that are conditionally dependent on another statement, and *data depdendencies*, which occur when two statements access the same memory location. Data dependencies are further broken down into four subtypes based upon whether the location is being read or written to. Given two statements S1 and S2, where S1 precedes S2, then S2 has a true dependency on S1 if S1 writes to a location that S2 later reads, and an antidependency if S1 reads a location that S2 later writes to. Likewise, S2 has an output dependency on S1 if they both write to the same location, and an input depdendency if they both read from the same location. How it might be possible to take advantage of read and write operations with dependencies to manage synchronisation buffers is explored in Sect. 3.

Finally, this same issue is also a concern in implementing Coarray Fortran (CAF) [7]. In CAF, the different processes in the system (referred to as *images*) may belong to arbitrary *teams* much like the ones proposed for OpenSHMEM. All images initially start off in a single *team* representing the world, and at any time new *teams* may be split off from an existing *team*. When this happens, the respective images then disassociate themselves from their current *team* in order to join the new one. There are collective operations in CAF as well, which similarly need memory for synchronisation, but it does not expose this memory or pass off its management to the user.

3   Design Considerations

If each pSync array (or particular portions of them) is treated like a cache line, where other PEs can invalidate it by using it in a collective operation, it can start to be seen how the underlying problem is relevant. Unfortunately, there are a number of critical assumptions that common cache coherency solutions have made thus far. One of the chief among them is that all cores are using a single uniform bus. The issue of cache management in non-uniform memory access (NUMA) systems further complicates matters by destroying that assumption. Not only is snooping not a possibility anymore for this reason alone, but the non-uniform access times make synchronisation substantially more difficult and costly. Comparing the problem to OpenSHMEM puts the library specification into the same category as NUMA systems, thus preventing any strategies relying on the ability to snoop from being useful. There is also enough work on cache coherence to recognise that there is already enough difficulty scaling coherence as it is [8, 9].

Additionally, the expectation when dealing with cache lines is to avoid as much as possible any situations where multiple sources are modifying the same cache line. However, here sharing the same "cache line" is one of the specific goals, since that is the point that multiple PEs synchronise on (and thus also can result in one of the worst performance scenarios for caches - excessive thrashing). For reasons such as these, implementing something akin to cache coherence is not good enough to meet the needs of OpenSHMEM, as it places even fewer restrictions on memory use and behaviour. However, the ultimate problem being addressed is still similar enough in nature to that of cache coherence to be able to draw wisdom from it. In particular, that this problem can not be automatically solved without incurring additional cost from potentially multiple sources of overhead, and that it is likely best to avoid conflicts entirely when possible.

We also are not able to use the same strategy employed by CAF, as it places far more restrictions on *teams* and collective operation which result in easier management of synchronisation memory. In particular, images may only belong to a single *team* at any given point (thus there can be no overlap between ongoing collective operations between different *teams*), and all collective operations have an implicit barrier at the end of their execution.

Fortunately, while algorithms taken directly from cache coherence protocols themselves are insufficient and likely to result in unsatisfactory performance if adapted, we can alleviate some issues by taking advantage of usage patterns, assumptions, or other qualities regarding use of synchronisation buffers within OpenSHMEM. For one, it is neither important nor desirable to maintain a single, consistent "main memory" value (nor is there such a location), so concepts like shared or exclusive values don't make sense and need not be addressed. Also, the memory locations in question no longer need to be defined by the code, but can be selected at run-time - if one synchronisation buffer is not available without conflicts, then another may be used instead.

If we observe that the greatest difficulty in determining reuse comes from multiple remote sources being capable of deciding to write to a given location at any time, we may consider the implications of altering this behaviour such that any particular buffer may only be written to by a single PE. This simplifies point to point synchronisation enough that the origin PE can always unambiguously know what writes are pending completion on which buffers without the need to query any external sources. All that is necessary in order to free an old buffer up for reuse at that point is receipt of something equivalent to an acknowledgement from the target PE, which can be received at any point, in any form, and apply to any set of buffers.

This makes it simple enough to do some form of run-time dependence analysis without incurring expensive communication costs and creating additional synchronisation points. However, the goal of finding dependencies in this case is not to facilitate reordering, but to determine the lifetime of variable instances and use it for determining when old instances (buffers) must then be safe for reuse. The focus here is on "satisfying" dependencies on synchronisation buffers, and doing so without having to rely on further synchronisation initiated by the user or the implementation. For instance, if writing to a synchronisation buffer is determined to be dependent on the contents of some user memory, and the implementation sees that said user memory is later written, then it can know that the synchronisation buffer must be safe to reuse again (as its dependency has been "satisfied").

We tried this strategy out, but there were two main problems. First, since the user could (and usually does) do whatever they want with memory outside of the implementation's knowledge, it generally was unable to get sufficient information on run-time data flow to properly exploit any dependencies found between synchronisation points. Second, there were no communication patterns found in testing that were unusual enough to conceivably benefit much from the additional analysis. Thus, satisfied dependencies would ultimately just trace back to various points of synchronisation.

With these considerations in mind, we focused our designs simply on different methods of exploiting synchronisation points to free used buffers. These designs are examined in full in Sect. 4.

4   Design

We present three possible methods for moving management of synchronisation buffers to the implementation. These all rely in some way upon maintaining multiple buffers and using a set of locks to determine which buffers are available for reuse.

4.1 Additional Synchronisation

This method involves maintaining n buffers for each *team* of PEs. These buffers can be internally managed the same way as pSync arrays traditionally have been, except that each has a lock associated with it managed by the local PE. When a collective operation on a *team* is started, the PE finds the first free buffer and uses it for the operation. After the operation is complete, it then needs to find the next free buffer to use for barrier synchronisation, effectively ensuring that no PE leaves the collective operation before they have all completed it. Thus, upon finishing the barrier, it is known that no prior operation is still using their respective buffers, so at this point their buffers may all be unlocked.

Without support for threads or non-blocking operations, $n = 3$ buffers per *team* is sufficient for this approach - two for each pair of implementation-added barriers, and one for the operation performed in between them. Adding thread support may require up to $n = 3t$ buffers, where t is the number of threads. Furthermore, the locks must then track not just the lock state of a buffer, but also which thread ID locked it. This ID must be used when unlocking buffers so that only those used by the active thread may be unlocked. However, since $n = 3t$ buffers are only needed if all threads are actively participating in collective operations at a given time, it is not necessary to allocate the maximum number of buffers all at once, but instead it is possible to dynamically add more as necessary. Since synchronisation is already being performed internally within each collective, this approach has the potential to also benefit from "free" allocation in the sense of not requiring an additional barrier, provided sufficient memory remains.

Further adding support for non-blocking collective operations requires n to become unbounded, as any number of operations may be started before previous ones have completed. As such, the pool of available buffers must be handled in a way that allocates more on demand when the pool is exhausted. The locked buffers must also be ordered by when their associated collective is waited on, such that a given synchronisation can only unlock buffers whose respective operations have already been waited on.

4.2 Unlock on User Barrier

This method is similar to the previous one, maintaining n pSync-style buffers for each *team*. However, unlike that method, this does not impose additional synchronisation operations. Instead, each collective merely obtains the first free buffer, locks it, and completes the collective before returning. These buffers may then only be unlocked when the user explicitly performs a barrier across all members of a given *team*. In this case, it is not necessary for such a barrier to exclusively contain only PEs from a particular *team* - so long as it includes at least all the PEs from a *team*, that *team's* previously locked buffers may be safely unlocked. As a result, the number of required buffers becomes dependent on the number of collective operations that come between any given pair of barriers in user code. Thus, using this method the pool of buffers must be dynamically resizeable even without support for threads or non-blocking operations.

The only change necessary for adding support for threads would be to similarly associate locks with thread IDs like in the previous method. Non-blocking operations likewise would work the same as well.

4.3   Pairwise Synchronisation

The final method is no longer based on pSync-style buffers at all, but instead each PE has n dedicated buffers for each remote PE that needs to write to it. Thus, if for a particular synchronisation operation, three PEs need to communicate with PE i, it will have three separate sets of buffers for each such PE. Each time that a PE needs to synchronise with a target, it uses and locks the first available buffer for that target, allocating more if none exist. However, the receiver may not know which buffer a sender chose to use for synchronising, so the sender must send a unique ID for the collective operation that can be used to match the receiving end, and the receiver must scan all buffers the sender could use for the same ID. When a PE locks a buffer, it keeps track of the ID associated with it, so that when a message is received from a given PE with a particular ID as previously described, it may unlock buffers for that PE associated with IDs of past operations. In other words, receipt of a message from a source PE with a particular operation ID is dependent on that PE having processed all buffers of past operations from the target PE.

This approach can be extended to support threads by also associating a thread ID with each operation/buffer, and only unlocking buffers from the same thread. The only necessary changes to add non-blocking operations are that buffer unlocking must again occur only when waiting on an operation to complete, and that care must be taken to not unlock buffers used for operations that have yet to be waited on.

A benefit to this approach is that not all PEs participating in a collective operation must use the same synchronisation buffers, and that the buffers need not be exclusively bound to any particular *team*. This opens up greater potential for reuse across *teams*, but may add the additional concern for when to destroy old memory to prevent unused buffers from never being deallocated. The potential concern over the lifetime of these buffers is left for future work.

In order to minimise memory use, the focus in implementing this method is to minimise the number of PEs that need to directly communicate with any given PE for any given *team*. Within the scope of particular *teams*, this becomes a question of how to handle particular algorithms. To demonstrate this issue, we will observe its impact on two main patterns for collective communication - that of tree and recursive doubling algorithms. Figure 1 illustrates how PEs are connected when using a recursive doubling algorithm. The edges of the graph represent which PEs actually communicate to which other PEs. Here, it can be seen that the communication pattern constructed by this algorithm effectively creates a hypercube. The interesting quality of this is that regardless of any parametres besides the *team*, the edges of the graph will always remain the same, so nothing different needs to be done.

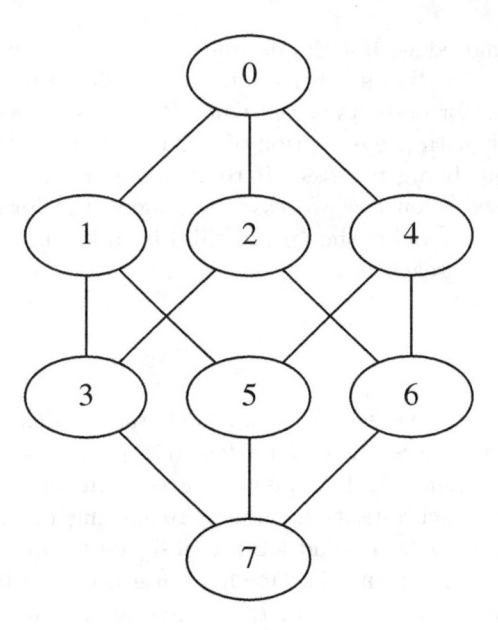

Fig. 1. Recursive doubling

However, this changes when looking at tree algorithms. If maintaining a balanced tree as most implementations ordinarily should, this would inevitably result in the tree's overal structure remaining the same, but the edges would connect different PEs for every different root. Thus, if making an effort to preserve these edges, then the tree must be rearranged so as to satisfy that requirement regardless of which PE is used as the root of the tree. Figure 2(a) shows a typical tree with PE 0 as the root, and Fig. 2(b) shows how it can be rearranged

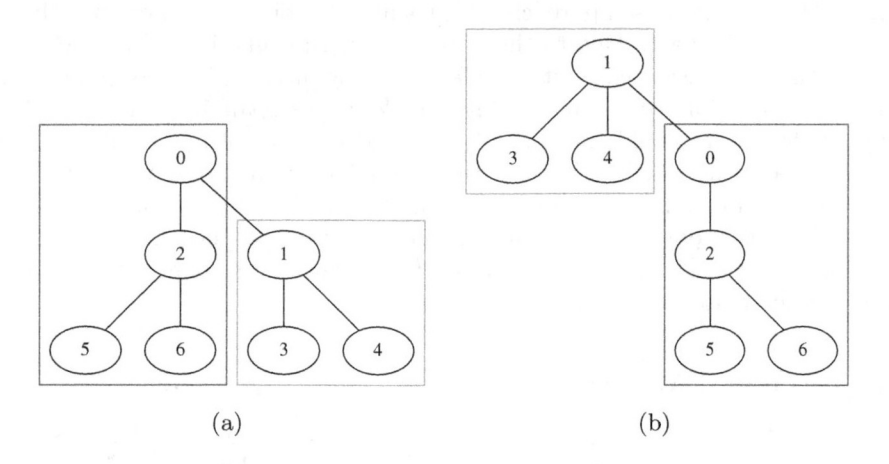

Fig. 2. Preserving edges in a tree algorithm

to maintain the same edges if PE 1 is made to be the root instead. This is accomplished by leaving PE 1's subtree intact, but adding a third child to communicate to what was formerly its parent when PE 0 was the root. PE 0's subtree is likewise left intact, with the exception of PE 1 being removed due to the parent/child relationship being inverted. If rearranging a tree around root PE n further down the tree, then the process of changing the former parent into a child and said parent removing the former child from its subtree continues until the original root of 0 is reached.

5   Evaluation

Before we can evaluate expected performance characteristics, we must first consider a few critical differences between the design choices presented. In particular, we must consider differences in how we can measure memory requirements and potential lifetime of synchronisation buffers. Regarding memory, the first two strategies described in Sects. 4.1 and 4.2 are designed to operate on traditional pSync-style buffers. This means that memory use needs to be looked at from the level of the number of pSync buffers created, as the size of them can vary between collective operations and implementations. On the other hand, for the third option described in Sect. 4.3, the unit of memory is effectively a single value (index) representing an address for synchronising with a specific target from a specific source. Thus, the memory used for each such buffer may be far less than what is needed to support a pSync buffer. In the case of an implementation supporting the recursive doubling algorithm as seen in Fig. 1, each pSync may need $\log n$ indices to support a *team* of size n. For the purposes of this analysis, we will be looking at total memory used across the system, so if each PE holds n buffers, the total memory use is that of n^2 buffers.

Similarly regarding the lifetime of buffers, the outlined strategies represent a rough division of lifetime expectancies. The simplicity of managing traditional pSync buffers make those approaches best suited for binding buffers strictly to the lifetime of the team. Due to the potential for run-time inconsistencies, the pSync of a parent *team* can not be safely used by any child *teams* created off of it. While multiple *pSync* buffers from child *teams* spanning across the full range of the parent could theoretically be used in place of a dedicated buffer for the parent, the benefits that could be reaped are minimal and not likely to justify the additional headache of attempting to exploit the possibility. Contrary to this, the nature of separating buffers from any direct reliance on *teams* in the pairwise synchronisation strategy makes it far easier to allow buffers to both live longer and be reused across different *teams*.

5.1   Theoretical Analysis

When introducing additional synchronisation or relying on user barriers, the same performance as can be achieved by the user supplying a buffer can be expected, with the addition of an extra barrier for synchronising after creation

of a pSync. The only significant difference is that the implementation may optionally choose to allocate and initialise more than one pSync at the same time in an
attempt to save on synchronisation costs. Nonetheless, this still means that the
worst case for communication cost when using tree or recursive doubling algo-
rithms for collectives is $\mathcal{O}(3 \log n)$ when adding synchronisation or $\mathcal{O}(2 \log n)$
when relying on user barriers. Memory, on the other hand, is the same when
using additional synchronisation and remains at $\mathcal{O}(n \log n)$, while falling back
on user barriers requires $\mathcal{O}(cn \log n)$, where c is the average distance between
barriers (measured in number of collective calls).

Looking at pairwise synchronisation, performance characteristics are affected
by the underlying algorithms used. For instance, memory and communication
costs required for performing recursive doubling are $\mathcal{O}(n \log n)$ and $\mathcal{O}(\log n)$,
respectively. In contrast, tree algorithms are less straightforward, as was detailed
in Sect. 4.3 and Fig. 2. If not preserving edges, the communication cost of
$\mathcal{O}(\log n)$ is preserved, but at the cost of $\mathcal{O}(n^2)$ memory use in the worst-case
scenario of all n roots being used. If only one root is ever used, or if preserving edges, the communication cost becomes $\mathcal{O}(2 \log n)$, but memory use can not
exceed a flat $3n$ buffers. Which approach to take may be a decision left to the
implementation or run-time.

However, this is looking only within the context of individual *teams*. One of
the more interesting aspects of this solution is the ability to recycle old buffers
for future use, including in different *teams*. To give an indication of how well this
can work, we will look at a particularly "bad" example and see that memory use
still scales linearly. First, we consider that most *teams* will either be traditionally
strided, or composable of such strided ranges. Then, we take a world of n PEs
and perform collectives over all such possible *teams* within the world. Figure 3
shows the total number of buffers needed to support all such *teams* for a world
of size $8 \leq n \leq 4096$.

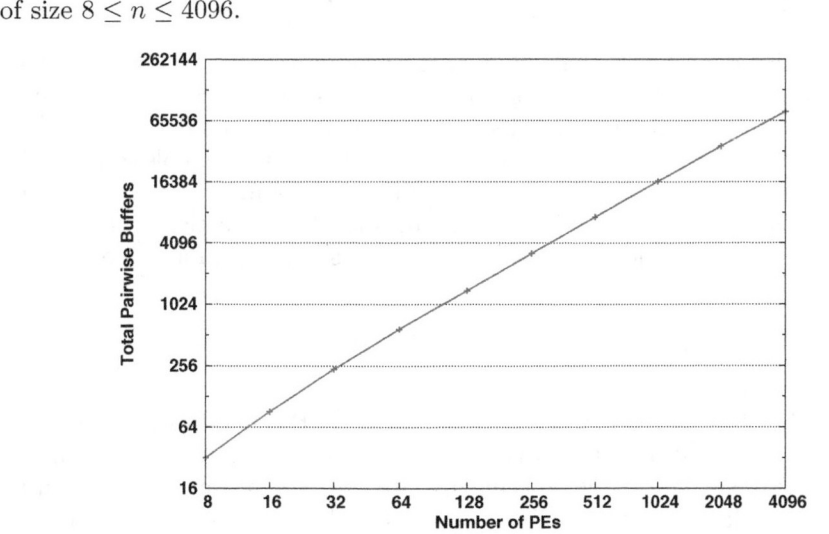

Fig. 3. Buffer use

This is obviously a very unrealistic scenario, but it is nonetheless obvious that it still scales slowly with respect to the size of the world. In contrast, Fig. 4 shows the number of total *team* configurations for the same test. With the other design strategies, each of these *teams* would need a separate pSync, and would additionally need to synchronise after *team* creation as necessary for each collective operation. It can be seen from the figure that the number of *teams* grows much faster than the number of necessary pairwise buffers, making it more appealing than the pSync-focused alternatives.

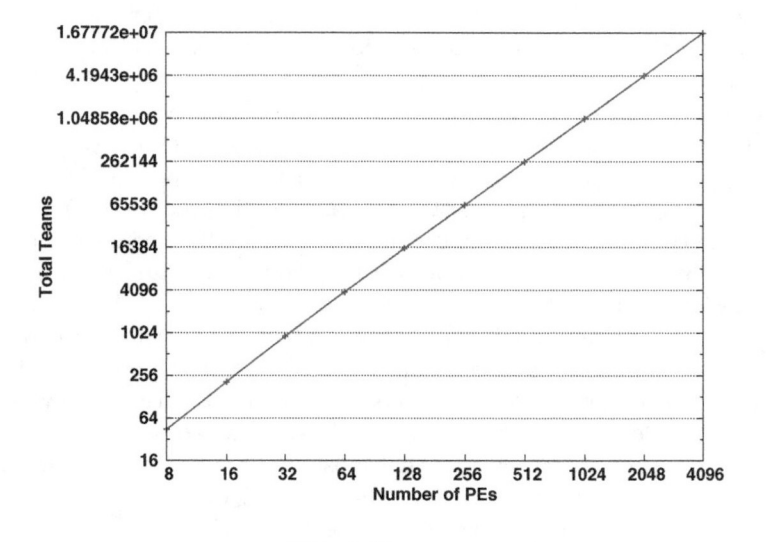

Fig. 4. Team use

It is worth noting again that while these results are still telling, they are nonetheless representing an unrealistic scenario - most applications are unlikely to come close to achieving these results, as they will only be present when creating all possible *teams* as previously described. In fact, we were unable to find any real-world tests whose needs were complex or unusual enough to merit concern, and any new use cases that may come from the formal introduction of *teams* are also unlikely to contain such exhausive use of them so as to exhibit the observed performance.

5.2   SHOC

Next, we will look at a more realistic scenario, in which this new feature is applied to a real-world application in the form of the Scalable Heterogeneous Computing (SHOC) benchmark suite [10]. Specifically, we will be looking at its quality threshold clustering benchmark. Tests within the SHOC suite are intended to be useful for comparison of heterogeneous systems containing multiple compute devices including GPU accelerators. Quality threshold clustering is a partitioning algorithm intended to find data clusters of a particular quality, rather than partitioning the data into k clusters.

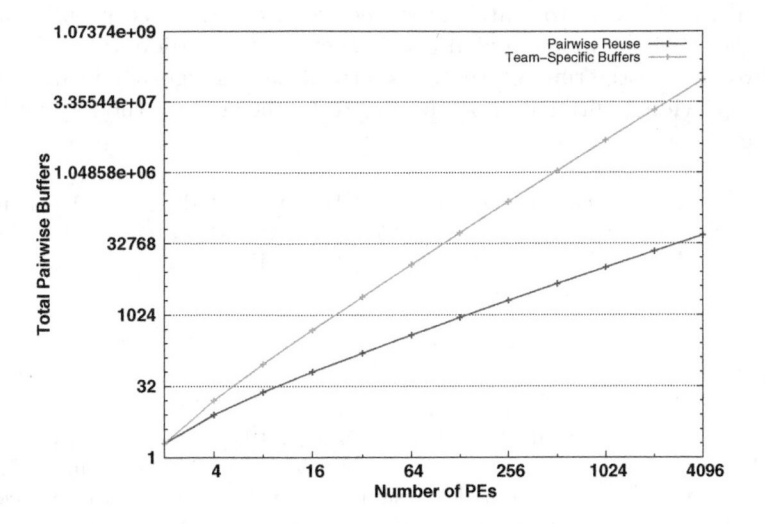

Fig. 5. Quality threshold clustering memory use

As the search space decreases, the benchmark successively removes processes from the original set of n processes from the computation until only one remains, eventually reducing down to a single process. The rate of this reduction can vary by input parametres, however in the "worst" case scenario, each such reduction results in the removal of a single PE. When this was tested for memory use using the pairwise strategy, this was shown to have $\mathcal{O}(n \log n)$ performance. In contrast, assuming $\log n$ memory use for each pSync buffer, using separate buffers for each *team* as the other strategies or a typical application might do results in $\mathcal{O}(n^2 \log n)$ performance. These results can be seen in Fig. 5. From this, it is clear that the pairwise strategy provides a more manageable and scalable alternative as the number of *teams* increase.

6   Conclusion and Future Work

In this paper we presented three alternatives for removing the burden of managing internal synchronisation memory within OpenSHMEM, and how they can affect execution. While there is no golden solution for getting around the potential loss of semantic information by hiding buffer management, it was shown that it can be done with set degrees of overhead, and scale linearly with respect to the number of PEs in the system.

For future work, it may be worth investigating whether and how old buffers should be destroyed when using the pairwise strategy. Additionally, it may be helpful to look at the utility of adding in some form of tags to collectives, as that may help add back some semantic knowledge that could be used to more easily match up different collective operations. This may especially be relevant in the case that threading support is introduced to the specification, as it could avoid the difficulties of trying to match up collectives from threads on different PEs without the need to enforce global consistency on thread identities. Finally, it may be worth investigating alternative synchronisation algorithms and whether some may provide additional opportunities to further reduce the required memory footprint.

Acknowledgments. This work is supported by the United States Department of Defense (DoD) and used resources of the Computational Research and Development Programs and the Oak Ridge Leadership Computing Facility (OLCF) at Oak Ridge National Laboratory.

References

1. OpenSHMEM Org.: OpenSHMEM specification (2011)
2. Welch, A., Pophale, S., Shamis, P., Hernandez, O., Poole, S., Chapman, B.: Extending the openshmem memory model to support user-defined spaces. In: Proceedings of the 8th International Conference on Partitioned Global Address Space Programming Models, PGAS 2014, pp. 11:1–11:10. ACM, New York (2014)
3. Ravishankar, C., Goodman, J.: Cache implementation for multiple microprocessors. IEEE, New York (1983)
4. Agarwal, A., Simoni, R., Hennessy, J., Horowitz, M.: An evaluation of directory schemes for cache coherence. SIGARCH Comput. Archit. News **16**, 280–298 (1988)
5. Papamarcos, M.S., Patel, J.H.: A low-overhead coherence solution for multiprocessors with private cache memories. SIGARCH Comput. Archit. News **12**, 348–354 (1984)
6. Bernstein, A.J.: Analysis of programs for parallel processing. IEEE Trans. Electron. Comput. **15**, 757–763 (1966)
7. Fortran Standards Committee: Fortran 2015 working document (2015)
8. Choi, B., Komuravelli, R., Sung, H., Smolinski, R., Honarmand, N., Adve, S.V., Adve, V.S., Carter, N.P., Chou, C.T.: DeNovo: rethinking the memory hierarchy for disciplined parallelism. In: 2011 International Conference on Parallel Architectures and Compilation Techniques (PACT), pp. 155–166 (2011)
9. Xu, Y., Du, Y., Zhang, Y., Yang, J.: A composite and scalable cache coherence protocol for large scale CMPS. In: Proceedings of the International Conference on Supercomputing, ICS 2011, pp. 285–294. ACM, New York (2011)
10. Danalis, A., Marin, G., McCurdy, C., Meredith, J.S., Roth, P.C., Spafford, K., Tipparaju, V., Vetter, J.S.: The scalable heterogeneous computing (SHOC) benchmark suite. In: Proceedings of the 3rd Workshop on General-Purpose Computation on Graphics Processing Units, GPGPU-3, pp. 63–74. ACM, New York (2010)

OpenSHMEM Implementation
and Use Cases

Design and Implementation of OpenSHMEM Using OFI on the Aries Interconnect

Kayla Seager[1](✉), Sung-Eun Choi[2], James Dinan[1], Howard Pritchard[3], and Sayantan Sur[1]

[1] Intel Corporation, Santa Clara, USA
kayla.seager@intel.com
[2] Cray Inc., Seattle, USA
[3] Los Alamos National Laboratory, New Mexico, USA

Abstract. Sandia OpenSHMEM (SOS) is an implementation of the OpenSHMEM specification that has been designed to provide portability, scalability, and performance on high-speed RDMA fabrics. Libfabric is the implementation of the newly proposed Open Fabrics Interfaces (OFI) that was designed to provide a tight semantic match between HPC programming models and various underlying fabric services.

In this paper, we present the design and evaluation of the SOS OFI transport on Aries, a contemporary, high-performance RDMA interconnect. The implementation of Libfabric on Aries uses uGNI as the lowest-level software interface to the interconnect. uGNI is a generic interface that can support both message passing and one-sided programming models. We compare the performance of our work with that of the Cray SHMEM library and demonstrate that our implementation provides performance and scalability comparable to that of a highly tuned, production SHMEM library. Additionally, the Libfabric message injection feature enabled SOS to achieve a performance improvement over Cray SHMEM for small messages in bandwidth and random access benchmarks.

1 Introduction

Current trends in high performance computing (HPC) system architecture pose new challenges and introduce new requirements for the system fabric. Dramatic increases in the number of cores and threads per node requires a host-fabric interface (HFI) that can process communication on behalf of many threads efficiently. At the same time, these *throughput-oriented* cores present new challenges to communication processing on the host processor [4]. Further, increases in the overall system scale in combination with a flattening trend in the amount of memory available per thread places additional stress on scalability requirements. In response to these challenges, a variety of novel solutions [11,13] and interfaces are being explored [5,9,14,27].

In addition to new techniques at the system fabric layer, the communication middleware and underlying communication software stack must also be

© Springer International Publishing AG 2016
M. Gorentla Venkata et al. (Eds.): OpenSHMEM 2016, LNCS 10007, pp. 97–113, 2016.
DOI: 10.1007/978-3-319-50995-2_7

adapted to leverage and expose new functionality. The OpenFabrics Alliance recently introduced the OpenFabrics Interfaces (OFI) framework as a new, open-source software ecosystem designed to enable efficient usage of evolving high-performance fabrics [14]. OFI's libfabric component provides a communication interface that is designed for scalability, flexibility, and extensibility. In particular, typical scalability challenges, such as endpoint addressing, connection management, message processing, and memory registration are encapsulated within libfabric, allowing them to be optimized using fabric- and system-specific capabilities.

The OpenSHMEM specification is a recent initiative directed toward standardizing and extending the SHMEM* parallel programming model for future systems. OpenSHMEM defines a partitioned global address space (PGAS) data access library that can be used to establish one-sided access to read, write, and atomically update remote data. OpenSHMEM applications commonly require high throughput and the ability to perform remote data accesses asynchronously, thereby placing significant demands on the underlying system fabric.

In this work, we document our experiences with the development of an Open-SHMEM software stack using OFI on a contemporary HPC interconnect. We present an open source implementation of the OpenSHMEM 1.3 specification that targets the OFI libfabric interface and describe how libfabric can be used to improve the efficiency of OpenSHMEM middleware. We further describe the implementation of libfabric for the Cray® XC40™ system with the Aries interconnect that utilizes the uGNI [8] API. We evaluate the performance of our software stack using several communication and application benchmarks. The results indicate that the performance of the open-source SHMEM and libfabric is comparable to the highly tuned, production Cray SHMEM library. In addition, we show that the libfabric message injection feature enabled a performance improvement over Cray SHMEM for small messages in bandwidth and random access benchmarks.

Our paper starts with a description of the relevant background information and related work in Sect. 2. Next, we describe the design of our OpenSHMEM implementation and underlying OFI implementation for the Aries interconnect in Sects. 3 and 4, respectively. We present an experimental evaluation in Sect. 5 and conclude with Sect. 6.

2   Background and Related Work

Our work describes and analyzes the implementation of the OpenSHMEM specification using a modern fabric interface. In this section, we provide an overview of these topics and some of the most closely related works.

2.1   Fabric Interfaces

A variety of low-level communication APIs have been used in HPC for high performance networking, including the OpenFabrics Alliance (OFA) Verbs API,

PAMI [19], Portals [2], and uGNI [8]. Often, such low-level APIs are customized to leverage specific system architectures. Recently, the industry has trended toward exchanging system-specific APIs for open, portable *fabric interfaces* that provide a low-level interface to fabric services while minimizing ties to specific architectures. This approach promises to provide better portability for communication middleware, such as OpenSHMEM, while maximizing the exposure of application-level communication semantics to the fabric to enable aggressive optimization.

OpenFabrics Interfaces. The OpenFabrics Alliance (OFA) provides open-source software for high-performance networking applications that demand low latency and high bandwidth. Historically, the only fabric interface offered by the OFA was the Verbs API as defined in the InfiniBand* specification. As the InfiniBand specification was originally envisioned as a generic system I/O interconnect, there are semantic differences between Verbs and the requirements of PGAS libraries and languages. These semantic mismatches require unnecessary adaptations in PGAS implementations, such as OpenSHMEM, resulting in significant software overhead [21].

The OFA has created a working group, called the OpenFabrics Interfaces Working Group (OFIWG), that aims to define a fabric interface that has a tight semantic map to various applications classes that use it, including PGAS programming models. Members of the PGAS community provided input into the design of the new fabric interfaces to help improve the mapping of PGAS features onto fabric interface features. The fabric library created from this effort is called *libfabric*. It consists of two logically distinct components: A set of fabric *providers* that implement the communication interfaces for a particular fabric hardware, and a general purpose *framework* that provides a plugin-like capability for providers. In the rest of the paper, we use the term *uGNI provider* to imply the specific implementation of libfabric interfaces for the Aries interconnect. Libfabric is freely available from Github [20], and is distributed via the OpenFabrics Enterprise Distribution (OFED) as well as popular Linux distributions.

Other Fabric APIs. The Portals interface [2] allows the user to describe actions that are performed on remote memory segments – possibly gated by message matching requirements – providing close alignment between HPC communication libraries and the underlying software or hardware implementation of the Portals layer. A variety of PGAS runtimes have been ported to use Portals, including OpenSHMEM [3]. The current Portals 4 specification [2] adds a lightweight non-matching interface to boost PGAS messaging rates. Additionally, it introduces logical rank-based addressing to simplify code paths, eliminate cache misses, and improve memory scaling. Members of the Portals community also participate in the effort to craft the OFI interface, resulting in adoption of multiple concepts from the Portals API.

OpenUCX [27], is another fabric framework that is being developed by as a collaboration outside the OpenFabrics umbrella. It aims to provide semantics that target data centric and HPC programming models. UCCS [26] is a predecessor to OpenUCX and a detailed study of OpenSHMEM performance on UCCS was recently conducted [28]. Additionally a study of UCCS over uGNI on Gemini was evaluated in [16]. The authors of these studies observed similar performance results as we present; however, because of differences in the hardware and software environments, our results cannot be directly compared.

2.2 OpenSHMEM

OpenSHMEM [23] is a parallel programming model that defines a Single-Program, Multiple-Data (SPMD) execution model and an accompanying partitioned global address space (PGAS) communication library. OpenSHMEM allows the programmer to expose regions of memory for remote access using one-sided read, write, and atomic access routines.

Recently, the OpenSHMEM specification was introduced in an effort to standardize and extend the SHMEM* communication library. SHMEM has been in use for over two decades, with implementations from most major HPC vendors, however the lack of an open specification has resulted in variations across implementations and has limited the ability of the user community to extend the programming model.

A reference implementation of the OpenSHMEM specification is available as open source [22] and is compatible with a wide range of system fabrics through the low-level GASNet API [6]. The OpenMPI communication middleware also recently added support for OpenSHMEM [12], called OSHMEM. OSHMEM leverages the MPI runtime and MPI collective implementations to provide a lightweight implementation. Mellanox* Scalable SHMEM is a proprietary implementation that is available as a part of the HPC-X toolkit distributed by Mellanox. It is designed to work on Mellanox InfiniBand fabrics. Similarly, the MVAPICH2-X [17,18] SHMEM distribution is a closed source implementation that targets only Mellanox fabrics.

In this work, we utilize the open source Sandia OpenSHMEM (SOS) library [25], which is based on the earlier Portals SHMEM library [3]. SOS extends Portals SHMEM with support for the new OpenSHMEM 1.3 specification, as well as adding support for the OpenFabrics Interface libfabric communication layer [21]. While existing libfabric support was recently added, supplementary work has refined the mapping of OpenSHMEM to OFI, yielding additional portability and performance benefits. Furthermore, the codebase continues to evolve alongside the OpenSHMEM community as a sandbox and proof-of-concept for the latest OpenSHMEM proposals.

3   Design of OpenSHMEM for OFI

As shown in Fig. 1, Sandia OpenSHMEM (SOS) defines internal network data transport and shared memory layers. The SOS transport layer was designed to reduce the number of functions that must be implemented for each fabric, while

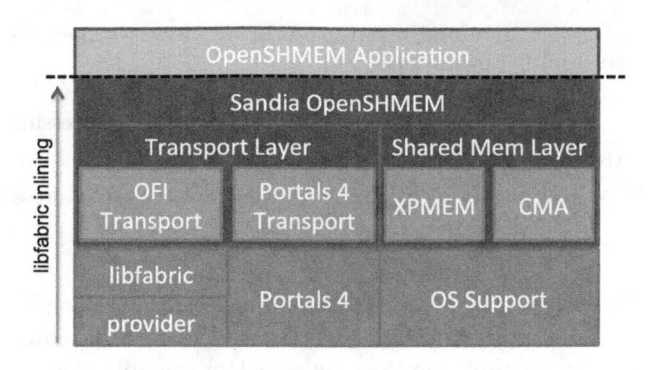

Fig. 1. Sandia OpenSHMEM library design, showing libfabric inlining to eliminate software overheads.

exposing core OpenSHMEM communication semantics so that the transport can optimize for scalability and performance. SOS provides support for both Portals 4 and OFI. This work focuses primarily on the OFI transport layer and extending it to support a broad range of libfabric capabilities and efficiently utilize the Aries system interconnect through the libfabric uGNI provider.

The SOS-OFI transport layer requires provider support for remote memory access (RMA) and remote atomics capabilities. The libfabric RMA and atomic APIs were designed to provide a direct mapping of performance sensitive PGAS operations to libfabric routines, with the intention of facilitating close alignment with fabrics that provide support for remote direct memory access (RDMA) and atomic capabilities. Libfabric further supports a direct build, shown in Fig. 1 where the implementation of the libfabric API routines are inlined into the middleware, enabling cross-call compiler optimizations and eliminating function call overheads. Sandia OpenSHMEM (SOS) also supports aggressive inlining within the implementation, which is used to reduce the middleware stack overheads to a single function call. In combination, these optimizations have been shown to significantly improve software overheads, and by extension small message latency and throughput [21].

3.1 Launch, Wire-Up, and Memory Registration

Careful setup and resource management is crucial for achieving scalability and reducing overheads. SOS supports the PMI-1 and PMI-2 process management interfaces (PMIs) [1], and we have added support for the Cray process manager. For stand-alone builds, SOS includes a built-in PMI-1 option that can be used to attach to any PMI-1 compliant job launcher.

Mapping of OpenSHMEM PE numbers to network addresses is typically facilitated through a scalable libfabric address vector (AV); however, for portability reasons, SOS supports both the *map* and *table* AV modes. The map mode provides the broadest compatibility; however, it requires the middleware to maintain a table that maps PE numbers to fabric interface (FI) addresses obtained

Table 1. Memory registration and remote addressing models supported by the SOS OFI transport and resulting overheads.

	Remote virtual addressing	Remote offset addressing
Scalable MR		Offset calculation
Basic MR	Key tables	Key tables, base address table, offset calculation

through the PMI exchange. When a communication operation is performed, the target PE number must be first converted to the corresponding FI address using this table. The AV table mode provides better scalability and performance opportunities by allowing the PE number to be used directly in communication operations and performing address resolution within the provider. For networks that require a translation table, the provider is able to map the table in a shared segment, improving the memory scalability. Further, the AV table mode provides a mechanism to take advantage of networks that offload or regularize address resolution. We use AV table in our study since it is supported by OFI-uGNI.

In libfabric, remote memory access (RMA) operations require both a protection key and a destination address. Libfabric provides two different models for exposing memory regions for remote access, referred to as *scalable* and *basic* memory registration (MR), that establish different key and destination address semantics. We have implemented support for both modes in SOS, and we further take advantage of systems that can support mapping the symmetric heap and data segments at the same base addresses across all PEs, referred to as remote virtual addressing. The combination of these two features results in the matrix shown in Table 1. In the scalable MR mode with remote virtual addressing, SOS exposes the full address space of the PE for efficient remote access. In all other modes, the heap and data segments are exposed separately.

Basic memory registration is the most portable model and allows the provider to determine the memory protection key, and requires the application to provide destination virtual address for the RDMA operation. This results in SOS exchanging protection keys and maintaining a key table as the key may be different on different PEs. Protection keys are required by some networks to enable access to remote memory. Additionally, basic memory registration support requires the SOS middleware to maintain tables containing the symmetric heap and data segment base addresses of all PEs. When performing an RMA operation, a local offset calculation is performed to convert the symmetric address passed to the OpenSHMEM routine into an offset relative to the symmetric heap or data segment base. This is then added to the target PE's base address before performing the libfabric communication operation.

In contrast, scalable memory registration allows the user to select the protection key, eliminating the key table overheads. Addressing in the scalable memory registration model is performed relative to the beginning of the memory segment exposed at the target PE. In the remote virtual addressing model, the full address space is exposed and the symmetric address passed to the OpenSHMEM routine can be directly used by libfabric. When remote virtual addressing is not available, the symmetric address is converted into an offset relative to the local base address and this offset is passed directly to the libfabric communication routine. Thus, scalable memory registration eliminates both the key and base address tables.

In this paper, we use the Basic memory registration path due to current uGNI provider limitations. In the future, we may explore adding the scalable memory registration feature to the provider in order to expose more optimal code paths in OpenSHMEM.

3.2   One-Sided Communication Operations

OpenSHMEM one-sided put operations are mapped to the libfabric write API and different strategies are used depending on the message size. OpenSH-MEM defines both blocking and nonblocking put operations; blocking operations return after local completion, whereas nonblocking operations provide no completion guarantee. For messages below the injection threshold of the fabric, the fi_inject_write routine is called; in all other cases, the fi_write routine is called. The inject-write routine provides immediate local completion and the provider is responsible for any buffering needed to ensure reliable message delivery. For blocking put operations whose message size is greater than the injection threshold and less than the user-selectable SMA_BOUNCE_SIZE parameter, the user's data is copied to a temporary bounce buffer and the operation provides immediate local completion. As shown in Sect. 5, we have observed that bounce buffering can provide significant performance improvements for applications that rely on blocking put operations; however, this optimization can be disabled when not needed to reduce the memory footprint of SOS. Finally, larger messages are issued directly using the fi_write operation and are fragmented according to the maximum transmission unit (MTU) of the fabric.

The OpenSHMEM atomic operations are divided into three categories, non-fetching, fetching, and comparison atomics. Currently, all OpenSHMEM atomic operations are blocking. The non-fetching atomics perform a remote update without returning a result and are implemented using the fi_inject_atomic and fi_atomic routines using the same strategy as described for blocking put operations. While all OpenSHMEM atomic routines are scalar and map to inject-atomics, SOS does implement vector atomics in the transport layer that is only utilized by the OpenSHMEM collectives API. The fetching atomic and comparison atomic operations are implemented using fi_fetch_atomic and fi_compare_atomic operations. However, since these blocking operations return the prior contents of the destination buffer, they cannot return until the operation has completed and neither message injection nor bounce buffering is used.

Finally, the OpenSHMEM get operations are implemented directly using the libfabric fi_read routine. The runtime must wait for blocking get operations to complete before returning. In the nonblocking case, the routine returns immediately and the application completes the get operation with a subsequent call to the shmem_quiet routine.

As shown in Fig. 1, SOS supports shared memory through XPMEM and Linux cross-memory attach (CMA). When enabled, shared memory is used to improve the performance of put and get operations. Atomic operations are always performed through the transport layer in order to ensure atomicity.

3.3   Ordering and Remote Completion Operations

All communication operations in libfabric are nonblocking; completion of issued operations is established using either event counters or completion queues. When they are created, the programmer selects which events will be captured by a particular event counter or completion queue. Event counters and completion queues are then bound to a fabric endpoint. Thus, for a given operation, the type of completion that will be generated is determined by the fabric endpoint on which the operation was issued and the type of event that the operation generates. In SOS we mainly use counters for completion, but a queue is used for bounce buffering and error handling.

Completion queues provide a full event structure for each completed operation, with detailed information including a "context" value that was supplied when the original operation was performed. The context is typically used to forward a reference to a middleware object (e.g. a request object) from the communication operation to the full event. In SOS, full events are used only when a put or non-fetching atomic operation utilizes a temporary bounce buffer. In this case, a pointer to the bounce buffer is included as the context and is used when processing the remote completion event to return the bounce buffer to a free pool. The number of operations issued using a bounce buffer is tracked by a variable within the SOS runtime and is used to wait for pending operations to complete when performing an OpenSHMEM fence or quiet operation.

Full completion events incur an overhead to allocate space in the event queue and populate the event with the information from the operation that completed. In contrast, event counters capture no information regarding specific operations that have completed. Instead, the counter is simply incremented upon completion of the operation, resulting in lower overhead than a full event. SOS establishes two counters for tracking completion of read and write operations separately. Operations that do not return a result, including puts and non-fetching atomics are accounted for using the write counter (with the exception of operations using a bounce buffer; those are tracked separately using a completion queue). All other operations are accounted for using the read counter. Within the SOS middleware, two variables are used as counters to track the number of operations of each kind that have been issued.

Separate read and write counters are used to optimize blocking communication operations. Blocking put and non-fetching atomic operations that are buffered using either the inject or bounce buffer method return immediately. Large blocking put operations must wait for completion before returning. Similarly, blocking fetching operations of any size must wait for completion prior to returning. By using separate counters for these classes of operations, we allow operations to overtake each other. This can provide significant benefit in cases where small fetching operations are combined with large puts. It is possible to use additional counters to optimize blocking operations based on the operation type and size (e.g. to separate fetching and comparison atomics from gets). We plan to investigate the impact of such refinements during future performance tuning.

The OpenSHMEM quiet operation must wait for remote completion of all pending blocking and nonblocking operations, whereas the fence operations must only ensure ordering of remote updates. Currently, SOS waits for completion of all pending communication in both quiet and fence operations. In the future, we plan to leverage the separation of read and write counters to optimize these operations. In this model, the quiet operation waits for completion of both remote writes and reads, whereas the fence operation waits only for completion of remote writes.

3.4   Notification API

The OpenSHMEM wait API allows the programmer to wait for an update to a location in symmetric memory. When shared memory optimizations are not used, all updates arrive through the network and the wait implementation can block on a network event rather than polling the target memory location. When supported by the OFI provider, the SOS OFI transport binds an event counter to one or more regions of exposed memory that is incremented whenever a remote update occurs. In this mode, the implementation of the OpenSHMEM wait operation blocks on a communication event, allowing the provider to optimize resource utilization.

4   Libfabric for the Aries Network

The libfabric provider, shown as the bottom-most layer in Fig. 1, is responsible for mapping the libfabric APIs to the underlying system. In this section we give an overview of the implementation of the libfabric API utilized by SOS. We refer readers to previous work for further details on the implementation [7, 24].

The provider implementation for the Aries interconnect utilizes the Generic Network Interface (uGNI) library [8], a low-level interface that exposes the capabilities of the Aries NIC. The uGNI provider utilizes the Aries NIC's fast memory access (FMA) hardware for small messages, as well as the bulk transfer engine (BTE) for offloading large message transfers. FMA descriptors are used to initiate remote loads, stores and atomic operations. FMA descriptors are bound to local Aries hardware-provided completion queues (hCQ) to enable notifications for the completion of remote memory access.

4.1   Addressing and Memory Registration

The uGNI provider supports both the OFI map and table address vector (AV) modes. For both modes, the address entry is represented by the uGNI device address and an identifier for utilizing the hardware protection, in combination with information about the endpoint and RDMA credentials. AV map mode uses a hash table to store address entries, whereas AV table mode uses a growable vector of address entries.

The uGNI provider supports the OFI basic memory registration (MR) mode, including a configurable memory registration cache. Memory regions are registered with uGNI via a call to uGNI_MemRegister, which returns a handle that is encoded in the key for the memory region. The memory registrations are stored in a red-black tree for fast access in cases where an existing registration satisfies the requested memory region. To further reduce the number of registrations with uGNI, all registrations are rounded up to the nearest page size. Additionally, adjacent memory regions are coalesced into a single, larger entry to further reduce the number of registrations. The memory registration cache also supports lazy deregistration when a memory region is closed. Lazy deregistration holds on to the uGNI memory handle until a configurable limit is reached, after which memory regions are deregistered via a call to uGNI_MemDeregister.

4.2   Issuing and Completing Communication Operations

The OFI RMA operations (fi_write and fi_read) with data size less than 8 KB in size are sent using Aries FMA functionality as a control message payload. Larger transfers are handled using the Aries BTE. The switch-over point can be adjusted using a GNI provider specific fi_open_ops method on a fi_domain object.

The Aries FMA hardware is also used to provide fast atomic operations. Currently, the uGNI provider only supports libfabric atomic operations that are implemented directly by the Aries hardware. This includes 32- and 64-bit versions of *min*, *max*, *sum*, bitwise *OR*, bitwise *AND*, bitwise *XOR*, read, write, *compare-and-swap* and masked *compare-and-swap*. In addition, the uGNI provider exposes the Aries *AND-and-XOR* atomic operation.

The uGNI provider checks for Aries completion events from all active hCQs upon most calls into the libfabric library as well as from an independent progress thread, if automatic progress is requested. Callback functions are used to generate a corresponding libfabric completion event, which is placed on the appropriate completion queue (represented by a singly-linked, double-ended list). The Aries hardware does not directly support completion counters. Completion counters are implemented similarly to completion queues; the callback simply increments the appropriate counter value.

5   Evaluation

We compare the performance of SOS using the OFI transport and uGNI provider with the performance of Cray's SHMEM implementation for the Aries network. Experiments were conducted on the NERSC "Cori" system, which is a Cray® XC40™ with 1,630 compute nodes. Compute nodes are comprised of two Intel® Xeon™ "Haswell" processors (E5-2698 v3) with 32 cores total (16 cores/socket) with hyperthreading disabled, and with 128 GB of memory per node.

The system was running Cray* Linux Environment (CLE) version 5.2up04 and Slurm* version 15.0.8.11. Libfabric (master@3dddae68) was used for the experiments. Libfabric was built using gcc version 5.2.0 with optimization level -O2. No special configuration options were used. Sandia OpenSHMEM (master@a3662791) was configured to use the uGNI provider, but otherwise no special optimizations were used. Cray MPT* 7.3.1 was used for the Cray SHMEM results.

We note that Cray SHMEM is built on top of DMAPP [8], rather than uGNI. DMAPP* is a communication API optimized to support the small (e.g. 8-byte) transfers typical of high-performance PGAS compilers. As a consequence of this, DMAPP relies on a different hardware mechanism in the Aries NIC for managing PCI-e downstream posted write credits (a deadlock avoidance mechanism (DLA)) than uGNI. In contrast, uGNI is optimized for larger transfers more typical of message passing applications including MPI and Lustre's LNET, as well for allowing efficient sharing of DLA resources and FMA descriptors among processes. Note the DLA mechanism was not present in older Cray® XE™ systems, thus making comparison of results presented here with apparently similar results from Cray® XE™ not particularly meaningful.

We conduct our evaluation using the SOS communication microbenchmark suite that is included in the SOS distribution, the scalable integer sort (ISX) benchmark [15], and the HPCC random access benchmark [10]. For communication microbenchmarks requiring just two nodes, measurements were taken using nodes connected to the same Aries router.

5.1   Latency Results Using SOS Microbenchmarks

The SOS put latency microbenchmark uses two processes, where one of the processes performs a loop of shmem_putmem() and shmem_quiet() operations. Figure 2a shows results for this test. The figure compares the PUT latency of Cray SHMEM with SOS with and without bounce buffering. Excluding the effects of buffering, the latency of SOS is about 150 nsecs more than that attained using Cray SHMEM. Trace data of the 8-byte put latency runs, in addition to comparison of comparable tests written directly to DMAPP and uGNI, indicate the major contributions to extra overhead for SOS can be attributed to the additional overhead within the uGNI library required to manage DLA credits and support sharing of hardware resources (FMA descriptors) between different processes.

The SOS buffering between 128 and 2048 bytes results in significantly higher overhead for SOS put operations compared to Cray SHMEM. As will be shown below for the streaming benchmark, the bounce buffers can sometimes lead to improved results for SOS.

The SOS get latency also uses two processes, where one of the processes performs a loop of shmem_getmem() operations. Figure 2b compares the results obtained using Cray SHMEM and SOS. Results for Cray SHMEM using an Aries BTE threshold at 8192 bytes are also shown. For small get operations between 4 and 64 bytes, SOS again shows an additional 150 nsecs compared to

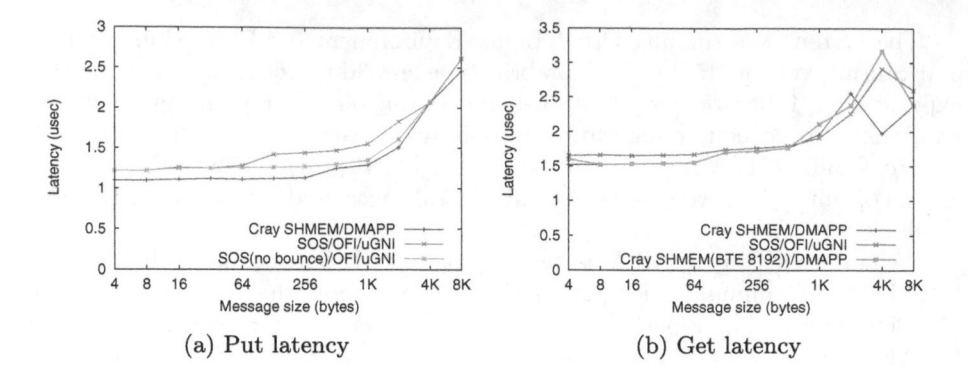

(a) Put latency   (b) Get latency

Fig. 2. Latency measurements for Sandia OpenSHMEM and Cray SHMEM.

Cray SHMEM. This overhead gradually decreases until the point where the respective implementations switch to using the Aries BTE - 4096 bytes for Cray SHMEM and 8192 bytes for SOS. Overall, SOS shows comparable performance with Cray SHMEM in terms of latency, with small overheads attributed to differences between DMAPP and uGNI on Aries.

5.2   Bandwidth Results Using SOS Microbenchmarks

The SOS bi-directional write bandwidth microbenchmark is performed on two processes, where both processes repeatedly perform a stream of shmem_putmem() operations within a fixed window size before performing a shmem_quiet() to ensure remote completion. Figure 3b shows the throughput results between nodes. For small message sizes, SOS utilizes the libfabric inject feature to accelerate the small message pathway through the uGNI provider. After reaching the inject threshold of 64 bytes, SOS switches to bounce buffering until 2 KB in order to immediately achieve local completion without stalling outgoing transactions. We find these two features give noticeable improvement, achieving an average of *61%* relative performance improvement compared to Cray SHMEM. At 4 KB the BTE engine is utilized by both SOS and Cray SHMEM. This transition levels out the results; SOS keeps pace with Cray SHMEM with a *2%* average relative deviation.

The SOS uni-directional read bandwidth microbenchmark is performed on two processes, where one process repeatedly reads from the remote process through a shmem_getmem() operation. In this case remote completion is implied upon return. Figure 3a shows that Cray SHMEM and SOS have comparable results. For get results SOS was tuned to exercise the BTE engine at 2 KB which enables a temporary performance gain over Cray SHMEM's default 4 KB BTE switch. Overall SOS shows competitive performance numbers that are on average within *5%* relative to Cray SHMEM's performance.

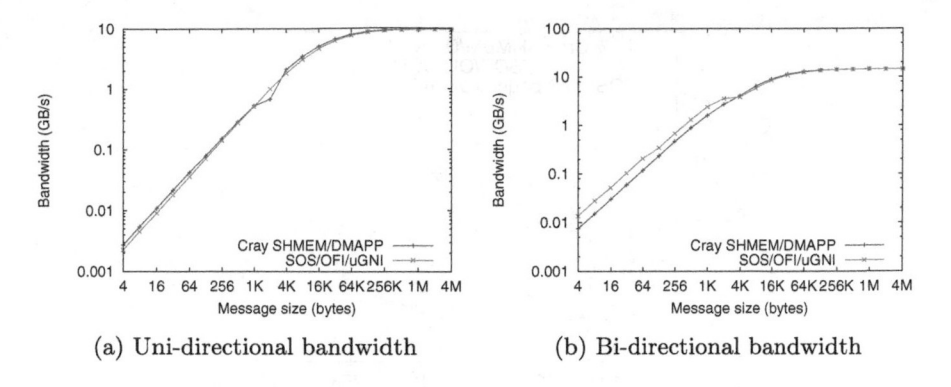

(a) Uni-directional bandwidth   (b) Bi-directional bandwidth

Fig. 3. Bandwidth measurements for Sandia OpenSHMEM and Cray SHMEM.

5.3   Random Access Benchmark (GUPs)

The Random Access Benchmark (GUPs) is intended to assess the ability of an interconnect and its associated network software stack to efficiently handle many small, concurrent load/store accesses to a data table distributed across multiple nodes in a systems. The modified version of the HPCC RandomAccess benchmark employs various aggregation algorithms, all of which encounter scalability challenges. Instead, a version of the benchmark was written based on the serial and OpenMP variants. In this version, each PE executes a series of shmem_longlong_g/shmem_longlong_p operations to load an element from the table, XOR the element with a locally generated value, then write the updated element back in to the table. The number of updates per PE scales as the size of the table. The global table size scales linearly as the number of PEs in the job.

The benchmark was run using a local table size of 32 MB, with each PE executing 16 million updates. Verification of the update run was accomplished by rerunning the algorithm, but using shmem_set_lock/shmem_clear_lock on an array nPES in size to implement a critical region around the update procedure. A run is considered successful if 1% or fewer elements are found to be inconsistent. Figure 4 presents the global update rate (giga-updates/sec) when using Cray SHMEM and SOS. For this experiment, SOS was enhanced to allow for backing the symmetric heap with large pages. Rather than calling mmap with MAP_ANON and a NULL file descriptor, a file was created on one of the node-local CLE large page file systems, and subsequently mapped in to the process address space using mmap. For GUPs style memory access patterns, the Aries I/O MMU works best with large pages. The Xeon 2 MB native large page size was used to back the SOS symmetric heap in these tests. Note Cray SHMEM backs the symmetric heap with large pages by default. For jobs using 32 PEs or fewer, the Aries network is not involved as all get/put operations are handled via XPMEM cross mappings. Above 32 PEs, the Aries network is used for a portion of the remote memory updates. As the job size grows, a greater proportion of the updates target off-node memory and hence exercise the Aries network. SOS performance compares favorably to the Cray SHMEM implementation, particularly when using large pages. The combi-

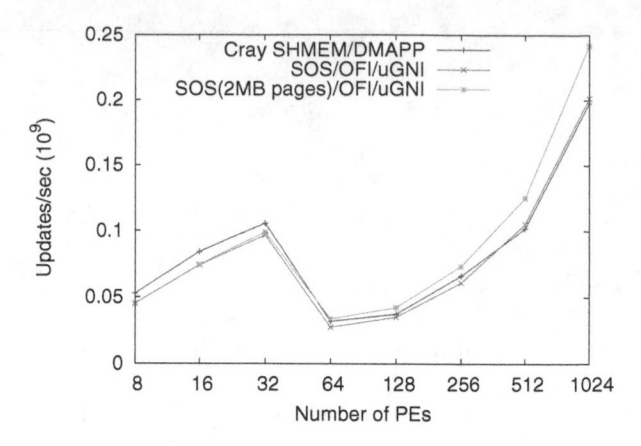

Fig. 4. Giga-updates per second (GUPs) for the RA benchmark on SOS and Cray SHMEM.

nation of the use of the libfabric fi_inject_writedata function in the implementation of shmem_longlong_p and the use of large pages for the symmetric heap, helps SOS to realize a higher update rate than Cray SHMEM at the larger job sizes.

5.4   Scalable Integer Sort Benchmark (ISx)

ISx [15] is a scalable integer sort benchmark using a bucket-sort algorithm. The core communication pattern is an all-to-all exchange of locally sorted keys. The all-to-all exchange is implemented using shmem_int_put to deliver the sorted keys to the target PE. The offset into the target array (allocated from the symmetric heap), is determined using a shmem_longlong_fadd. A final shmem_barrier_all call is invoked to ensure all data has been exchanged. The benchmark allows for both strong and weak scaling. With weak scaling, the number of keys per PE is fixed. For these experiments, ISx was built both with Cray SHMEM and SOS. Except for specifying dynamic linking, no special compiler or linker options were used.

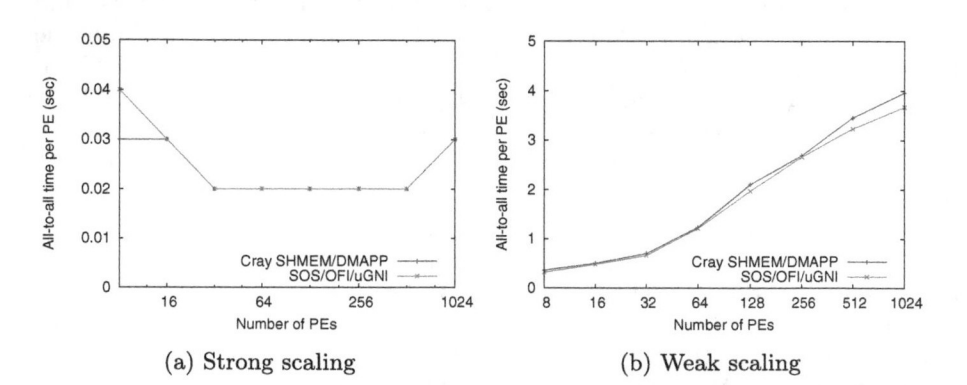

(a) Strong scaling   (b) Weak scaling

Fig. 5. Performance of ISx using Sandia OpenSHMEM and Cray SHMEM.

Figure 5a presents the time spent in the all-to-all exchange in the case of strong scaling, sorting a total of 2^{27} keys. Except for the 8 PE run, the time spent in the all-to-all exchange pattern is the same whether using Sandia SHMEM or Cray SHMEM. Figures 5b shows the time spent in the all-to-all exchange pattern for the weak scaling case. For weak scaling, the time in the all-to-all operation is essentially the same, with SOS showing a small performance improvement.

6   Conclusions and Future Work

Sandia OpenSHMEM (SOS) is the first PGAS middleware to demonstrate the new OpenFabrics Interface communication API on a modern HPC system. Significant effort was invested in both SOS and the uGNI provider to broaden the set of supported performance and portability features, including support for additional memory registration and addressing modes. Overall we found OFI to be closely aligned with the requirements of OpenSHMEM, yielding efficient mappings between the OpenSHMEM middleware and the lower-layer libfabric interfaces.

We evaluated the performance of our implementation on a Cray® XC40™ system and demonstrated comparable latency and scalability to the production Cray SHMEM library. SOS with OFI achieved comparable or better bandwidth and random access (GUPs) performance than Cray SHMEM. For small messages, the OFI inject functionality used by SOS resulted in an improvement of up to *61%* in bi-directional bandwidth. In addition, the SOS bounce buffering optimization enabled further improvements in the small-to-medium message regimes. We hope to further improve upon these results with additional performance and scalability tuning.

The OpenSHMEM community is actively working to extend the OpenSHMEM model with new tools that will allow users to leverage future extreme scale systems. We hope that the new, open source platform that we have presented will provide a useful environment for evaluating and developing new extensions to the OpenSHMEM parallel programming model.

Acknowledgements. This research used resources of the National Energy Research Scientific Computing Center, a DOE Office of Science User Facility supported by the Office of Science of the U.S. Department of Energy under Contract No. DE-AC02-05CH11231. We also thank the OpenFabrics Interfaces Working Group (OFIWG) and its attendees, whose participation has enabled the cooperative design of the libfabric interfaces. This publication has been approved for public, unlimited distribution by Los Alamos National Laboratory, with document number LA-UR-16-24359.

*Other names and brands may be claimed as the property of others.
Intel and Xeon are trademarks of Intel Corporation in the U.S. and/or other countries. Software and workloads used in performance tests may have been optimized for performance only on Intel microprocessors. Performance tests, such as SYSmark and MobileMark, are measured using specific computer systems, components, software, operations and functions. Any change to any of those factors may cause the results to vary. You should consult other information and performance tests to assist you in fully

evaluating your contemplated purchases, including the performance of that product when combined with other products. For more information go to http://www.intel.com/performance.

References

1. Balaji, P., Buntinas, D., Goodell, D., Gropp, W., Krishna, J., Lusk, E., Thakur, R.: PMI: a scalable parallel process-management interface for extreme-scale systems. In: Keller, R., Gabriel, E., Resch, M., Dongarra, J. (eds.) EuroMPI 2010. LNCS, vol. 6305, pp. 31–41. Springer, Heidelberg (2010). doi:10.1007/978-3-642-15646-5_4
2. Barrett, B.W., Brightwell, R., Hemmert, S., Pedretti, K., Wheeler, K., Underwood, K., Riesen, R., Maccabe, A.B., Hudson, T.: The portals 4.0.2 network programming interface. Technical report SAND2013-3181, Sandia National Laboratories, April 2013
3. Barrett, B.W., Brigthwell, R., Hemmert, K.S., Pedretti, K., Wheeler, K., Underwood, K.D.: Enhanced support for OpenSHMEM communication in Portals. In: 19th Annual Symposium on High Performance Interconnects, August 2011
4. Barrett, B.W., Hammond, S.D., Brightwell, R., Hemmert, K.S.: The impact of hybrid-core processors on MPI message rate. In: Proceedings of 20th European MPI Users' Group Meeting, EuroMPI 2013, pp. 67–71 (2013)
5. Birrittella, M.S., Debbage, M., Huggahalli, R., Kunz, J., Lovett, T., Rimmer, T., Underwood, K.D., Zak, R.C.: Intel ® Omni-path architecture: enabling scalable, high performance fabrics. In: Proceedings of 23rd Annual Symposium on High-Performance Interconnects, pp. 1–9, August 2015
6. Bonachea, D.: GASNet specification, v1.1. Technical report UCB/CSD-02-1207, University of California, Berkeley, October 2002
7. Choi, S.E., Pritchard, H., Shimek, J., Swaro, J., Tiffany, Z., Turrubiates, B.: An implementation of OFI libfabric in support of multithreaded PGAS solutions. In: Proceedings of 9th International Conference on Parititioned Global Address Space Programming Models, PGAS 2015, September 2015
8. Cray Inc.: Using the GNI and DMAPP APIs. Technical report S-2446-3103, Cray Inc. (2011)
9. Derradji, S., Palfer-Sollier, T., Panziera, J.P., Poudes, A., Atos, F.W.: The BXI interconnect architecture. In: Proceedings of IEEE 23rd Annual Symposium on High-Performance Interconnects, pp. 18–25, August 2015
10. Dongarra, J., Luszczek, P.: Introduction to the HPCChallenge benchmark suite. Technical report ICL-UT-05-01, ICL (2005)
11. Flajslik, M., Dinan, J., Underwood, K.D.: Mitigating MPI message matching misery. In: Kunkel, J.M., Balaji, P., Dongarra, J. (eds.) ISC High Performance 2016. LNCS, vol. 9697, pp. 281–299. Springer, Heidelberg (2016). doi:10.1007/978-3-319-41321-1_15
12. Gabriel, E., et al.: Open MPI: goals, concept, and design of a next generation MPI implementation. In: Kranzlmüller, D., Kacsuk, P., Dongarra, J. (eds.) EuroPVM/MPI 2004. LNCS, vol. 3241, pp. 97–104. Springer, Heidelberg (2004). doi:10.1007/978-3-540-30218-6_19
13. Girolamo, S.D., Jolivet, P., Underwood, K.D., Hoefler, T.: Exploiting offload enabled network interfaces. In: Proceedings of 23rd Annual Symposium on High-Performance Interconnects. IEEE, August 2015

14. Grun, P., Hefty, S., Sur, S., Goodell, D., Russell, R., Pritchard, H., Squyres, J.: A brief introduction to the OpenFabrics interfaces - a new network API for maximizing high performance application efficiency. In: Proceedings of 23rd Annual Symposium on High-Performance Interconnects, August 2015
15. Hanebutte, U., Hemstad, J.: ISx: a scalable integer sort for co-design in the exascale era. In: 2015 9th International Conference on Partitioned Global Address Space Programming Models (PGAS), pp. 102–104, September 2015
16. Janjusic, T., Shamis, P., Venkata, M.G., Pool, S.W.: OpenSHMEM reference implementation using UCCS-uGNI transport layer. In: Proceedings of 8th International Conference on Partitioned Global Address Space Programming Models, PGAS 2014 (2014)
17. Jose, J., Kandalla, K., Luo, M., Panda, D.K.: Supporting hybrid MPI and OpenSHMEM over InfiniBand: design and performance evaluation. In: Proceedings of 41st International Conference on Parallel Processing, ICPP 2012, pp. 219–228, September 2012
18. Jose, J., Zhang, J., Venkatesh, A., Potluri, S., Panda, D.K.D.K.: A comprehensive performance evaluation of OpenSHMEM libraries on InfiniBand clusters. In: Poole, S., Hernandez, O., Shamis, P. (eds.) OpenSHMEM 2014. LNCS, vol. 8356, pp. 14–28. Springer, Heidelberg (2014). doi:10.1007/978-3-319-05215-1_2
19. Kumar, S., Mamidala, A.R., Faraj, D.A., Smith, B., Blocksome, M., Cernohous, B., Miller, D., Parker, J., Ratterman, J., Heidelberger, P., Chen, D., Steinmacher-Burrow, B.: PAMI: a parallel active message interface for the Blue Gene/Q supercomputer. In: Proceedings of 26th International Parallel Distributed Processing Symposium, IPDPS 2012, pp. 763–773, May 2012
20. Libfabric. http://ofiwg.github.io/
21. Luo, M., Seager, K., Murthy, K.S., Archer, C.J., Sur, S., Hefty, S.: Early evaluation of scalable fabric interface for PGAS programming models. In: Proceedings of 8th International Conference on Partitioned Global Address Space Programming Models, PGAS 2014 (2014)
22. Reference OpenSHMEM implementation. https://github.com/openshmem-org/openshmem
23. OpenSHMEM application programming interface, version 1.3, February 2016. http://www.openshmem.org
24. Pritchard, H., Harvey, E., Choi, S.E., Swaro, J., Tiffany, Z.: The GNI provider layer for OFI libfabric. In: Proceedings of Cray User Group Meeting, CUG 2016, May 2016
25. Sandia OpenSHMEM. https://www.github.com/Sandia-OpenSHMEM/
26. Shamis, P., Venkata, M.G., Kuehn, J.A., Poole, S.W., Graham, R.L.: Universal common communication substrate (UCCS) specification, version 0.1. Technical report ORNL/TM-2012/339, Oak Ridge National Laboratory (2012)
27. Shamis, P., Venkata, M.G., Lopez, M.G., Baker, M.B., Hernandez, O., Itigin, Y., Dubman, M., Shainer, G., Graham, R.L., Liss, L., Shahar, Y., Potluri, S., Rossetti, D., Becker, D., Poole, D., Lamb, C., Kumar, S., Stunkel, C., Bosilca, G., Bouteiller, A.: UCX: an open source framework for HPC network APIs and beyond. In: Proceedings of IEEE 23rd Annual Symposium on High-Performance Interconnects, pp. 40–43, August 2015
28. Shamis, P., Venkata, M.G., Poole, S., Welch, A., Curtis, T.: Designing a high performance OpenSHMEM implementation using universal common communication substrate as a communication middleware. In: Poole, S., Hernandez, O., Shamis, P. (eds.) OpenSHMEM 2014. LNCS, vol. 8356, pp. 1–13. Springer, Heidelberg (2014). doi:10.1007/978-3-319-05215-1_1

OpenSHMEM-UCX: Evaluation of UCX for Implementing OpenSHMEM Programming Model

Matthew Baker[1]([✉]), Ferrol Aderholdt[1], Manjunath Gorentla Venkata[1], and Pavel Shamis[2]

[1] Computer Science and Mathematics Division,
Oak Ridge National Laboratory (ORNL), Oak Ridge, USA
bakermb@ornl.gov
[2] ARM Research, Cambridge, UK

Abstract. The OpenSHMEM reference implementation was developed towards the goal of developing an open source and high-performing OpenSHMEM implementation. To achieve portability and performance across various networks, the OpenSHMEM reference implementation uses GASNet and UCCS for network operations. Recently, new network layers have emerged with the promise of providing high-performance, scalability, and portability for HPC applications. In this paper, we implement the OpenSHMEM reference implementation to use the UCX framework for network operations. Then, we evaluate its performance and scalability on Cray XK systems to understand UCX's suitability for developing the OpenSHMEM programming model. Further, we develop a benchmark called SHOMS for evaluating the OpenSHMEM implementation. Our experimental results show that OpenSHMEM-UCX outperforms the vendor supplied OpenSHMEM implementation in most cases on the Cray XK system by up to 40% with respect to message rate and up to 70% for the execution of application kernels.

Keywords: OpenSHMEM · UCX

Notice of Copyright

1 Introduction

OpenSHMEM is a Partitioned Global Address Space (PGAS) programming library interface. The specification has evolved from version 1.0, which has

© Springer International Publishing AG 2016
M. Gorentla Venkata et al. (Eds.): OpenSHMEM 2016, LNCS 10007, pp. 114–130, 2016.
DOI: 10.1007/978-3-319-50995-2_8

created an open specification of SHMEM, to version 1.3, which provides very useful functionality for modern architectures. As the specification has evolved, so has the availability of implementations. Multiple proprietary implementations have always been available from vendors such as SGI and Cray. Besides the open source implementation of *OpenSHMEM* from Oak Ridge National Laboratory (ORNL) and the University of Houston (UH), only recently has there been the availability of other open source implementations through the efforts of the Open-MPI community [1], the Portals community [2], the Ohio State University (OSU) with MVAPICH-X [3], and Mellanox [4]. Though historically the open source implementations have not been high-performant, they are working towards providing high-performance and high-scalability [5–7] by leveraging high-performing network layers such as Unified Communication X (UCX), Universal Common Communication Substrate (UCCS), Libfabrics, as well as network capability layers such as Portals.

The *OpenSHMEM* reference implementation is a simple and essential layer over a PGAS compatible network layer to provide an open source implementation of *OpenSHMEM*. The simplicity of the layer has resulted in keeping the performance overhead low while achieving portability with the aid of network layers. Previously, it was implemented utilizing GASNet and UCCS to achieve portability and performance over a wide variety of network such as Cray's *Gemini* and *Aries*, InfiniBand, Ethernet and Shared Memory transports. In this paper, we port the reference implementation to use UCX, which has shown the promise of providing high-performance and high-scalability for parallel programming models.

The reason for choosing UCX is the fact that it was developed in a close collaboration between the *OpenSHMEM* community and hardware vendors. UCX is a framework of network APIs and protocol implementations for implementing parallel programming models such as *OpenSHMEM*, Message Passing Interface (MPI), and task-based models. It provides two levels of APIs, the low-level transport API called UC-Transports (UCT) and high-level protocol API called UC-Protocols (UCP). The UCT layer provides a set of interfaces for transferring data efficiently over multiple high-performance networks including InfiniBand, *Gemini*, *Aries*, and various types of shared memory. It is designed to provide low-overhead and portable interfaces over the native network drivers and hardware abstraction layers. The UCP layer provides messaging layer functionality and protocols such as eager, rendezvous protocols, tag matching, and support for multi-rail network, which is required to support parallel programming models. This two-level design suits well for function rich and portability driven models such as MPI and high-performance driven programming models such as *OpenSHMEM*.

In the rest of the paper, we provide details of the design and implementation of the *OpenSHMEM* reference implementation using UCX. Particularly, we focus our implementation on the *uGNI* conduit, which provides data transport functionality over Cray's network interface *Gemini* and *Aries*. In Sect. 4, we provide details of UCX relevant for implementing PGAS programming models; in

Sect. 6, we provide details of *uGNI* Transport Layer (TL); in Sect. 8, we provide an evaluation of the implementation using Titan at ORNL as a testbed.

2   Related Work

Since the 1.0 API specification of *OpenSHMEM*, there have been numerous open source implementations of the *OpenSHMEM* specification up to the 1.3 release [1–4,8]. With respect to these implementations, there has been a primary motivation of providing the community with *OpenSHMEM* implementations including those with both portable and high-performance conduits for networking operations.

The first open source implementation of the *OpenSHMEM* specification was the *OpenSHMEM* reference implementation completed by both ORNL and the UH. This implementation utilized the GASNet conduit and provided both performance and portability. Shamis et al. [5] later updated the reference implementation to support UCCS as a conduit to provide a high-performance conduit for the *OpenSHMEM* programming model. Hammond et al. [8] explored the utilization of the one-sided operations in MPI-3 as a conduit for *OpenSHMEM* with the intent of leveraging MPI implementations to provide high-performance and portability. The Portals interface was another conduit explored by the implementation of *OpenSHMEM* by Sandia National Laboratory [2]. Open-MPI also provides an implementation of *OpenSHMEM* bundled with their MPI implementation [1]. Additionally, the OSU and Mellanox both provide an implementation of *OpenSHMEM* in the MVAPICH-X [3] implementation and in HPC-X [4], respectively. In addition to the open source implementations, there are also many proprietary implementations of SHMEM including those by SGI, Cray, and HP, which are specific to the systems deployed by those companies.

This work focuses on implementing the *OpenSHMEM* reference implementation to utilize the UCX networking framework. Unlike other conduits for the reference implementation, UCX is a collaboration between both the *OpenSHMEM* community and hardware vendors allowing for both portability and high performance.

3   OpenSHMEM Reference Implementation

The *OpenSHMEM* reference implementation is an open source implementation of the *OpenSHMEM* specification. The main components of the implementation are Atomics, Remote Memory Access (RMA), Collectives, Symmetric Memory, and Utils components. The central component responsible for all data transfer is the *COMMS* layer.

The *COMMS* layer separates network-agnostic and network-specific code bases for all of the communication driven operations including puts, gets, and atomics. Operations that require no communication are implemented outside of the communication layer. This can be seen in Fig. 1. This separation allows the reference implementation to leverage many PGAS friendly network layers. Currently, the reference implementation can take advantage of GASNet, UCCS, and UCX.

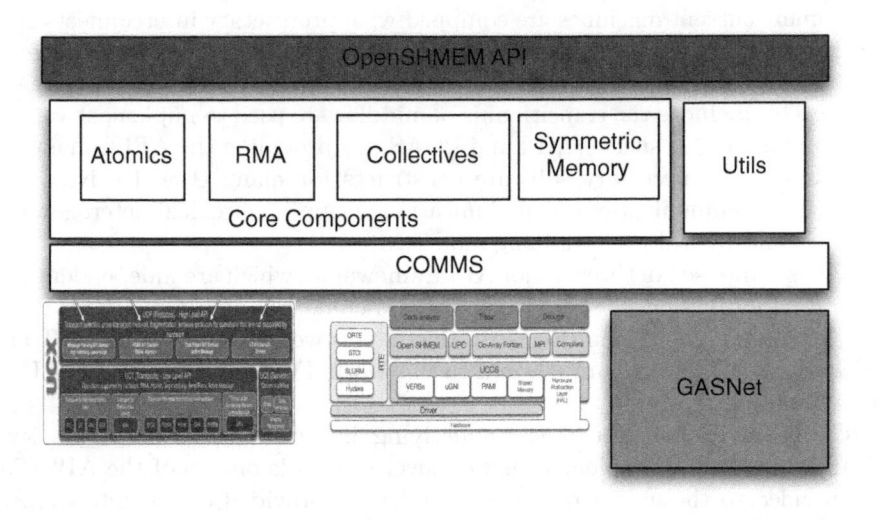

Fig. 1. Various components in the *OpenSHMEM* reference implementation

The *COMMS* layer is a thin layer that implements the functionality to bridge the gap between *OpenSHMEM* requirements and the functionality provided by UCX's UCP. For example, shmem_get blocks until the completion of the operation since the UCX operations are non-blocking. Similarly, other RMA and Atomic operations map directly to UCP interfaces. In this implementation, we specifically use the UCP interfaces rather than the UCT interfaces. However, It should be noted that one could also only leverage the UCT interfaces for implementing *OpenSHMEM*.

The initialization of UCX with *OpenSHMEM* involves several steps. Initially, the Run Time Environment (RTE) is initialized and used to bring up the initial state of the individual Processing Element (PE). This is done so each PE has some base state including an index, or PE number, groups, and heap size. Anchormen interfaces with UCX through the UCP layer. This includes the initialization of the UCX library and the creation of a UCP worker thread, which is a unit UCX uses to make progress in communication requests.

After each PE has a worker, all PEs within the job exchange their data to obtain each PE's worker's address for later communication. After the addresses are determined, endpoints are created. Finally, the atomics handlers and collectives are initialized and ready for use. After initialization, UCP is interfaced by *OpenSHMEM* for the underlying networking capabilities.

4   UCX Design

UCX is a network API framework focused on providing a portable and high performance library over the underlying networking components. This is important as many current machines are equipped with proprietary interconnects each with their own interfaces. The differences between interfaces is costly as a significant amount time must be used to port a piece of software from one interface to another. This includes the transitioning of middleware used to implement various programming models such as MPI and PGAS. By providing the API framework, UCX exposes the necessary software constructs for many thread driven high performance communications, communication within hierarchical heterogeneous memories, and hybrid programming models.

UCX is composed of three major API frameworks, which are independent and can be used individually. These frameworks include UC-Services (UCS), UCT, and UCP and can be seen in Fig. 2. In this paper, we will detail both UCT and UCP as these frameworks are relevant to this work. Further information on UCS can be found in [9].

UCT is an abstraction of the underlying hardware providing a low-level API allowing users to implement higher-level protocols on top of the API. The API provided to the user is driven by the drivers provided by the interconnect manufacturers. Additionally, the UCT API provides the necessary functionality for communication context management, device specific memory allocation and management, and interfaces for various types of messages.

UCP provides an abstraction of higher-level protocols that may be used by common programming models such as MPI or PGAS. This is possible by leveraging the transports provided by UCT and selecting the correct transport for the desired communication. Additionally, UCP will initialize the library, allow for message fragmentation, and provide multi-rail communication. The API also provides interfaces for various operations including initialization, RMA, *Atomic Memory Operations* (AMO), active messages, and collectives.

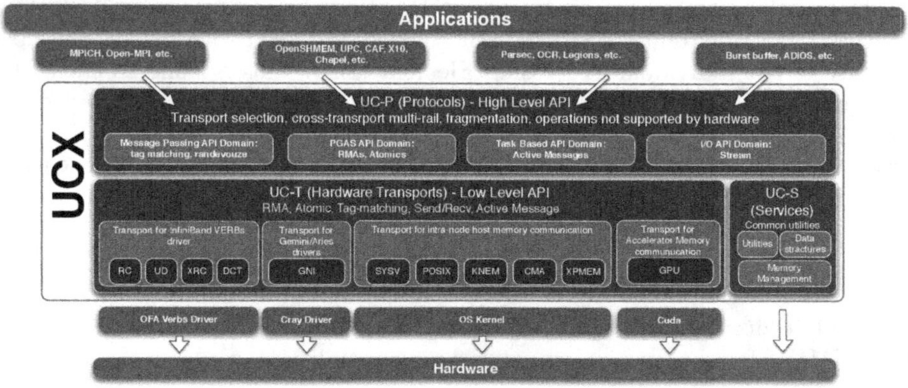

Fig. 2. The UCX architecture [9]

5   UCX Core Components

In order to provide the scalability needs present in modern and future extreme-scale systems, it is imperative the networking library presented by UCX provides the basic mechanisms to support these needs. This is accomplished through the use of workers, interfaces, and arbiters. The use of these mechanisms allow for an ease of scalability within the networking paths of execution.

5.1   Workers

Applications are abstracted on top of UCX through the use of application contexts. These contexts allow for a conceptual separation between multiple jobs as well as provide an isolation of communication resources such that there is no interference between jobs. For application contexts, a significant amount of the abstraction of applications is provided by workers.

Workers are an abstraction of multiple components including the processes or threads executing within a parallel job, the communication resources necessary to complete a parallel job, and the progress made by the communication resources to complete the requests of the application. This abstraction is useful as the architectures of current and future systems suggest a shift towards workloads that consist primarily of threads, which may or may not be communicating threads across node boundaries.

Workers exist across multiple layers of UCX having a presence in both UCT and UCP. In both layers, the conceptual duties are similar with the primary functionality within UCT consisting of ensuring the progress of communication, while in UCP the functionality includes the abstraction of communication resources. With the worker's responsibility in UCP focused on the abstraction of communication resources, this implies that workers are able to communicate with other each other.

Communication between workers is possible after the workers become addressable. To become addressable, the worker must be coupled with an endpoint, which provides the addressing mechanisms and attributes. Afterwards, communication may commence between processes and threads locally and remotely. To ensure the ability to perform both synchronous and asynchronous communication in an independent manner with the ability to complete communications efficiently, a progress engine is used, which keeps track of outstanding requests and completes them.

5.2   Interfaces

While workers abstract computational elements such as processes and threads as well as the communication resources, the elements abstracted have certain capabilities and components that may be exposed to the applications making use of UCX. This is accomplished through the use of interfaces, which abstract the physical device while exposing features of the device for usage by the application. Examples of the exposed elements include short and buffered copy capabilities, send and receive queues, keys for use with infiniband, device overhead, latency, and bandwidth as well as other features. By exposing a set of features to the user while abstracting the individual characteristics of the device, the user can make informed decisions about the communication between PEs without concern of future changes should the underlying network device change.

5.3   Arbiter

In order to maintain scalability and perform a fair distribution of requests, an arbiter is used within the interface to a device. The arbiter mediates the requests attempting to be fair with respect to request dispatches. This allows for requests to be dispatched when prior requests have yet to complete.

6   Design and Implementation of uGNI TL

The *uGNI* TL provides interfaces and implementations to transfer data over Cray's Gemini and Aries networks. To support PGAS and MPI programming models, it provides interfaces for *Remote Direct Memory Access* (RDMA) and Send/Recv type message transfers as well as atomic operations. The *OpenSH-MEM* layer along with the UCP layer chooses the appropriate interfaces and implements the missing semantics to satisfy the programming model semantic requirements. The rest of the section describes the initialization of the *uGNI* TL and various protocols for data transfers and atomic operations.

6.1   Initialization and Connection Setup

The UCP layer in co-ordination with the UCT layer initialize the *uGNI* protocols. The UCP layer provides two different wire-up mechanisms to serve different network semantics. In our experience, these two mechanisms are enough to serve various protocols of *InfiniBand*, *Gemini*, *Aries*, and Shared Memory.

- For networks that requires only the interface information for wire-up such as *uGNI*'s Fast Memory Access (FMA) and Block Transfer Engine (BTE) interfaces and *InfiniBand*'s datagram protocols, the UCP layer uses the out-of-band mechanisms to exchange the interface information. In our experiments for Cray systems, the *uGNI* TL uses Cray's Process Manager Interface (PMI) to exchange the interface information.
- For networks that require endpoint information in addition to interface information, it provides mechanisms to exchange the endpoint information using other protocols on the network. This is achieved in two stages. In the first stage, it sets up a datagram connection between different PEs or *MPI Ranks* using *uGNI*'s endpoint datagrams for Cray systems. Then it uses this connection for exchanging endpoint connection information. Though it is not scalable, this approach is required for using some protocols such as *uGNI*'s Short message (SMSG) interfaces.

To alleviate some of the scalability impact of this approach, we exchange the endpoint information only on-demand. For the *OpenSHMEM* reference implementation, we do not exercise this code path. This is because the *OpenSHMEM* operations are one-sided and can efficiently be mapped onto the FMA and BTE interfaces and do not require use of the *SMSG* protocol. For a MPI implementation, only connections that actively exchange data are wired up using this approach.

6.2   Short Data Transfers

The functions *uct_ugni_ep_put_short* and *uct_ugni_ep_put_bcopy* are the interfaces for small and medium data transfers. They use *uGNI*'s FMA interface, which is optimized for RDMA small data transfers as it copies the data from the source buffer to library buffers. The function *uct_ugni_ep_put_short* returns after posting the FMA operation, and completion is learnt as required by the upper layer. For example, if this interface is used for implementing the shmem_put operation of the *OpenSHMEM* programming model, the *OpenSHMEM* layer will wait for global completion event by progressing the worker and flushing the endpoint. On the other hand, if this interface is used for shmem_put_nbi, the *OpenSHMEM* layer will return as soon as the operation is posted and waits for completion during the shmem_quiet or shmem_barrier calls. Thus, the interfaces along with the abstraction of endpoints, workers, and interfaces enable implementing various semantics.

6.3   Large Data Transfers

The function *uct_ugni_ep_put_zcopy* implements the interface for large data transfers. It uses *uGNI*'s BTE interface, *GNI_PostRdma()*, with post type GNI_POST_ RDMA_PUT or GNI_POST_RDMA_GET. The interface is optimized for RDMA large data transfers as it copies data from the source buffers to the network using DMA engines without CPU intervention. The interface has semantics similar to the short data transfer interfaces.

The mapping onto *uGNI*'s interface is straightforward when the data is 4-byte aligned and the data length is a multiple of 4-bytes. However, because of BTE's Get interface's constraints on the message length and alignment, a protocol was developed for unaligned messages. For example, when the data length is not a multiple of 4-bytes, we pad the data and transfer the data using the appropriate protocols as shown in Fig. 3.

6.4   Active Messages

The interface *uct_ugni_smsg_ep_am_short* provides an implementation of the active message semantics, particularly useful to implement MPI_Send and MPI_Recv interfaces. The implementation leverages *uGNI*'s GNI_SmsgSendWTag() for data transfer. After the posting of the message using this interface, it maintains the list

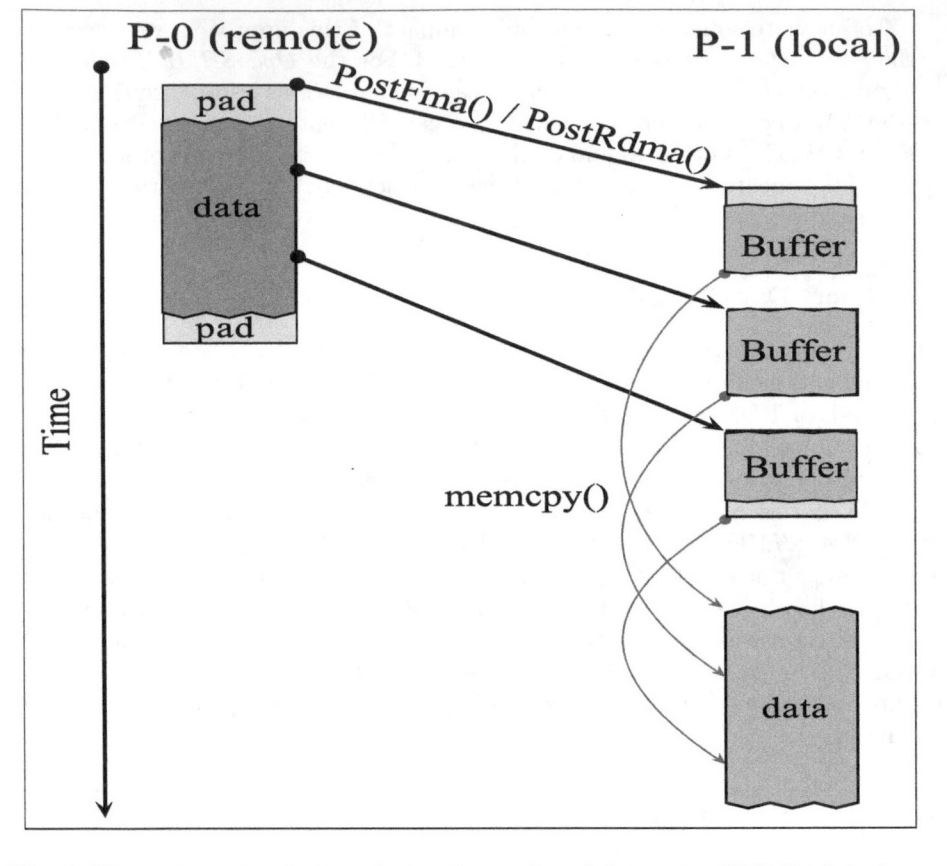

Fig. 3. The various steps in transferring the unaligned data using BTE Get interfaces

of posted messages and eventually frees the descriptors and consumes the completions. It uses this interface only for small data transfers because of the performance advantages and resources consumed by the SMSG interfaces.

6.5   Atomic Operations

The *uGNI* TL provides complete support for atomics in the *OpenSHMEM* programming model including 32-bit and 64-bit atomic operations. Aside from swap, the 64-bit atomic operations are supported using the native atomic operation interfaces provided by *uGNI*. Additionally, 32-bit atomic operations and 64-bit swap operations are emulated using the *cswap* operation.

A swap operation can be emulated using *fetch* and *cswap* operations. The swap operation is emulated in two steps, which are similar to the implementation in UCCS [5]. First, the original value in the remote address is fetched. Then, the *cswap* operation is used to swap in the new value using the fetched value as the condition operand. If the *cswap* operation fails because the value in the remote address changed, then the emulation operation loops to fetch the new value and attempt the *cswap* operation again. This can cause higher latencies than a native swap operation but will result in the correct behavior. All of the 32-bit operations can be similarly emulated. In all operations, the remote value is fetched, cast into a 32-bit integer, operated on, then replaced with *cswap*.

7 Experiments

This work focuses on the development of a reference implementation of *OpenSH-MEM* on top of the UCX networking framework. This involves a considerable amount of work at the network level in order to properly design and implement such a work. Thus, the evaluation of this work will focus on measuring the necessary communication paths encountered by an *OpenSHMEM* application. The experimental evaluation includes the execution of multiple micro-benchmarks including a synthetic ping-pong benchmark, the *OpenSHMEM Put* message rate benchmark from the Ohio State University (OSU) benchmark suite [10], the SHOMS benchmark, and the HPCS Scalable Synthetic Compact Applications (SSCA) 1 benchmark from [11]. In order to validate the work, the results of these experiments will be compared against the Cray SHMEM implementation, which is a proprietary implementation specific to the underlying network.

The ping-pong benchmark allows us to measure the latency overhead of the communication between PEs. This is accomplished by having a PE sending a token to another PE, which will then return the token. With respect to *Open-SHMEM*, this is done by putting data from an originator to a recipient and then the recipient returning the data.

The OSU benchmark suite allows us to determine the performance of the networking layer as an increasing amount of PEs are added to the application. The *Put* benchmark measures the message rate of the *Put* operation between pairs of PEs. Thus, the message rate from a particular node can be measured by increasing the amount of PEs on two nodes. We do this in order to stress the networking layer on a particular node obtaining a reasonable performance measurement.

The SHOMS benchmark, as described in Sect. 8, performs a benchmark on the functionality described in the *OpenSHMEM* specifications. Making use of this test allows us to obtain a complete view of UCX's performance with respect to *OpenSHMEM*. The primary factors we are concerned with are *Put* and *Get* performance in terms of latency as well as bandwidth.

The HPCS SSCA 1 benchmark makes use of the *Smith-Waterman* algorithm, which determines the similarity between two large sequences. For the HPCS SSCA 1 benchmark, the sequences being compared are DNA/RNA protein sequences, which is a common use case in Bioinformatics. This allows us to observe the execution of a real world application. The implementation used for this experiment is the same as found in [11].

The experimental setup included an allocation on the Titan machine at ORNL. Titan contains 18,688 physical compute nodes each composed of 16 compute cores and 32 GB of RAM, which is a total of 299,008 cores and 598 TB of memory. Each node is connected via a *Gemini* interconnect.

8   Evaluation

The validation of this work was completed by making use of multiple benchmarks. The synthetic ping-pong benchmark, OSU, and SHOMS micro-benchmarks were used to evaluate the performance of basic OpenSHMEM routines. Then we used the OpenSHMEM version of the HPCS SSCA 1 benchmark to evaluate the overall quality of the implementation in the context of a real-life computational kernel.

The results of these benchmarks will be detailed and analyzed in this section.

8.1   Short Message Latency

To measure the short message latency, we implemented a simple ping-pong benchmark. Each execution of the benchmark was completed with 1 PE across two nodes. A *Put* operation of varying size is done between each PE, where the remote PE is waiting for the message. When the message is received, the receiver will write a message back to the originating PE. The results of the experiment can be seen in Fig. 4.

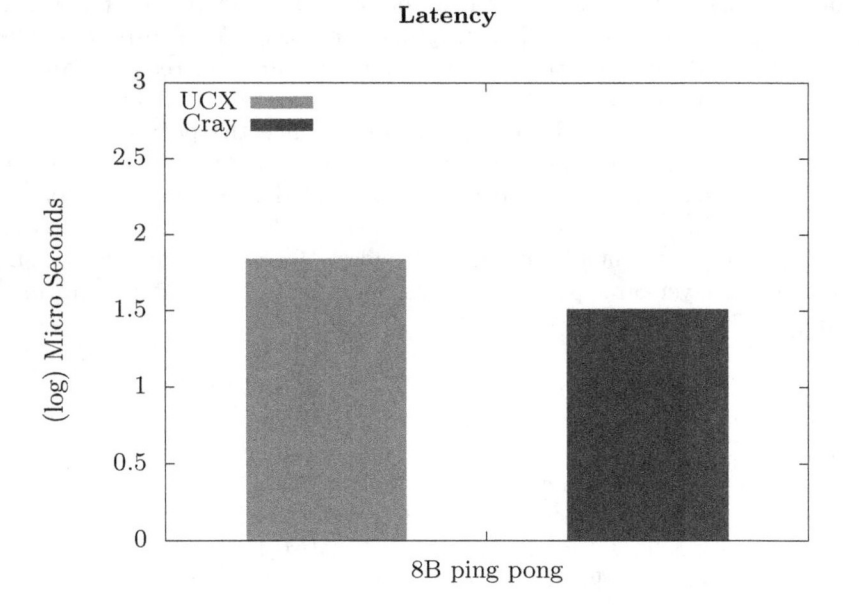

Fig. 4. Ping pong results. Lower is better.

The performance of Cray SHMEM is a slightly better than the OpenSHMEM-UCX implementation. The round-trip latency of OpenSHMEM-UCX and Cray

SHMEM is $1.84\,\mu s$ and $1.51\,\mu s$ respectively. We believe the performance difference is due to the difference in the completion semantics of both implementations. The advantages of our approach can be seen in the message rate.

8.2   Message Rate

We use the micro benchmark suite from OSU [10] for measuring the message rate. Each execution of the benchmark was completed on two nodes with an increasing amount of PEs being placed on each node beginning with 1 PE per node and ending with 16 PEs per node. Each PE was paired with another PE on the neighboring node. The message rate was measured with the use of repeated *Put* operations over time. The results of the experiment can be seen in Fig. 5.

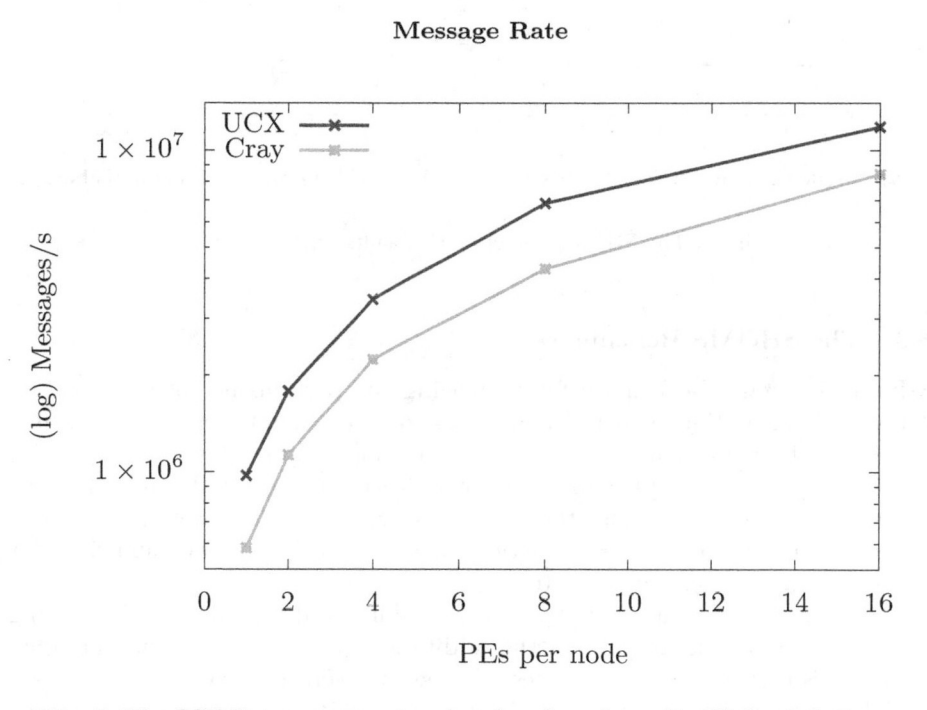

Fig. 5. The OSU Put message rate micro-benchmark results. Higher is better.

The results showed a considerable difference between OpenSHMEM-UCX and Cray's implementation with an increasing amount of PEs per node. Both implementations appear to scale reasonably well, however, the UCX implementation consistently maintains a higher performance with respect to messages being sent per second. As the number of PEs per node increases from one to 16, the difference between both approaches is between roughly 59% and 24% with respect to message rate. Due to the proprietary nature of Cray OpenSHMEM implementation, it is challenging to identify the exact reason for such substantial performance differences. Nevertheless, it is worth pointing out that one of the core differences between the two implementations is the underlying communication driver. Cray's OpenSHMEM implementation is based on the DMAPP driver while UCX leverages a more generic uGNI driver. In addition, the UCX design was focused on the optimization of the communication path for high-injection rates, which is one of the core requirements emerging from OpenSHMEM applications (Fig. 6).

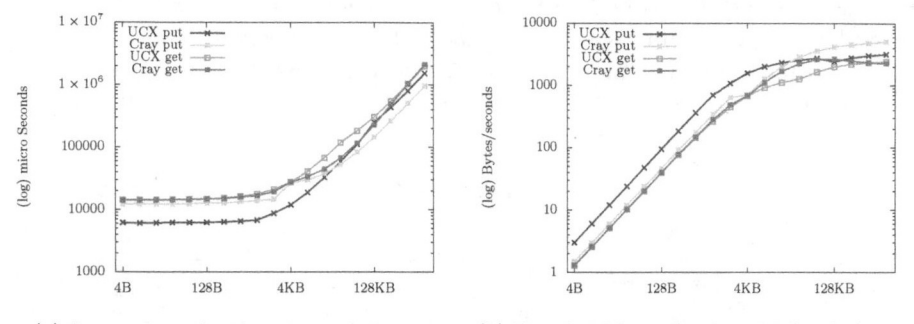

(a) Latency evaluation, lower is better.   (b) Bandwidth evaluation, higher is better.

Fig. 6. The SHOMS benchmark results with 4096 PEs.

8.3   The SHOMS Benchmark

SHOMS is a microbenchmark for evaluating the performance of an OpenSH-MEM implementation. The design goal was to have a simple benchmark capable of testing the performance of all of the functions of the latest OpenSHMEM specification. It is designed to iterate over each function with multiple messages lengths. It will produce the minimum, maximum, and average overhead for issuing a message with each function. It will also calculate the bandwidth for functions where this is appropriate.

SHOMS is also designed to be highly modular and configurable. Extending SHOMS is simplistic and allows the addition of new functions with minimal effort. This reduces the effort for testing new experimental features.

The SHOMS benchmark showed interesting results when compared to the ping-pong benchmark. In the ping-pong benchmark, a chunk of data at an increasing size was put from a single sender node to a receiver and then the receiver sent the data back. In SHOMS, for this experiment there is one sender node and 4095 receivers. Each receiver gets a certain number of bytes, from 4 bytes to 1 MB. The sender is simply performing a sequence of multiple Open-SHMEM *Put* operations to each node and a quiet operation on the receiver without a reply. Thus, there are differences in the results.

The *Put* latency and *Get* latency for UCX when compared to Cray's implementation showed a 76% and 33% improvement in performance. However, Cray showed higher bandwidth than UCX with UCX performing within 17% and 6%

of Cray for Put and Get bandwidth respectively. This evaluation highlights the differences of underlying implementations.

8.4   Evaluation Using HPCS SSCA 1

HPCS SSCA1 is an implementation of Smith-Waterman local sequence alignment algorithm [12]. The communication characteristics of the benchmark stresses the important characteristics of many OpenSHMEM applications. The crux of the communication in the benchmark is within two loops - an outer and inner loop. The inner loop in each iteration issues many *Get* operations and few *Put* operations. Both the *Get* and *Put* operations are used to transfer small data. The algorithm requires only the *Get* operations complete in each iteration, and *Put* operations do not block the progress of the inner loop. It needs to be completed by the start of next outer loop. As a consequence of this characteristic, the benchmark is sensitive to small message latency and message rate.

For this benchmark, the application was run on a varying amount of PEs, which were spread across multiple nodes with a range from 4 to 256 nodes with eight PEs per node. In this experiment, the time taken to complete the experiment was measured, where lower times are better. The results of this experiment can be seen in Fig. 7. The benchmark was also executed at a larger scale with 16K nodes. The results of the 16K nodes are in Fig. 8.

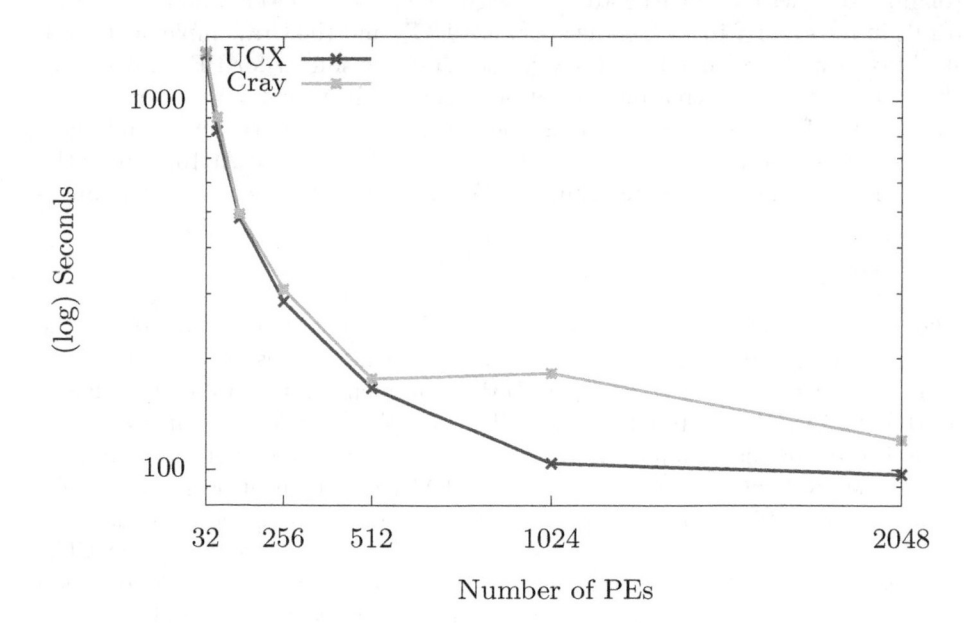

Fig. 7. The time to completion of the Smith-Waterman algorithm from the HPCS SSCA 1 benchmark. Lower times are better.

Smith-Waterman 16k node runtime

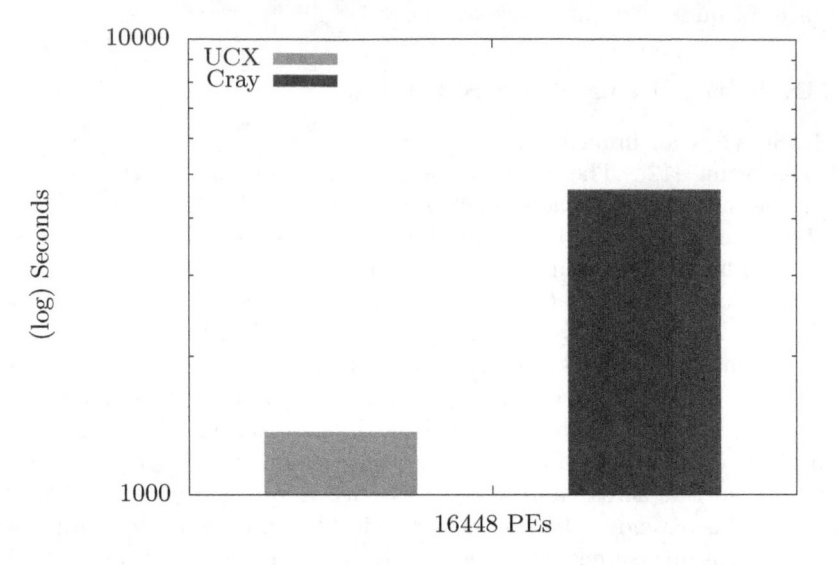

Fig. 8. The Smith-Waterman algorithm from the HPCS SSCA 1 benchmark with 16,448 PEs. Lower times are better.

The results of the benchmark show a significant increase in performance when UCX is used rather than the Cray implementation. These differences range from roughly 20% with 2048 PEs to 43% with 1024 PEs. Lower amounts of PEs result in less than a 10% difference between UCX and the Cray implementation. Additionally, the scaling of both UCX and Cray are similar for PE counts lower than 512, with each increasing allocation reducing the time taken to completion by nearly half. At 1024 and 2048 PEs, the reduction in time to completion lessens and becomes marginal at those scales for both UCX and Cray. At 16K nodes the differences become even more dramatic. With a 70% difference in performance.

8.5   Analysis

The above evaluation highlights some of the core differences between the two implementations. The OpenSHMEM implementation using UCX leverages Cray's uGNI driver, while the OpenSHMEM implementation by Cray is based on the DMAPP driver. In addition, the UCX implementation was driven by the optimization of the communication path for *Put* and *Get* operations. Specifically, the UCX uGNI transport leverages FMA communication semantics for short messages. This enables in-place completion of *Put* operations as those are buffered and transferred by the underlying uGNI layer. As a result, the UCX injection rate for *Put* operations as well as the latency of the *Get* operation is substantially better than Cray SHMEM. This leads to the acceleration of HPCS SSCA1 benchmark, which leverages small *Put* and *Get* operations for data exchanges.

9   Conclusion

To understand the suitability of UCX as a communication layer for implementing OpenSHMEM, in this paper, we provide a prototype implementation, OpenSHMEM-UCX, and evaluate its performance characteristics on a Cray XK system. Towards this end, we implement a uGNI TL that provides protocols for RMA operations, active messages, and atomic operations. Then, we port the OpenSHMEM reference implementation to use UCX, which involves implementing OpenSHMEM interfaces using UCP interfaces. Our experimental results demonstrate the benefits of using UCX as a communication layer for OpenSHMEM. The prototype OpenSHMEM-UCX outperformed the matured vendor provided OpenSHMEM implementation, particularly it demonstrated a higher message rate and better application performance. However, we also identified some performance bottlenecks in OpenSHMEM-UCX leading to slightly worse bandwidth. This we expect can be improved by introducing a caching of the memory registrations that is used to optimize large message transfers.

Acknowledgments. This work is supported by the United States Department of Defense and used resources of the Extreme Scale Systems Center located at the Oak Ridge National Laboratory.

References

1. Open-MPI: Open source high performance computing (2016)
2. Barrett, B.W., Brigthwell, R., Hemmert, K.S., Pedretti, K., Wheeler, K., Underwood, K.D.: Enhanced support for OpenSHMEM communication in portals. In: 2011 IEEE 19th Annual Symposium on High Performance Interconnects, pp. 61–69 (2011)
3. The Ohio State University: MVAPICH2-X: Unified MPI+PGAS communication runtime over OpenFabrics/Gen2 for Exascale Systems (2014)
4. Mellanox: HPC-X OpenSHMEM (2016)
5. Shamis, P., Venkata, M.G., Poole, S., Welch, A., Curtis, T.: Designing a high performance OpenSHMEM implementation using universal common communication substrate as a communication middleware. In: Poole, S., Hernandez, O., Shamis, P. (eds.) OpenSHMEM 2014. LNCS, vol. 8356, pp. 1–13. Springer, Heidelberg (2014). doi:10.1007/978-3-319-05215-1_1
6. Pophale, S., Nanjegowda, R., Curtis, A.R., Chapman, B., Jin, H., Poole, S.W., Kuehn, J.A.: OpenSHMEM performance and potential: a NPB experimental study. In: 6th Conference on Partitioned Global Address Space Programming Models (PGAS 2012). OSTI (2012)
7. Jose, J., Kandalla, K., Zhang, J., Potluri, S., Panda, D.: Optimizing collective communication in OpenSHMEM. In: 7th International Conference on PGAS Programming Models (PGAS 2013), pp. 185–196 (2013)
8. Hammond, J.R., Ghosh, S., Chapman, B.M.: Implementing OpenSHMEM using MPI-3 one-sided communication. In: Poole, S., Hernandez, O., Shamis, P. (eds.) OpenSHMEM 2014. LNCS, vol. 8356, pp. 44–58. Springer, Heidelberg (2014). doi:10.1007/978-3-319-05215-1_4

9. Shamis, P., Venkata, M.G., Lopez, M.G., Baker, M.B., Hernandez, O., Itigin, Y., Dubman, M., Shainer, G., Graham, R.L., Liss, L., Shahar, Y., Potluri, S., Rossetti, D., Becker, D., Poole, D., Lamb, C., Kumar, S., Stunkel, C., Bosilca, G., Bouteiller, A.: UCX: an open source framework for HPC network APIs and beyond. In: 2015 IEEE 23rd Annual Symposium on High-Performance Interconnects, pp. 40–43 (2015)
10. The Ohio State University: OSU micro-benchmarks (2016). http://mvapich.cse.ohio-state.edu/benchmarks/
11. Baker, M., Welch, A., Gorentla Venkata, M.: Parallelizing the Smith-Waterman algorithm using OpenSHMEM and MPI-3 one-sided interfaces. In: Gorentla Venkata, M., Shamis, P., Imam, N., Lopez, M.G. (eds.) OpenSHMEM 2014. LNCS, vol. 9397, pp. 178–191. Springer, Heidelberg (2015). doi:10.1007/978-3-319-26428-8_12
12. Bader, D., Madduri, K., Gilbert, J., Shah, V., Kepner, J., Meuse, T., Krishnamurthy, A.: Designing scalable synthetic compact applications for benchmarking high productivity computing systems. Cyberinfrastruct. Technol. Watch **2**, 1–10 (2006)

SHMemCache: Enabling Memcached on the OpenSHMEM Global Address Model

Huansong Fu$^{(\boxtimes)}$, Kunal SinghaRoy, Manjunath Gorentla Venkata,
Yue Zhu, and Weikuan Yu

Oak Ridge National Laboratory, Florida State University, Tallahassee, USA
{hsfu,singharo,yzhu,yuw}@cs.fsu.edu, manjugv@ornl.gov

Abstract. Memcached is a popular key-value memory store for big data applications. Its performance is directly related to the underlying run-time systems including the communication protocols. OpenSHMEM is a strong run-time system that supports data access to both local and remote memory through a simple shared-memory addressing model. In view of the communication compatibilities between Memcached and OpenSHMEM, we propose to integrate the programmability and portability of OpenSHMEM for supporting Memcached on a wide variety of HPC systems. In this paper, we present the design and implementation of SHMemCache, an OpenSHMEM-based communication conduit for Memcached, which can expand the deployment scope of Memcached to various leadership facilities with OpenSHMEM run-time.

Keywords: SHMemCache · OpenSHMEM · Memcached · Global Address Space models

1 Introduction

One grand challenge nowadays is a deluge of digital data, so called *Big Data*. Many organizations are deploying different MapReduce implementations such as Hadoop [1], Spark [26], and Memcached [3] to meet their needs of analyzing enormous datasets. Among the aforementioned software systems that process and analyze the explosion of big data, Memcached particularly plays a critical role as a key-value memory store for distributed user applications. Its performance and scalability is directly related to the underlying run-time systems including the communication protocols and the storage stack. Global Address Space (GAS) or Partitioned Global Address Space (PGAS) models have been very popular for large-scale computing because of their capabilities of supporting data access to both local and remote memory through a simple shared-memory addressing model. OpenSHMEM has evolved into a strong run-time system that supports PGAS semantics.

In the meantime, the capability of High Performance Computing (HPC) systems is growing rapidly. While the IT industry is embracing this modern rush for gold from data, HPC system providers need to evolve their systems to meet the

© Springer International Publishing AG 2016
M. Gorentla Venkata et al. (Eds.): OpenSHMEM 2016, LNCS 10007, pp. 131–145, 2016.
DOI: 10.1007/978-3-319-50995-2_9

demands of data analytics applications while continuing to support existing HPC applications and customers. This is particularly important for the users and administrators at the leadership computing facilities who have been relying on traditional HPC (High-Performance Computing) systems for their scientific applications.

In this project, we have examined the compatibilities of communication interfaces between Memcached and OpenSHMEM. Accordingly, we propose to integrate the programmability and portability of OpenSHMEM for supporting Memcached on a wide variety of HPC systems. Such integration is particularly attractive because of the common use of memory-style addressing model in OpenSHMEM and Memcached. It can lend a great portability for Memcached to be deployed on various leadership facilities with OpenSHMEM run-time. As an initial attempt to demonstrate the feasibility, we have designed an OpenSHMEM-based communication conduit for Memcached, which we refer to as SHMemCache. Through an extensive code examination and architecture analysis in collaboration with researchers from Oak Ridge National Lab, we have implemented an prototype of SHMemCache and evaluated its performance using a variety of benchmarks.

The paper is organized as follows. First we introduce the background of this research in Sect. 2 and the design of SHMemCache in Sect. 3. Next we elaborate the implementation details of SHMemCache in Sect. 4. The performance evaluation of SHMemCache is provided in Sect. 5. Finally, we provide a review of other related works in Sect. 6 and conclude our paper in Sect. 7.

2   Background

2.1   Memcached

Memcached is a popular open-source, distributed caching system. It has been designed to address the web server's caching demand. In the Memcached architecture, there are two key components: a *server* that stores *key/value* pairs and a *client* that can query and populate the key/value pairs. The clients can interact with multiple Memcached servers to perform a SET operation, i.e. storing the key value tuples or GET operation, i.e. retrieving the value associated with the key. Memcached uses a two stage hashing procedure for unbiased data disposition. In the first step, it hashes the value of the key to decide on which server to store the tuple. In the second step, the key is further hashed to the server's local hash table which stores the address of the key value pair. Memcached uses TCP/IP to send and receive the data. LibMemcached, on the other hand, is a powerful Memcached client library that can support both synchronous and asynchronous transport, tunable hashing and many other features. It includes *memslap*, a widely-used Memcached benchmark that can generate key/value pairs, evaluate SET/GET performance and provide configurable benchmark settings.

2.2   OpenSHMEM

Partitioned Global Address Space (PGAS) models provide an abstraction of global shared memory. In this model, each Processing Element (PE) has a local memory space and a shared memory space. This model facilitates the programming of applications that have irregular communication patterns. OpenSHMEM is a standardized library that realizes the PGAS model. Each PE has *symmetric memory* and local memory. The symmetric memory contains symmetric variables, which exist with the same name, type and relative address across all PEs. OpenSHMEM library routines use one-sided communication paradigm for transferring data from one PE to the symmetric memory of other PE. OpenSHMEM's `put` operation returns as soon as the data has been copied out from the local memory of the sending PE. The data delivery to the symmetric memory of receiving PE is ensured by point to point communication operations or collective synchronization routines.

3   SHMemCache: Enabling Memcached on OpenSHMEM

This section introduces the design of SHMemCache. We will describe the overall structure, key components, and our design choices for SHMemCache.

3.1   Overview of SHMemCache Design

First of all, SHMemCache has a communication backbone that utilizes the communication and programming routines of OpenSHMEM. The communication backbone consists of many OpenSHMEM *delegators*. Each OpenSHMEM processing element (PE) constitute as a delegator and it resides on one of the participating nodes running SHMemCache. Each of those delegators acts like a proxy for network communication, running alongside with one or more SHMemCache *server* and *client*. It is dedicated to handle all the communication between SHMemCache servers and clients. The delegators can use one-sided point-to-point communication primitives, e.g., `shmem_putmem()` in the OpenSHMEM library to communicate with each other. Note that, we do not use the OpenSHMEM primitives to directly operate the key/value pairs in Memcached because that requires a complete re-design of cache management, transaction protocols, etc., which actually deserves another paper. However, we will show that the design of SHMemCache can achieve optimal performance for Memcached operations even with the delegators dedicated for communication. In addition, based on the existing design of Memcached server and client, we have proposed and implemented the design of our SHMemCache server and client. SHMemCache client uses transaction-like memory operations instead of setting up socket connections between the server and client. Since the OpenSHMEM delegators have initialized the communication channels between all participating hosts, the costly connection setup is completely avoided in SHMemCache client and server. The SHMemCache server uses a master-slave architecture that takes the incoming Memcached operations and process them in a multi-threaded fashion.

The aforementioned structure of SHMemCache is depicted in Fig. 1. The right hand side of the figure shows four OpenSHMEM PEs running on four different computer nodes. In addition, two servers and four clients are also collocated on

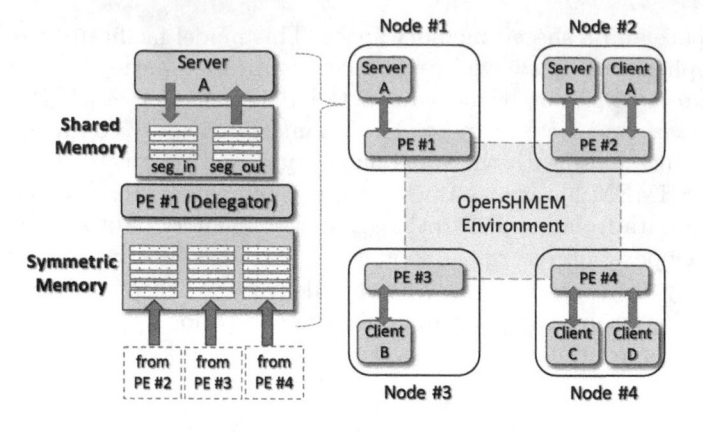

Fig. 1. Overview of structure. It shows an example that consist of 4 nodes, each of which runs with an OpenSHMEM PE and some SHMemCache server/client.

those nodes. The server or client can communicate with each other through the delegators that are present on the same node. The delegators can communicate with each other in the OpenSHMEM environment, which forms the communication backbone of SHMemCache. The left hand side of the figure shows the data structure used on Node #1. There are two different types of memory regions being used for message passing: shared memory and symmetric memory. For each server or client, there is a shared memory region that is shared between itself and the delegator. This shared memory region consists of two segments: a *seg_in* that is responsible for receiving messages from server/client and another *seg_out* partition that is responsible for receiving messages from the delegator. In addition, every delegator has a symmetric memory region which is also divided into multiple pools. This symmetric memory region is only used for receiving data from other PEs. Hence, if there are N PEs in a SHMemCache system, the symmetric memory region on each node will have N pools, each of which receiving message from a specific PE. Such design ensures that, for both symmetric and shared memory communications there are two dedicated memory buffers for any pair of PE-to-PE or PE-to-server/client. Thus, no complex write-write race control is required while the memory use is efficient.

Figure 2 demonstrates the operation process flow in SHMemCache. As the communication backbone of SHMemCache, the delegators need to be initialized before any server or client comes in. Thus, it needs to be implemented as a long-running daemon and its resource needs to be recycled properly. Symmetric memory is initialized during initialization of the delegators. Then, SHMemCache server or client can be launched without strict ordering. The collocated client and server will synchronize with each other before they start processing the operations. After being launched, server or client will make inquiry about the shared memory allocation via pipe. The delegator will assign the identifier of available shared memory region and both sides will then initialize the shared memory region. After its initialization, the client generates an *operation item*

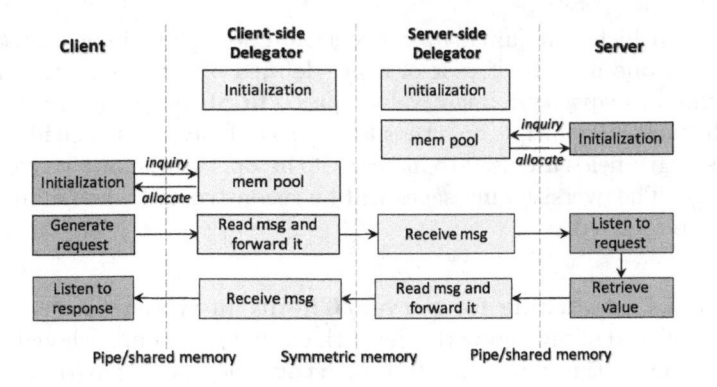

Fig. 2. The flow of a Memcached get operation between a client and a server. The boxes show basic steps during the process. Arrows show the message passing. The blue barriers show the means of communication. (Color figure online)

(i.e., op_item), which is the name we use to denote an operation instance in SHMemCache, e.g., SET or GET. The request op_item that the client generates will be transmitted through the delegators and processed by the server. The response op_item will be transferred to the client through those same delegators following the same procedure.

3.2 OpenSHMEM Delegator

The OpenSHMEM delegator is the central communication component of SHMemCache. As mentioned previously, it is solely responsible for the network communication, ensuring the networking to be *transparent* to the server and the client. Moreover, it will orchestrate the transferring of op_items between the server and the client, which requires careful consideration for data synchronization, since we are using a global *shared memory pool* for the passing of op_items. We also have a *Symmetric Ring Buffer* that can accommodate multiple concurrent op_item operations for their data transfers. Last but not least, we divided the processing of operations in the delegator into several stages and formulate a pipeline for overlapping of processing in different stages. In the rest of the section, we will first introduce the op_item, then we will describe the aforementioned techniques in detail.

op_item. Each op_item represents an instance of the SHMemCache operation. It illustrates the memory-like semantics for communication in SHMemCache, which differs sharply from the connected-oriented communication in existing Memcached. An op_item is created by the client using a certain size of contiguous memory space. It consists of properly aligned different fields which contains all the needed information about the operation, e.g., command type, server name, key/value lengths and values. By using the same data structure, the server, client and delegator can seamlessly exchange and utilize op_items across the SHMem-Cache framework. This eliminates the need of complex message concatenation or separation which is required by conventional string or binary message passing. However, one negative factor of a pre-defined op_item structure is that it has a maximum capacity for key/value space. In SHMemCache, we solve this issue by dispatching multiple op_items for oversized messages. The identifier and key/value length fields are used to indicate if the op_item is for a whole or a part of a message. The oversized messages will be reconstructed when all its member op_items are received.

Transparent Networking for Server/Client. In SHMemCache, clients and servers are relieved of managing the network communication. Although still need to indicate the destination node of an op_item, they do not participate in the actual network transferring. They only need to place an op_item to the corresponding shared memory segment that is shared between the delegator and itself. On the other hand, when receiving an op_item, it only needs to fetch from another shared memory segment when the item becomes available. Thus, the delegator is responsible to translate the destination node's host name to a PE id, which can be used for OpenSHMEM communication primitives. The delegator does so by referring to a mapping table that maps all participating host names to the corresponding PE ids. The table is created by an OpenSHMEM routine shmem_broadcast(), which broadcasts a PE's host name and PE id to every other PEs.

Enforcing the transparent networking for the server and client not only reduces the amount of work imposed on the server and client, it also greatly increases the concurrency of the SHMemCache execution. For connection-based operation, the client needs to maintain a connection with the server for every operation, which is often handled by a separate thread. However, in SHMemCache, servers and clients can both send out or receive in many requests via memory operations with only one single thread. Although this certainly increases the amount of work imposed on the delegators, with the OpenSHMEM one-sided communication capabilities, we can conveniently pipeline the communications between delegators for optimal network performance. To this end, we have also designed a *Symmetric Ring Buffer* for the communication between delegators, which will be discussed later.

Shared Memory Pool. Between the delegator and server/client, all the op_items pass through shared memory. Since only one delegator is available on every node but multiple clients or even servers can be launched on the same node, we need to gracefully handle the concurrency of read/write of many op_items from different servers and clients. In SHMemCache, we have a *shared memory pool* that contains multiple shared memory *regions* of uniform size. When a server/client is launched, it will communicate with the delegator through a reserved pipe for any available regions that it can use. The identifier of the memory region is then passed to the server/client by the delegator. The initialization of the shared memory pool happens at the startup phase of the delegator so it would not affect the performance of the client. The only cost it incurs during the execution of an `op_item` is the searching and assigning of available region, both of which require negligible time. The delegator will recycle the region when the client exits.

Therefore, each server/client can use a dedicated shared memory region without worrying about race condition with other server/client. However, we still need to take care of data synchronization for one single server/client. For example, a client can send out many request `op_items` in a short amount of time and can also receive multiple response `op_items` at the same time. Thus, to better ensure the synchronization of sending and receiving, we divide each shared memory region into two *segments*, each handling either reading from the delegator or writing to the delegator, namely `seg_out` and `seg_in` based on the direction of data movement in the SHMemCache structure (Fig. 1). Then, we use a flag in the segment to indicate if it is *empty*, *ready*, or *been-fetched*. Additionally, since we use two threads in the delegator for either reading from client/server or writing to them, two dedicated segments can provide better overlapping of processing in the two threads.

Symmetric Ring Buffer. The OpenSHMEM one-sided communication can greatly benefit the concurrency of execution if designed properly. In SHMemCache, we use a *symmetric ring buffer* to accommodate transferring of multiple concurrent `op_items`. The structure of the ring buffer is illustrated in Fig. 3. A ring buffer consists of a number of symmetric memory *chunks*. Each chunk can be used to send an `op_item`. Every delegator owns a number of symmetric ring buffers that equals to the number of PEs in the system. The ith buffer will be receiving data from PE i. For example, PE 1 will be sending data to Pool[1] of all other nodes. In addition, Pool[1] on PE 1 is not wasted but can be used for broadcasting. The delegator also keeps the *head* and *tail* chunk numbers of its corresponding receiving ring buffer of every other delegator. Moreover, to saturate the sending latency, the delegator collects a group of `op_items` of a *window* size and sends them all at once. When a client-side delegator wants to send a group of `op_items`, it claims the equal amount of chunks starting from the head chunk in the ring buffer of the server-side delegator. The server-side delegator, on the other hand, keeps fetching from the tail chunk in its ring buffer and after that

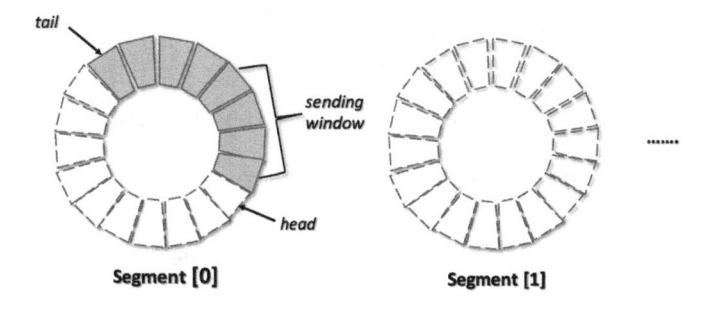

Fig. 3. Symmetric ring buffer.

op_item has been processed in the server, it sends the response op_item to its corresponding receiving buffer on the client-side delegator. Once the client-side delegator gets the response, it will move the tail forward. Therefore, in SHMem-Cache, each pair of delegators has two dedicated buffers for communication, each handling the communication from one direction between the two delegators. By doing so, we only need to synchronize the *read-write race* between the two delegators, i.e., reading incorrect item while it is being written. We do not have to worry about more complex *write-write* race between two or more delegators, i.e., updating the same item at the same time. In fact, the same idea is applied to the shared memory region as well.

Operation Stages and Pipelined Processing. One of the key challenges in ensuring high parallelism of data transfers based on OpenSHMEM put/get memory semantics is the *operation pipelining*, i.e. dividing the processing of an operation into stages and formulating a pipeline for the stages. Based on the processing flow of an operation shown in Fig. 2, we divide an operation into a number of different stages as shown in Fig. 4: *request* from the client, *notify* to the delegator, *forward* by the delegator, *receive* by another delegator, *transfer* to the server, *listen* of the request in the server and *process* of the request in the server. Note that the processing stages for a server response to a client are arranged in a similar manner but in reverse direction. Hence, not all stages are shown in the figure. Each stage is handled by one or more threads so they can be well pipelined with each other.

For every client or server that is launched on the same node with a delegator, there are two threads being spawned in the delegator. One *request* thread is responsible for getting and forwarding the request op_item and another *response* thread is responsible for getting and forwarding the response op_item. Each thread will copy the op_items in only one direction. For example, a request thread for a client only copies the op_item from the client to the symmetric ring buffer, but a request thread for a server only copies the op_item from the ring buffer to the server. After the completeness of the copying, the thread will start fetching the next item when it becomes available.

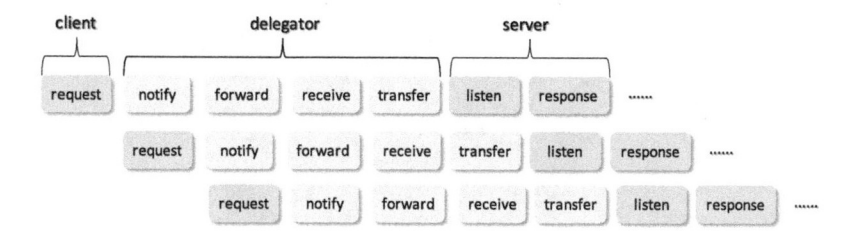

Fig. 4. The pipelining of operation stages.

3.3 Server and Client

Compared to the delegator, the SHMemCache server and client are developed by mostly maintaining the design of an existing Memcached client and server. However, a number of implementation work is still needed, which will be discussed in Sect. 4. For our SHMemCache client, we have implemented two basic Memcached primitives, i.e., SET and GET. Both SET and GET will leverage the shared memory region to pass the corresponding op_item to the delegator. We make sure that the new implementations are compliant the with existing Memcached applications by adding pluggable modules to *memslap*, which is a popular Memcached benchmark being used in many prior studies [12–14,19].

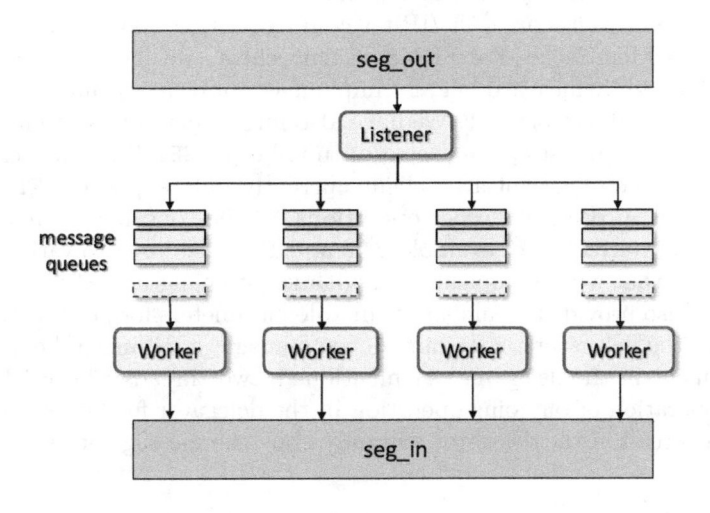

Fig. 5. SHMemCache server structure.

We have also developed the SHMemCache server by modifying the Memcached server. The existing Memcached server design uses heavy-weight connection setup and complex event switch for every operation. In contrast, our communication does not enforce any connection setup or event switches on the server. The server structure is shown in Fig. 5, SHMemCache server has a listener thread and a number of worker thread (currently four). The listener thread monitors the seg_out of the assigned shared memory region for incoming op_item. When there is one, it pushes the data into the *operation queue* owned by one of the worker threads. The worker thread to use is chosen in a round-robin manner. After it have processed the op_item, the response message is incorporated in an op_item and then written to seg_in of the shared memory region. We make sure that our modification is modularized and pluggable. The old interfaces of the Memcached server are intact from our modification. Thus, both connection or transaction protocols are supported at the same time in SHMemCache. The underlying key/value stores are shared by both protocols.

4   Implementation

Based on the design described in Sect. 3, we have built a proof-of-concept proto-type of SHMemCache. We use the latest versions of OpenSHMEM, Memcached and libMemcached to implement our prototype. Specifically, we use the Open-SHMEM implementation in OpenMPI v1.10.3 [4], Memcached v1.4.25 [3] and libMemcached 1.0.18 [2]. We will also present a few details for the challenges we faced during the implementing and tuning of SHMemCache.

For SHMemCache server, we still leverage the caching system of the existing Memcached but implement our own communication interface, thread manage-ment, etc. The code changes are modularized and pluggable according to user's wish. None of the existing Memcached interfaces have been altered so other clients who use conventional TCP/IP for communication may still function cor-rectly with SHMemCache. For SHMemCache client, we leverage the hashing functions of the libMemcached but also implement our own communication inter-face, multi-thread functions, etc. We have also implemented more tunable para-meters, e.g., the value size, the execution number of GET (libMemcached only supports SET), etc. SHMemCache client currently only supports SET and GET operations. But in principle, other operations can be conveniently made avail-able given our interfaces. For example, ADD and INCR are just two variants of the SET operation that will be implemented with slight changes to SET.

We have also provided a number of tunable parameters for performance opti-mizations of the delegators. For example, we manage to minimize the number of data movement in the delegator. As mentioned, two threads will handle either incoming operation or outgoing operation in the delegator for a client or server. Thus, each thread in the delegator will only copy the message once.

5   Evaluation

5.1   Experimental Environment

Experimental Testbed. Our experiments are conducted on a cluster of 21 server nodes. Each machine is equipped with dual-socket, 10 Intel Xeon(R) cores and 64 GB memory. All nodes are connected through an FDR InfiniBand inter-connect. The software versions have been introduced in Sect. 4. Unless otherwise specified, on each machine we run only one Memcached client or Memcached server.

Benchmarks. We use *memslap* to generate test workload that consists of either SET or GET operations. We also use memslap to provide varying factors for eval-uation (data size, execution count, etc.).

Metrics. In this paper, we focus on evaluating the operation latency of SHMem-Cache. For baseline comparison, we use the unmodified Memcached server and libMemcached client of the same versions that we used for implementing our

SHMemCache server and client. We first test the average latency of the SET and GET operations against the baseline Memcached. Then, we dissect the latency of SET and GET using dummy components. For each set of experiment, we run it one hundred thousand times and report the average result. Throughout this section, we use **SMC** to denote the results of SHMemCache and **MCD** to denote the baseline Memcached.

5.2   Operation Latency

Firstly, we test the latency of SET and GET operations generated by memslap. In this experiment, we use only one client to generate requests and one server to process the requests. We vary the message size, i.e., size of the value in the key/value pairs in the experiment. The results are shown in Fig. 6. Both SHMemCache's SET and GET latency are much lower than the baseline Memcached's SET and GET for all data sizes. In specific, SHMemCache achieves less than 10 ms of latency of both SET and GET for small messages (e.g., less than 1 KB), and less than 30 ms of latency for large message such as 16 KB. These latency results of SHMemCache are comparable to other RDMA-based distributed key/value stores as reported in [9,13,17]. Moreover, SHMemCache's performance also shows less variation and more predictability than the baseline Memcached.

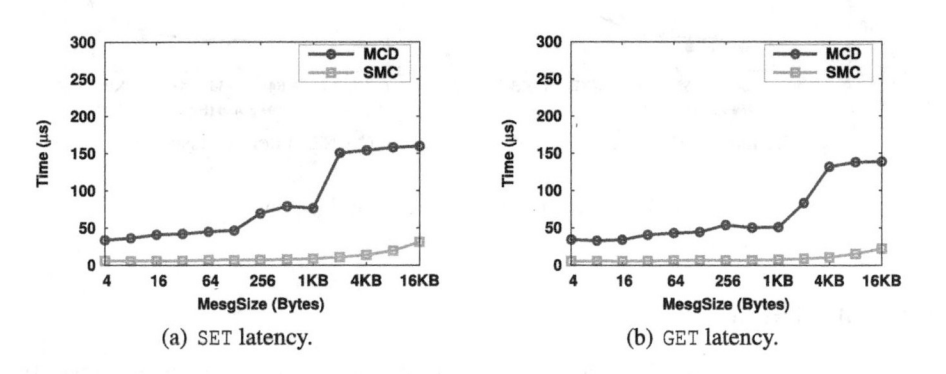

(a) SET latency.   (b) GET latency.

Fig. 6. Results of operation latency.

5.3   Latency Dissection

We have further studied the SHMemCache operation latency by dissecting the time spent in each component. We accomplish this by creating some *dummy* components in SHMemCache, i.e., dummy client-side delegator (*dum-cli-del*), dummy server-side delegator (*dum-serv-del*) or dummy server (*dum-serv*). A dummy component will response to a request op_item as soon as it receives the op_item without forwarding the op_item further. For example, a dummy server-side delegator will immediately reply with a response when it receives an request op_item but not forward the op_item to the server. We make sure that such response op_item has the same size as in the no-dummy case so the difference in performance does not result from different size of message passing. The results are shown in Fig. 7. As seen from the figure, for both SET and GET, the latency of *dum-cli-del* is extremely small, which shows that local data transfer via shared memory is really fast. Then, the difference between *dum-cli-del* and *dum-serv-del* is the network transferring of the op_item, which has the largest portion of the latency. Moreover, the difference between *dum-serv-del* and *dum-serv* is the time spent on processing in server-side delegator and also data transferring via local shared memory. This part also takes only a small portion of time. Finally, the difference between *dum-serv* and *no-dum* is the time spent on server processing, which takes longer for SET than GET because the former involves memory allocation and copying while the latter only requires memory reads. The results show that our implementation adds negligible overheads to the irreducible time costs such as the network transferring and server processing.

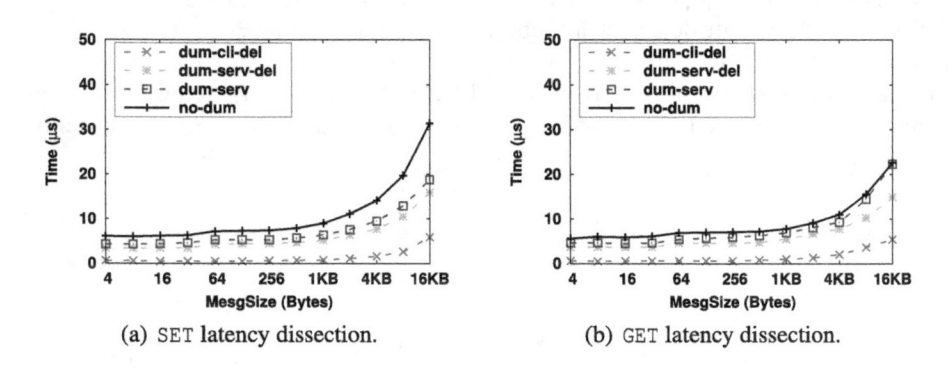

(a) SET latency dissection.   (b) GET latency dissection.

Fig. 7. The time dissection of the latency.

5.4   Discussion

During the test, we also find that the size of message affects the performance. In our early implementation, every message incorporates a fixed size of header fields (id, lengths, flag, key, etc.) plus a value field of varying size. Setting the value field to as low as 4 B does not give better performance than setting it to 4 KB. However, when setting it to 16 KB or larger, the performance will degrade drastically. This is because OpenSHMEM will temporarily buffer the data when sending to other nodes. Moreover, it is not possible to dynamically adjust the message size because many system variables such as the shared memory region size depends on the message size. Adjustment of that may cause difficulty in orchestrating different components of SHMemCache. Thus, in the current implementation, we fix the size of message to 4 K. For bigger size of operations we will divide it into multiple messages and send out sequentially. We also make sure that only the valid part of a message is copied everytime a message is being transferred across memory or network. For example, if value size is 4 B, we only copies the size of header fields plus 4 B. This has limited effect to the OpenSHMEM communication, but can reduce time for memory copying.

6 Related Works

Leveraging high performance capabilities in HPC domain for big data analytics frameworks are becoming increasingly popular among both the HPC and big data communities in recent years. To name a few, Jose *et al.* [13] presented an Memcached design on high-speed interconnects. They implemented a communication library called Unified Communication Runtime (UCR) that provided interfaces for the Remote Direct Memory Access (RDMA) on the high-speed interconnects. Similarly, Mitchell *et al.* [17] also exploited RDMA capability for fast key/value store such as Memcached. However, they proposed an idea that was for the client to directly access in-memory key/value stores without involving the server at all, thus completely bypassing any CPU overhead. Moreover, Appavoo *et al.* [7] took an early effort on leveraging one-sided RDMA reads for Memcached and running Memcached with high-speed interconnects on supercomputers. Wang *et al.* presented a design of RDMA-aware cache management for distributed key/value store in [22] and a complete design of RDMA-driven distributed middleware [23] for accelerating big data analytics frameworks, e.g., Hadoop, Spark and G2 Sensemaking.

On the other hand, exploiting the distributed in-memory key/value stores for designing a fast PGAS-like distributed computing programming model also attracted much attention. Aguilera *et al.* [5] described a distributed programming paradigm that is built with a linear addressing space, which provided ease for programmers to write parallel programs without handling the complexities of message passing themselves. Similarly, Dragojevic *et al.* [9] presented an memory distributed computing platform that utilizes the memory of all machines to form a PGAS for storing data and facilitating transactions. In addition, it uses RDMA-enabled ACID transactions for better performance and consistency. Greenberg *et al.* [11] gave a brief introduction to MDHIM, a middleware that could integrate some of the popular HPC programming models such as MPI with other popular data analytics tools such as Cassandra. By conveniently leveraging the high-speed capability of InfiniBand interconnect, it had shown to greatly improve the performance of Cassandra.

More generally, there were a lot of efforts for fast distributed memory transaction [8,18,20,21,24]. Particularly, Wei *et al.* [24] improved distributed in-memory transaction system by leveraging strong consistency between RDMA and HTM and offloading concurrency control with HTM. There were also abundant studies for the architectural or algorithmic optimization of Memcached or other key/value stores [6,10,15,16,25]. For example, Fan *et al.* [10] did not touch upon the communication venues but instead improved Memcached's hashing algorithm and had shown dramatic performance advantages.

7   Conclusion

In this paper, we have examined the compatibilities of communication interfaces between Memcached and OpenSHMEM. Accordingly, we have designed and implemented a software framework that integrates the programmability and portability of OpenSHMEM with the power of Memcached for supporting big data applications. SHMemCache can be leveraged to help deploy Memcached on various leadership facilities with OpenSHMEM run-time. We have also leveraged a set of test benchmarks to validate our design and evaluate the performance of SHMemCache. Our experimental results show that SHMemCache achieves low latency and adds negligible overheads to network trasferring and operation processing.

Acknowledgment. We are very thankful for the insightful comments from the anonymous reviewers. This work was supported in part by a contract from Oak Ridge National Laboratory to Florida State University.

References

1. Apache Hadoop Project. http://hadoop.apache.org/
2. Libmemcached. http://libmemcached.org/libMemcached.html
3. Memcached. https://memcached.org/downloads
4. OpenMPI. https://www.open-mpi.org/
5. Aguilera, M.K., Merchant, A., Shah, M., Veitch, A., Karamanolis, C.: Sinfonia: a new paradigm for building scalable distributed systems. ACM SIGOPS Oper. Syst. Rev. **41**, 159–174 (2007)
6. Andersen, D.G., Franklin, J., Kaminsky, M., Phanishayee, A., Tan, L., Vasudevan, V.: Fawn: a fast array of wimpy nodes. In: Proceedings of the ACM SIGOPS 22nd Symposium on Operating Systems Principles, pp. 1–14. ACM (2009)
7. Appavoo, J., Waterland, A., Da Silva, D., Uhlig, V., Rosenburg, B., Van Hensbergen, E., Stoess, J., Wisniewski, R., Steinberg, U.: Providing a cloud network infrastructure on a supercomputer. In: Proceedings of the 19th ACM International Symposium on High Performance Distributed Computing, pp. 385–394. ACM (2010)
8. Corbett, J.C., Dean, J., Epstein, M., Fikes, A., Frost, C., Furman, J.J., Ghemawat, S., Gubarev, A., Heiser, C., Hochschild, P., et al.: Spanner: Googles globally distributed database. ACM Trans. Comput. Syst. (TOCS) **31**(3), 8 (2013)
9. Dragojević, A., Narayanan, D., Castro, M., Hodson, O.: Farm: fast remote memory. In: 11th USENIX Symposium on Networked Systems Design and Implementation (NSDI 2014), pp. 401–414 (2014)
10. Fan, B., Andersen, D.G., Kaminsky, M.: Memc3: Compact and concurrent memcache with dumber caching and smarter hashing. Presented as part of the 10th USENIX Symposium on Networked Systems Design and Implementation (NSDI 2013), pp. 371–384 (2013)
11. Greenberg, H., Bent, J., Grider, G.: Mdhim: a parallel key/value framework for HPC. In: 7th USENIX Workshop on Hot Topics in Storage and File Systems (HotStorage 2015) (2015)

12. Issa, J., Figueira, S.: Hadoop and memcached: performance and power characterization and analysis. J. Cloud Comput. **1**(1), 1–20 (2012)
13. Jose, J., Subramoni, H., Luo, M., Zhang, M., Huang, J., Wasi-ur Rahman, M., Islam, N.S., Ouyang, X., Wang, H., Sur, S., et al.: Memcached design on high performance RDMA capable interconnects. In: 2011 International Conference on Parallel Processing (ICPP), pp. 743–752. IEEE (2011)
14. Kapoor, R., Porter, G., Tewari, M., Voelker, G.M., Vahdat, A.: Chronos: predictable low latency for data center applications. In: Proceedings of the Third ACM Symposium on Cloud Computing, p. 9. ACM (2012)
15. Lim, H., Fan, B., Andersen, D.G., Kaminsky, M.: Silt: a memory-efficient, high-performance key-value store. In: Proceedings of the Twenty-Third ACM Symposium on Operating Systems Principles, pp. 1–13. ACM (2011)
16. Mao, Y., Kohler, E., Morris, R.T.: Cache craftiness for fast multicore key-value storage. In: Proceedings of the 7th ACM European Conference on Computer Systems, pp. 183–196. ACM (2012)
17. Mitchell, C., Geng, Y., Li, J.: Using one-sided RDMA reads to build a fast, CPU-efficient key-value store. In: USENIX Annual Technical Conference, pp. 103–114 (2013)
18. Narula, N., Cutler, C., Kohler, E., Morris, R.: Phase reconciliation for contended in-memory transactions. In: 11th USENIX Symposium on Operating Systems Design and Implementation (OSDI 2014), pp. 511–524 (2014)
19. Ruan, W., Vyas, T., Liu, Y., Spear, M.: Transactionalizing legacy code: an experience report using GCC and memcached. ACM SIGARCH Comput. Architect. News **42**, 399–412 (2014)
20. Thomson, A., Diamond, T., Weng, S.-C., Ren, K., Shao, P., Abadi, D.J.: Calvin: fast distributed transactions for partitioned database systems. In: Proceedings of the 2012 ACM SIGMOD International Conference on Management of Data, pp. 1–12. ACM (2012)
21. Tu, S., Zheng, W., Kohler, E., Liskov, B., Madden, S.: Speedy transactions in multicore in-memory databases. In: Proceedings of the Twenty-Fourth ACM Symposium on Operating Systems Principles, pp. 18–32. ACM (2013)
22. Wang, Y., Meng, X., Zhang, L., Tan, J.: C-hint: an effective and reliable cache management for RDMA-accelerated key-value stores. In: Proceedings of the ACM Symposium on Cloud Computing, pp. 1–13. ACM (2014)
23. Wang, Y., Zhang, L., Tan, J., Li, M., Gao, Y., Guerin, X., Meng, X., Meng, S.: Hydradb: a resilient RDMA-driven key-value middleware for in-memory cluster computing. In: SC 2015, p. 22. ACM (2015)
24. Wei, X., Shi, J., Chen, Y., Chen, R., Chen, H.: Fast in-memory transaction processing using RDMA and HTM. In: Proceedings of the 25th Symposium on Operating Systems Principles, pp. 87–104. ACM (2015)
25. Wu, X., Zhang, L., Wang, Y., Ren, Y., Hack, M., Jiang, S.: Zexpander: a key-value cache with both high performance and fewer misses. In: Proceedings of the Eleventh European Conference on Computer Systems, p. 14. ACM (2016)
26. Zaharia, M., Chowdhury, M., Das, T., Dave, A., Ma, J., McCauley, M., Franklin, M.J., Shenker, S., Stoica, I.: Resilient distributed datasets: a fault-tolerant abstraction for in-memory cluster computing. In: Proceedings of the 9th USENIX Conference on Networked Systems Design and Implementation, NSDI 2012, p. 2. USENIX Association, Berkeley (2012)

An OpenSHMEM Implementation for the Adapteva Epiphany Coprocessor

James Ross[1(✉)] and David Richie[2]

[1] U.S. Army Research Laboratory,
Aberdeen Proving Ground, MD 21005, USA
james.a.ross176.civ@mail.mil
[2] Brown Deer Technology, Forest Hill, MD 21050, USA
drichie@browndeertechnology.com

Abstract. This paper reports the implementation and performance evaluation of the OpenSHMEM 1.3 specification for the Adapteva Epiphany architecture within the Parallella single-board computer. The Epiphany architecture exhibits massive many-core scalability with a physically compact 2D array of RISC CPU cores and a fast network-on-chip (NoC). While fully capable of MPMD execution, the physical topology and memory-mapped capabilities of the core and network translate well to Partitioned Global Address Space (PGAS) programming models and SPMD execution with SHMEM.

Keywords: OpenSHMEM · Network-on-chip (NoC) · Single-board computer · Performance evaluation

1 Introduction and Motivation

The OpenSHMEM communications library is designed for computer platforms using Partitioned Global Address Space (PGAS) programming models [1]. Historically, these were large Cray supercomputers, but now the OpenSHMEM interface may also be used on commodity clusters. The Adapteva Epiphany architecture represents a divergence in computer architectures typically used with OpenSHMEM and is just one of many emerging parallel architectures that present a challenge in identifying effective programming models to exploit them. While some researchers may be considering how the OpenSHMEM API may interact with coprocessors, the work presented here leverages the API for device-level operation. In some aspects, the Epiphany architecture resembles a symmetric multiprocessing (SMP) multi-core processor with a shared off-chip global memory pool. However, each core can directly address the private address space of neighboring cores across an on-chip 2D mesh network. Thus, the architecture also has the characteristics of a PGAS platform. Previous proof-of-concepts demonstrated that message passing protocols could achieve good application performance on the Epiphany architecture [2,3]. However, it was unclear if the

© Springer International Publishing AG 2016
M. Gorentla Venkata et al. (Eds.): OpenSHMEM 2016, LNCS 10007, pp. 146–159, 2016.
DOI: 10.1007/978-3-319-50995-2_10

OpenSHMEM 1.3 standard could be fully implemented within the platform limitations and achieve high performance using a standard programming model without resorting to non-standard software extensions.

Existing open source OpenSHMEM implementations are inadequate within the constraints of the Epiphany architecture, so a new C language implementation named *ARL OpenSHMEM for Epiphany* was developed from scratch. The design emphasizes a reduced memory footprint, high performance, and simplicity, which are often competing goals. This paper discusses the Epiphany architecture in Sect. 2.1, the OpenSHMEM implementation and performance evaluation in Sect. 3, and a discussion of future work and potential standard extensions for embedded architectures in Sect. 4.

2   Background

The 16-core Epiphany-III coprocessor is included within the $99 ARM-based single-board computer and perhaps represents the low-cost end of programmable hardware suitable for SHMEM research and education. Many universities, students, and researchers have purchased the platform with over 10,000 sales to date. Despite this, programming the platform and achieving high performance or efficiency remain challenging for many users. Like GPUs, the Xeon Phi, and other coprocessors, typical applications comprise host code and device code. Only a minimal set of communication primitives exist within the non-standard Epiphany Hardware Utility Library (eLib) for multi-core barriers, locks, and data transfers [4]. The barrier and data transfer routines are not optimized for low latency. Other primitives within eLib use unconventional 2D row and column indexing, which cannot easily address arbitrary numbers of working cores or disabled cores. More complicated collectives, such as those in the OpenSHMEM specification, are left as an exercise for the application developer.

Although not discussed in detail in this paper, the CO-PRocessing Threads (COPRTHR) 2.0 SDK [5] further simplifies the execution model to the point where the host code is significantly simplified, supplemental, and even not required depending on the use case [6]. There are essentially two modes of possible execution. The first mode requires host code with explicit Epiphany coprocessor offload routines. The second mode uses a host-executable coprocessor program with the conventional main routine provided. The program automatically performs the coprocessor offload without host code. Combined with the work presented in this paper, the COPRTHR 2.0 SDK enables many OpenSHMEM applications to execute on the Epiphany coprocessor without any source code changes. Execution occurs as if the Epiphany coprocessor is the main processor driving computation. COPRTHR 1.6 was used to present the Threaded MPI model for Epiphany [2] as well as a number of applications [7,8].

2.1   Epiphany Architecture

Many modern computer architectures address the "memory wall problem" by including increasingly complex cache hierarchies and core complexity, wider memory buses, memory stacking, and complex packaging to maintain the SMP hardware and software architecture. The Epiphany architecture unwinds decades of these types of changes – it is a cache-less, 2D array of RISC cores with a fast network-on-chip (NoC) that can an be simply described as a "cluster on a chip". Each core within the Epiphany-III architecture contains 32 KB of SRAM which is shared between instructions and local data. The Epiphany architecture can scale to one megabyte of SRAM per core, but there is a linear design trade-off between the number of cores and available memory for a fixed die space. The core local memory is memory-mapped, and each core may directly access the local memory of any core within the mesh network. Each core has shared memory access to off-chip global DRAM, although this access is significantly slower than local memory or non-uniform memory access (NUMA) to neighboring core memory. The highest performance and most energy-efficient applications leverage inter-core communication and on-chip data reuse. Like many high performance computing (HPC) clusters, the inter-core communication is generally explicit in order to achieve highest performance. The architecture is also scalable by tiling multiple chips without additional "glue logic". The tight coupling between the core logic and the on-chip mesh network enables very low-latency operation of OpenSHMEM routines. An architectural overview appears in Fig. 1. Unlike most application programming interfaces for communication, there is no additional software layer to handle networking for hardware abstraction. As we will discuss in further detail, the OpenSHMEM implementation for Epiphany performs network operations directly.

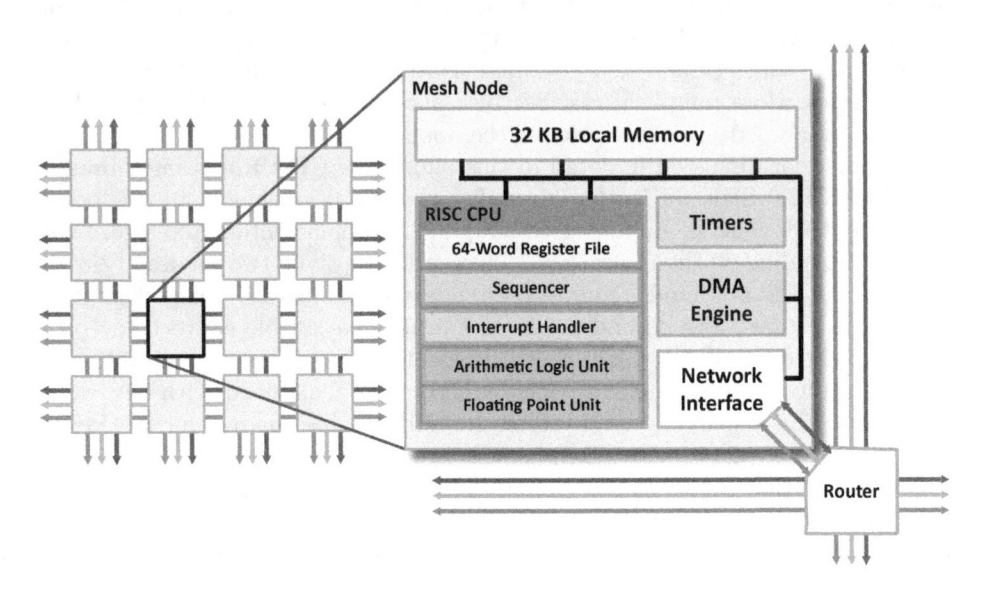

Fig. 1. The 16-core Epiphany-III architecture is a 2D array of RISC CPU cores. It contains a 64-word register file, sequencer, interrupt handler, integer and floating point units, timers, and DMA engines for the fast network-on-chip

3 Implementation and Performance Evaluation

Due to the tight memory constraints of the Epiphany memory and availability of specialized hardware features, the OpenSHMEM reference implementation built on GASNet was not suitable for deployment on the Epiphany cores. As a credit to the OpenSHMEM specification and the Adapteva Epiphany architecture documentation, the full OpenSHMEM 1.3 implementation was written and optimized over a period of a few weeks. The entire library, including the optional extensions described in detail later, is approximately 1800 lines of code and does not require additional software. The software directly targets the underlying hardware features and was designed to be extremely lightweight in order to compile to small binaries expected with embedded architectures.

Linear scaling algorithms were avoided, and many of the collective routines use dissemination or recursive doubling algorithms, optimized for low-latency on the Epiphany network. The remote memory access routines, shmem_*TYPE*_put and shmem_*TYPE*_get, use hand-tuned memory-mapped load and store primitives with a hardware loop feature specific to the Epiphany architecture. The non-blocking remote memory access routines use the dual-channel Direct Memory Access (DMA) engine on each processor network node. The distributed locking and atomic routines leverage an atomic TESTSET instruction that performs an atomic "test-if-not-zero" and conditional write. An optional hardware barrier implementation was also developed for a specialized shmem_barrier_all for extremely low-latency global barriers. An optional inter-processor interrupt and corresponding interrupt service routine (ISR) enable faster shmem_*TYPE*_get operations by interrupting the remote core to use the optimized shmem_*TYPE*_put.

Many of the OpenSHMEM routines have some component that is hardware accelerated on the Epiphany architecture such as zero-overhead hardware loops for copying data, memory-mapped loads and stores, the TESTSET instruction for remote locks and atomics, a wait on AND (WAND) instruction for a low-latency shmem_barrier_all. The MULTICAST experimental feature would enable energy-efficient, low-latency broadcasts but is presently unused. The point-to-point synchronization routines are among the simplest to implement and do not have a section dedicated to discussion. Generally, they spin-wait on local values until they meet the criteria defined by the routine. The memory ordering routines need only verify that both DMA engines have an idle status by spin-waiting on the relevant special register. There are no intermediate data copies in this implementation.

The performance evaluation of the Epiphany OpenSHMEM implementation began with the OpenSHMEM micro-benchmark codes. The timing code had to be modified because the gettimeofday routine is only accurate to a microsecond, and many of the operations operate in the sub-microsecond regime.

Many of the communication routines in the performance evaluation include the parameters α and β^{-1} in the figure subtitle along with their standard deviations. These two parameters are from the "α-β model" for communication in HPC. They neatly summarize the communication time (T_c) to include the latency (α) and marginal cost (β) to transfer a message (of size L) in Eq. 1. The β^{-1} parameter is the peak effective core bandwidth for the routine.

$$T_c = \alpha + \beta \cdot L \tag{1}$$

3.1 Library Setup, Exit, Query Routines

The shmem_init routine retrieves or calculates the local processing element (PE) number (for shmem_my_pe) and number of PEs (for shmem_n_pes), configures the optimized hardware barrier or collective dissemination barrier arrays, obtains the SHMEM heap memory offset, and precalculates a few other addresses for improved runtime performance. The shmem_ptr routine can directly calculate remote memory locations using simple logical shift and bitwise operations.

3.2 Memory Management Routines

Memory management on the Epiphany processor is atypical. Each Epiphany-III core has a flat 32 KB local memory map from address 0x0000 to 0x7fff. Programs are typically loaded starting at 0x0100 if extremely constrained for memory, or 0x0400 if using the COPRTHR 2 interface. The stack pointer typically moves downward from the high address. Data used for the application, including the SHMEM data heap, begins directly after the program space. Figure 2 shows the typical memory layout of an Epiphany-III core using the COPRTHR 2 interface as it relates to the PGAS model. The static or global variables that are typically defined within the application appear below the free local memory address within the symmetric heap. They are still symmetrical across all Epiphany cores as the program binary is identical.

Due to the tight memory constraints, a more modern memory allocator was not addressed in this work. The basic memory management system calls brk and

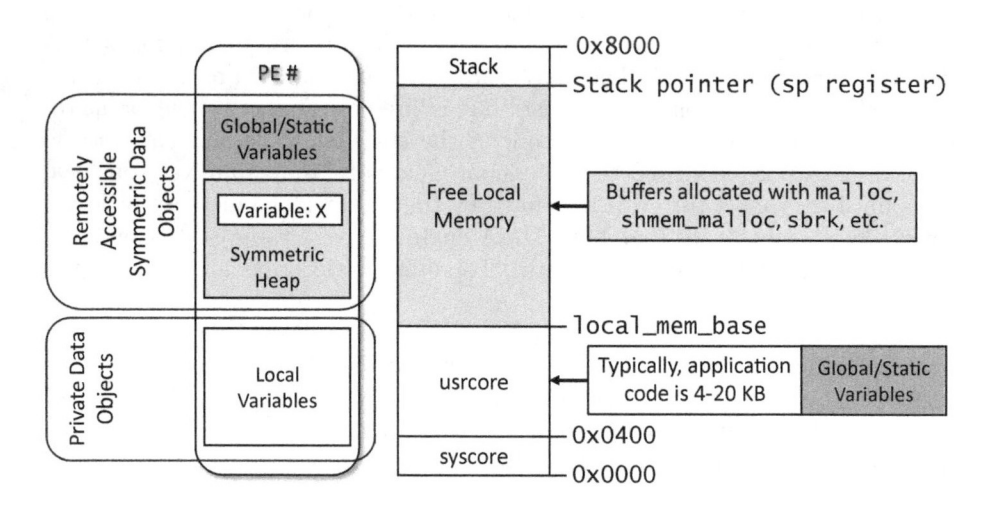

Fig. 2. The PGAS memory model (left) and the equivalent typical memory layout on an Epiphany-III core (right)

sbrk are more suited for controlling the amount of memory allocated from the
SHMEM data heap for each process element because there is no virtual address
abstraction. Instead, there is a local base memory tracking pointer that stores
the current free memory base address and incremented with each allocation. The
memory management routines build on these calls, but care must be taken to
adhere to the following rules:

1. shmem_free must be called in the reverse order of allocation if making subsequent allocations
2. shmem_realloc can only be used on the last (re)allocated pointer
3. shmem_align alignment must be a power of 2 greater than 8 (default is 8)

This is a pragmatic approach that we feel is reasonable and won't even be
noticed on most codes. Calling shmem_free moves the local base memory tracking
pointer to the address in the function argument so most routines only need
to call it once for the first allocated buffer in a series if freeing all memory.
The shmem_realloc routine could be designed to copy the contents of the old
buffer to the new buffer, however, this would waste the memory space in the
original allocation (a precious commodity on the Epiphany architecture). Future
developments with COPRTHR 2 may address these deficiencies by exporting the
COPRTHR host-side memory management to the coprocessor threads.

3.3   Remote Memory Access Routines

Inter-process memory copying on the Epiphany is trivial, and a simple loop over
incrementing source and destination arrays can be done in C code. However,
like many optimized memcpy routines, high-performance copies are non-trivial.
A high-performance inter-processor memory copy routine does not appear to be
in the eLib library. So after quite some time of hand-tuning in assembly, a put-
optimized method was written that makes use of a "zero-overhead" hardware
loop and four-way unrolled staggered double-word loads and (remote) stores.
A specialization for the edge case of unaligned memory is also included since
the Epiphany architecture requires loads and stores to be memory aligned to
the data size. Assuming the fast path is taken, the core can transfer a double-
word (8 bytes) per clock cycle. However, since the 8 byte load operation requires
an additional cycle, the effective peak network copy is 8 bytes every two clocks.
For a clock rate of 600 MHz, peak contiguous network transfers may achieve
up to 2.4 GB/s. Having the NoC and core clocks pinned ensures that application communication performance scales with the chip clock speed. The same
put-optimized memory copy subroutine is used for get operations. This is sub-
optimal, but remote read operations will never be as high-performance as remote
write operations on the Epiphany architecture, so they should generally be
avoided. Remote direct read operations are slower than equivalent remote direct
write operations because the read request must first traverse the network to the
receiving core network interface, then the data must traverse the network back to
the requesting core. Unlike a remote direct write operation which can issue store

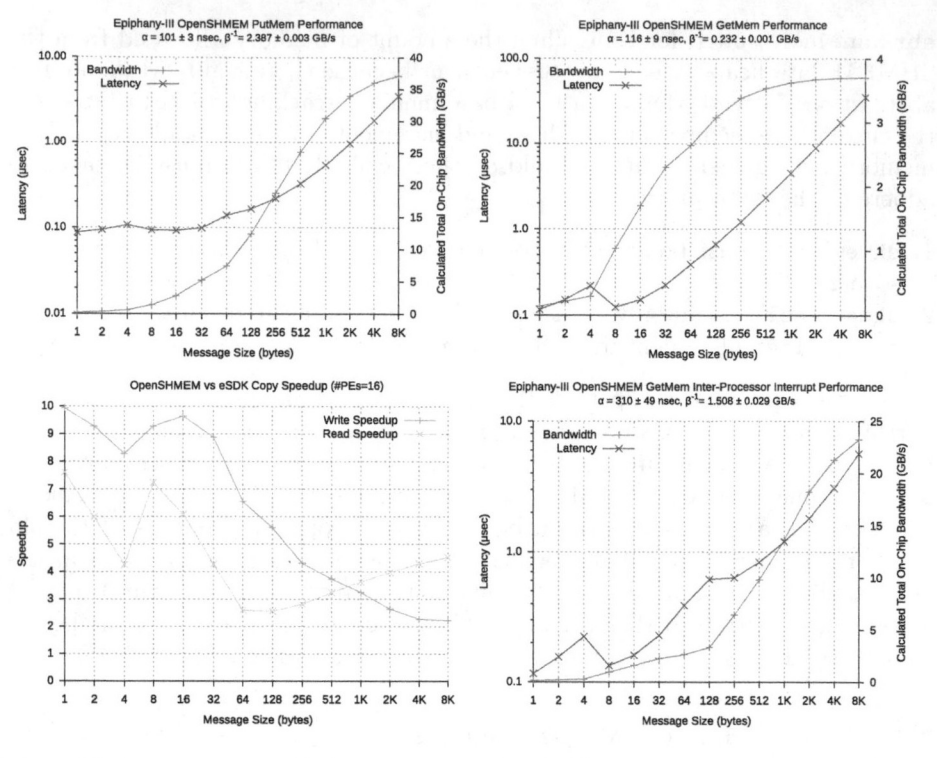

Fig. 3. Performance of optimized `shmem_put` (top left) and `shmem_get` (top right) for contiguous data exchange operations for 16 processing elements, speedup comparison with eLib (bottom left), and experimental inter-processor user interrupt for high-performance `shmem_get` (bottom right).

instructions without a response, the read operation stalls the requesting core until the load instruction returns data to a register. Issuing multiple requests does little to mitigate this performance issue, thus, the throughput of the optimized `shmem_put` is approximately an order of magnitude greater than `shmem_get` as shown in Fig. 3.

In order to address this performance disparity with contiguous remote reads, an inter-processor interrupt is configured and signaled by the receiving core, causing an equivalent fast write to be executed. The receiving core is then signaled to continue upon completion of the inter-processor ISR. This is an experimental feature because it uses the user interrupt and must be enabled with `SHMEM_USE_IPI_GET` during compilation. It has the greatest performance impact for large transfers. The method has a turnover point for buffers larger than 64 bytes so that smaller transfers are read directly and larger transfers use the inter-processor interrupt. All results for contiguous block transfers and a performance comparison with the equivalent eLib interface in the eSDK are shown in Fig. 3.

3.4   Non-blocking Remote Memory Access Routines

The set of non-blocking remote memory access routines (shmem_put_nbi and shmem_get_nbi) makes use of the on-chip DMA engine. The DMA engine has two independent DMA channels per processor node so that two non-blocking transfers may execute concurrently. Each channel has a separate DMA specification of the source and destination address configuration. The configuration is capable of 2D DMA operations with flexible stride sizes. This could support an extension to the OpenSHMEM 1.3 standard for non-blocking strided remote memory access routines if needed. The performance results for the non-blocking remote memory access routines appear in Fig. 4.

Application performance improvement may be realized for large non-blocking transfers by splitting transfers into two portions and calling two non-blocking transfers, however, the performance benefit is marginal and often worse. Due to hardware errata in the Epiphany-III, the DMA engine is throttled to less than half of the peak bandwidth of 8 bytes per clock, or 4.8 GB/s [9]. If fully enabled, as expected in future chips, the DMA engine would be used for the blocking remote memory access routines rather than remote load/store instructions. In general, it may be faster to use blocking transfers because the DMA engine setup overhead is relatively high, and there are often bank conflicts with

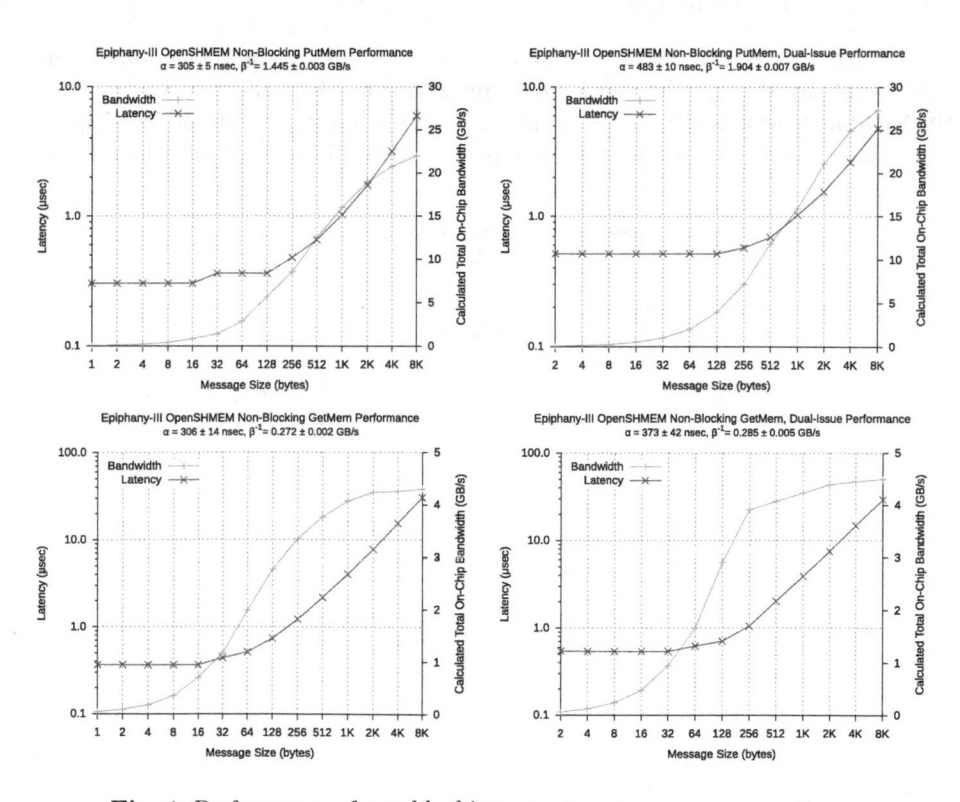

Fig. 4. Performance of non-blocking remote memory access routines.

the concurrent computation and DMA engine access, hindering fully overlapped communication and computation. The blocking operation, shmem_quiet, spin-waits on the DMA status register. Alternatively, a DMA ISR could be used to continue the shmem_quiet operation, but it is not clear how this could be higher performance.

3.5   Atomic Memory Operations

The Epiphany-III ISA does not have support for atomic instructions, but the TESTSET instruction used for remote locks may be used to define other atomic operations in software. With the current code design, it is trivial to extend to other atomic operations with a single line of code if additional atomic operations are defined by the OpenSHMEM specification in the future. At a core level, memory access for both fetch and set operations completes in a single clock cycle and is therefore implicitly atomic. The fetch operation still must traverse the network to the remote core and return the result. Each data type specialization uses a different lock on the remote core as per the specification. The performance results for the 32-bit integer atomic routines appear in Fig. 5.

3.6   Collective Routines

Multi-core barriers are critical to performance for many parallel applications. The Epiphany-III includes hardware support for a fully collective barrier with the WAND instruction and corresponding ISR. This hardware support is included as an experimental feature within the OpenSHMEM library and must be enabled

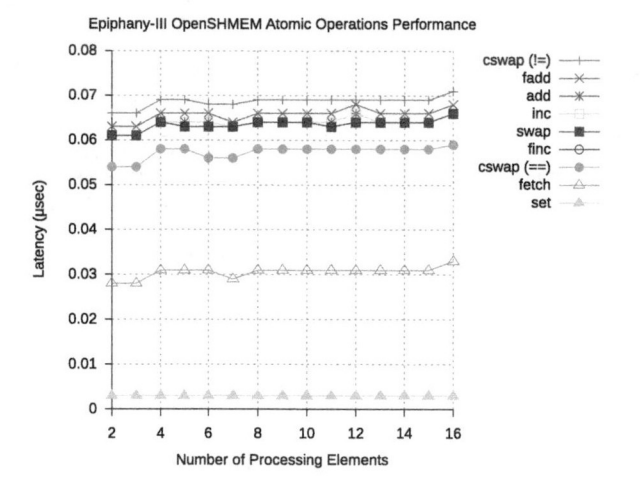

Fig. 5. Performance of OpenSHMEM atomic operations for 32-bit integers and a variable number of processing elements. Atomic operations are performed in a tight loop on the next neighboring processing element.

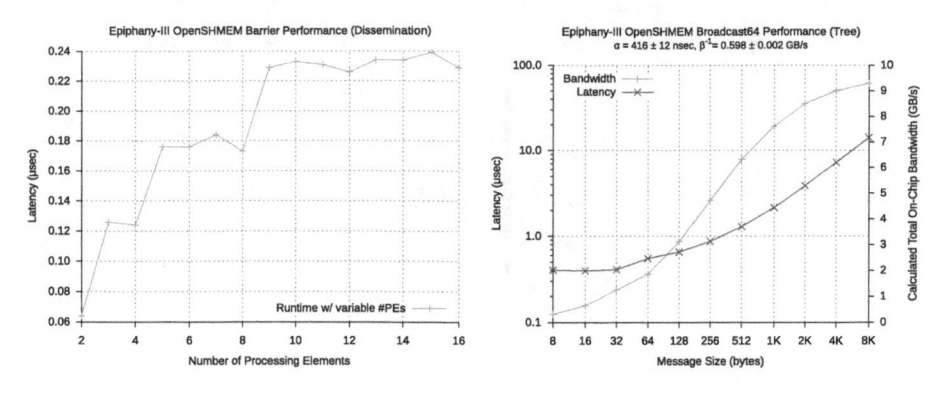

Fig. 6. Performance of `shmem_barrier` for variable number of processing elements (left) and the performance of `shmem_broadcast64` for variable message sizes (right)

by specifying `SHMEM_USE_WAND_BARRIER` at compile time. After several implementations of barrier algorithms, it was determined that a dissemination barrier was the highest-performing software barrier method. It is not clear if this algorithm will continue to achieve the highest performance on chip designs with a larger number of cores; alternative tree algorithms may be needed. The eLib interface in the eSDK uses a counter-based collective barrier and requires a linearly increasing amount of memory with the number of cores. The dissemination barrier requires $8 \cdot log_2(N)$ bytes of memory, where N is the number of processing elements within the barrier. The use of this synchronization array mitigates the need for signaling by locks at each stage of the barrier. The collective eLib barrier completes in $2.0\,\mu s$ while the WAND barrier completes in $0.1\,\mu s$. The performance for group barriers for a subset of the total processing elements is shown in Fig. 6. The latency of the dissemination barrier increases logarithmically with the number of cores so that more than eight cores take approximately $0.23\,\mu s$.

Broadcasts are important in the context of the Epiphany application development in order to limit the replication of off-chip memory accesses to common memory. It is faster to retrieve off-chip data once and disseminate it to other processing elements in an algorithmic manner than for each processing element to fetch the same off-chip data. The data are distributed with a logical network tree, moving the data the farthest distance first in order to prevent subsequent stages increasing on-chip network congestion. The broadcast routines use the same high-performance memory copying subroutine as the contiguous data transfers. Effective core bandwidth approaches the theoretical peak performance for this algorithm and is approximately $2.4/log_2(N)$ GB/s. Figure 6 shows collective broadcast performance for variable message sizes.

The `shmem_collect` and `shmem_fcollect` routines use ring and recursive doubling algorithms for concatenating blocks of data from multiple processing elements. Each uses the optimized contiguous memory copying routine. There is likely room for improvement with these routines; the measured performance appears in Fig. 7.

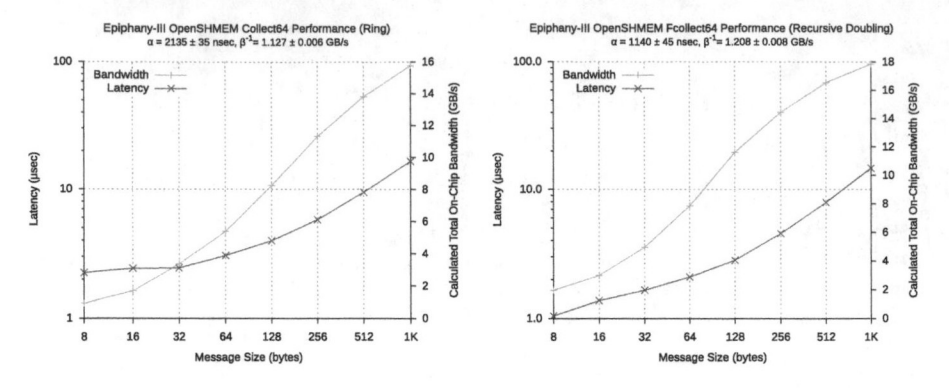

Fig. 7. Performance of linear scaling `shmem_collect64` and recursive doubling `shmem_fcollect64` for variable message sizes on 16 processing elements

The `shmem_TYPE_OP_to_all` reduction routines are important for many multi-core applications. The routines use different algorithms depending on the number of processing elements. A ring algorithm is used for processing elements that number in non-powers of two and a dissemination algorithm for powers of two. The symmetric work array is used for temporary storage and the symmetric synchronization array is used for multi-core locks and signaling. The performance of `shmem_int_sum_to_all` appears in Fig. 8. Other routines vary marginally in performance due to data types and the arithmetic operation used. Reductions that fit within the symmetric work array have improved latency as seen in the figure.

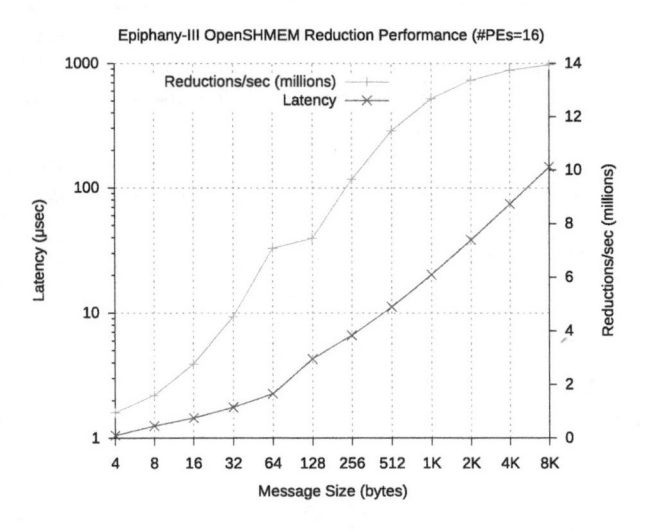

Fig. 8. Reduction performance for `shmem_int_sum_to_all` for all 16 processing elements. The latency and the number of collective reductions per second are shown. The effect of the minimum symmetric work array size for reductions, defined as `SHMEM_REDUCE_MIN_WRKDATA_SIZE` per the OpenSHMEM specification, is apparent for small reductions

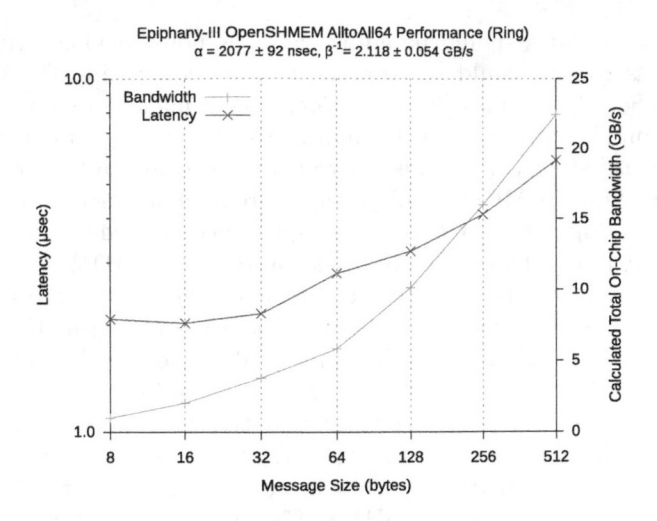

Fig. 9. Performance of the new (to version 1.3) contiguous all-to-all data exchange operation, shmem_alltoall, for 16 processing elements

The performance of the contiguous all-to-all data exchange, shmem_alltoall, appears in Fig. 9. This routine has a relatively high overhead latency compared to other collectives.

3.7   Distributed Locking Routines

The distributed locking routines, shmem_set_lock and shmem_test_lock, are easily supported by the atomic TESTSET instruction. The actual lock address is defined in the implementation to be on the first processing element. These locking mechanisms are also the basis for the atomic operations detailed in Sect. 3.5 but for multiple processing elements. The shmem_clear_lock routine is a simple remote write to free the lock. Although this scheme works well for the 16 processing elements on the Epiphany-III, the performance bottleneck will likely be a problem scaling to much larger core counts. Application developers should avoid using these global locks.

4   Future Work and Discussion of Extensions for Embedded Architectures

It is our intention to release *ARL OpenSHMEM for Epiphany*, as well as the performance evaluation codes and benchmarks used in this paper, as open source software through the U.S. Army Research Laboratory's GitHub account [10] for Parallella community input and further development. The Epiphany architecture may also be updated in the future to add more hardware support for many of the existing OpenSHMEM routines. Many of the currently proposed OpenSHMEM extensions and updates should be addressable. A non-blocking strided remote memory access routine could be supported with the existing DMA engine as mentioned in Sect. 3.4. Some other extensions do not make sense for the architecture. For example, Epiphany is not a multithreaded architecture and, although it can be performed via software, is not the ideal mechanism for improving performance. The OpenSHMEM standard should remain sufficiently lightweight to address low-level operations without relying on specific architectural features.

One of the more challenging portions of the OpenSHMEM standard for the Epiphany architecture and other embedded architectures are the memory management routines. It makes some sense for some platforms to have a pre-allocated symmetric heap from which memory allocations will be made. Within an Epiphany local core, there is no memory virtualization between the physical address and the memory address returned by the allocation routines as available memory is linearly removed from the symmetric heap. The limitations of the available core space make it challenging to introduce a Linux-like abstract model of virtual memory. As OpenSHMEM is a low-level interface and application developers are already accustomed to explicitly managing memory, it may make some sense to improve memory management interfaces, such as those discussed in Sect. 3.2, for embedded architectures.

5   Conclusion

OpenSHMEM provided an effective and pragmatic programming model for the Epiphany architecture. The header-only implementation enabled compiler optimizations for program size and application performance that is difficult to achieve using a standard pre-compiled library. We demonstrated improved performance and many useful features compared to the current eLib library despite the additional software abstraction with the OpenSHMEM interface. The *ARL OpenSHMEM for Epiphany* demonstrated high-performance execution while approaching hardware theoretical networking limits, and low-latency operation for many of the OpenSHMEM routines.

References

1. Chapman, B., Curtis, T., Pophale, S., Poole, S., Kuehn, J., Koelbel, C., Smith, L.: Introducing OpenSHMEM: SHMEM for the PGAS community. In Proceedings of 4th Conference on Partitioned Global Address Space Programming Model, PGAS 2010, pp. 2:1–2:3. ACM, New York (2010)
2. Richie, D., Ross, J., Park, S., Shires, D.: Threaded MPI programming model for the Epiphany RISC array processor. J. Comput. Sci. **9**, 94–100 (2015). Computational Science at the Gates of Nature
3. Ross, J., Richie, D.: Implementing OpenSHMEM for the Adapteva Epiphany RISC array processor. Proc. Comput. Sci. **80**, 2353–2356 (2016). International Conference on Computational Science, ICCS 2016, San Diego, California, USA, 6–8 June 2016

4. GitHub - Adapteva/Epiphany-libs: Epiphany runtime libraries and utilities. https://github.com/adapteva/epiphany-libs. Accessed 24 May 2016
5. COPRTHR-2 Epiphany/Parallella Developer Resources. http://www.browndeertechnology.com/resources_epiphany_developer_coprthr2.htm. Accessed 01 July 2016
6. Richie, D., Ross, J.: Advances in run-time performance and inter-operability for the Adapteva Epiphany coprocessor. Proc. Comput. Sci. **80**, 1531–1541 (2016). International Conference on Computational Science, ICCS 2016, San Diego, California, USA, 6–8 June 2016
7. Ross, J.A., Richie, D.A., Park, S.J.: Implementing image processing algorithms for the Epiphany many-core coprocessor with threaded MPI. IEEE, September 2015
8. Ross, J.A., Richie, D.A., Park, S.J., Shires, D.R.: Parallel programming model for the Epiphany many-core coprocessor using threaded MPI. Microprocess. Microsyst. **43**, 95–103 (2016)
9. Adapteva, Inc.: E16G301 Epiphany^{TM} 16-Core Microprocessor Datasheet, Rev 14.03.11, June 2013
10. US Army Research Laboratory - GitHub. https://github.com/USArmyResearchLab. Accessed 24 May 2016

Hybrid Programming and
Benchmarking with OpenSHMEM

An Evaluation of Thread-Safe and Contexts-Domains Features in Cray SHMEM

Naveen Namashivayam$^{(\boxtimes)}$, David Knaak, Bob Cernohous, Nick Radcliffe,
and Mark Pagel

Cray Inc., Seattle, USA
{nravi,dknaak,bcernohous,nradclif,pags}@cray.com

Abstract. There is increasing use of multithreading in High Performance Computing (HPC) programs in order to maximize the use of hardware resources of multi-core compute nodes. The latest version of the OpenSHMEM API Specification does not standardize the interaction between threads and OpenSHMEM routines in multithreaded applications. In this paper, we evaluate two proposals that have been put forward to try to address this deficiency: "Thread-Safe" and "Contexts-Domains". Both of these proposals have been implemented, at least in part, in Cray SHMEM, a vendor-specific OpenSHMEM implementation from Cray Inc. We provide a design overview of the two proposals and give some experimental results showing significant performance benefits of each. To the best of our knowledge, this is the first paper to compare and contrast these two proposals.

1 Introduction

SHMEM is a popular library-based Partitioned Global Address Space (PGAS) [6] programming model. The original SHMEM library was developed by Cray Research, the predecessor of Cray Inc., and in due course different vendor-specific closed source and other open source implementations of SHMEM were developed. OpenSHMEM [8] is an effort driven by Extreme Scale Systems Center (ESSC) at ORNL and University of Houston, with significant inputs from the SHMEM programming community, to standardize the SHMEM programming library interface with an API specification. OpenSHMEM provides the means to develop light-weight, portable, and scalable applications.

As modern compute processors contain a larger number of compute cores, multithreading in HPC applications is becoming more common in order to better utilize all of the compute resources.

But, with the current OpenSHMEM API, Version 1.3, interaction between OpenSHMEM routines and threads are not yet standardized. Hence, there is no explicit support for the use of OpenSHMEM routines in multithreaded applications. To be thread-safe in such applications, all calls to OpenSHMEM routines

---

D. Knaak and B. Cernohous—Contributed equally to this work.

© Springer International Publishing AG 2016
M. Gorentla Venkata et al. (Eds.): OpenSHMEM 2016, LNCS 10007, pp. 163–180, 2016.
DOI: 10.1007/978-3-319-50995-2_11

must be made only by the thread that initiated the call to `shmem_init`. This severely limits overall concurrency of the application.

Cray SHMEM is a vendor-specific OpenSHMEM implementation from Cray Inc. Released versions of Cray SHMEM support increased concurrency of some OpenSHMEM calls with explicit support for multithreaded applications. In this paper, we will refer to this feature, proposed and implemented by Cray Inc., as "Thread-safe" [18]. It is available as non-standard `SHMEMX`-prefixed extensions.

Another proposal for addressing this need comes from Intel [9]. We will refer to this feature as "Contexts-Domains". As a part of the work described in this paper, we developed a prototype version of some of the Contexts-Domains features in Cray SHMEM. Both of these proposed features are evaluated in this paper.

The contributions of this work are:

- implementation of a Contexts-Domains prototype in Cray SHMEM;
- compare and contrast the two different threading proposals based on effect of Thread Local Storage(TLS), support for different available thread-levels, usage of explicit and implicit non-blocking communication operations, differences in memory ordering, and efficient resource utilization;
- performance analysis of these extensions using modified multithreaded OSU Microbenchmarks [5]; and
- performance analysis with context and thread-safe implementations of all-to-all collective communication pattern.

This paper is organized as follows. In Sect. 2, we provide overviews of the Thread-Safe and Contexts-Domains proposals. In Sect. 3, we provide details of the Thread-Safe and Contexts-Domains design in Cray SHMEM. In Sect. 4, we compare and contrast different features of these two proposals. Performance results of an all-to-all collective communication pattern implemented with these two features are provided in Sect. 5. We discuss related work in Sect. 6, future work in Sect. 7, and conclude in Sect. 8.

2   Background

In this section, we provide brief introductions to Cray SHMEM and two different proposals for multithreading in OpenSHMEM applications. In brief, these proposals try to support safe and efficient interaction between OpenSHMEM calls and threads with standard APIs.

The main motivation is to take advantage of the power of combining different programming models in the same HPC application to increase concurrency, reduce communication overhead within nodes, and provide better scalability. Common hybrid programming approaches include use of threading models like OpenMP [16], OpenACC [15], or pthread [13] with distributed memory models like MPI [10], or OpenSHMEM.

In this paper we use the phrase "threaded region" to be a region of code where more than one thread may be running concurrently and use the phrase

"SHMEM threaded region" to be a threaded region where multiple threads make independent SHMEM communication calls.

2.1 Cray SHMEM

Cray SHMEM is a closed source vendor-specific OpenSHMEM implementation from Cray Inc. It is part of the Message Passing Toolkit (MPT) [1] software stack from Cray Inc. Other software libraries that are part of this software stack include Cray-MPICH, Cray-Global Arrays [3], and DMAPP [17]. Cray SHMEM is at version 7.4.0 and it is compliant with OpenSHMEM specification version-1.3 [4]. In addition to providing support for standard OpenSHMEM features, Cray SHMEM has support for thread-safe extensions, flexible PE subsets creation and management, point-to-point put operation with signal, and local shared memory pointers. As required by the OpenSHMEM standard, these extra features [11] are supported as SHMEMX-prefixed extensions.

2.2 Overview of Thread-Safe Proposal

The proposed extensions for thread-safety in OpenSHMEM supports calls to RMA and AMO routines in SHMEM threaded regions, with restrictions on using SHMEM collectives in these regions.

In a thread-safe OpenSHMEM implementation, the SHMEM Processing Element (PE) is an OS process that can be multithreaded. With respect to the symmetric heap; it is a per PE resource and hence the threads of a PE do not separately address symmetric data objects. Rather, the address space is shared by all threads of a PE.

The routines associated with this proposal are listed in Fig. 1.

Similar to shmem_init, shmemx_init_thread is used to initialize OpenSH-MEM resources. In addition, it specifies the thread-level usage of the application. SHMEM_THREAD_SINGLE and SHMEM_THREAD_MULTIPLE are the two currently proposed thread levels. This is discussed in detail in Sect. 4.4.

shmemx_query_thread is used to query the current thread-level used by an application.

Though applications may use multiple threads per PE, it is not necessary for all threads to make OpenSHMEM calls. Any thread that will make OpenSHMEM

```
int  shmemx_init_thread (int  required_threading_type );
int  shmemx_query_thread ( void );
void shmemx_thread_register ( void );
void shmemx_thread_unregister ( void );
void shmemx_thread_quiet ( void );
void shmemx_thread_fence ( void );
```

Fig. 1. OpenSHMEM extensions for thread-safe proposal

calls must call `shmemx_thread_register` to register it with the OpenSHMEM library. This allows the library to map threads to network resources.

Similar to `shmem_fence` and `shmem_quiet`, memory ordering is done with `shmemx_thread_fence` and `shmemx_thread_quiet`. `shmemx_thread_fence` orders communication for a particular thread. `shmemx_thread_quiet` waits for completion of all outstanding operations for a particular thread, while `shmem_quiet` waits for completion of all outstanding operations on all registered threads associated with a PE.

2.3   Overview of Contexts-Domains Proposal

Dinan *et al.* [9] proposed a new feature called Contexts and Domains to allow the programmer to generate independent streams of communication. This feature separates message injection resources from remote completion tracking.

OpenSHMEM extensions associated with this proposal are provided in Fig. 2. Domains are essentially a group of Contexts with a similar property. They are created and destroyed with `shmemx_domain_create` and `shmemx_domain_destroy`. While a list of properties on which these groups can be formed are not yet completely defined, SHMEM thread-level can be considered as an example property.

Each Context created through `shmemx_ctx_create` is associated with a particular domain and there is no limit on the number of contexts created per domain. `shmemx_ctx_t` and `shmemx_domain_t` are opaque handles to access contexts and domains respectively.

Relation Between Threads and Contexts. By definition, threads are not mapped to a particular context. Contexts and threads are two separate entities in an application. Contexts are network resource objects with a particular property and domains are group of contexts with similar property.

```
typedef int shmem_ctx_t;
typedef int shmem_domain_t;
void shmemx_domain_create(int thread_level, int num_domain,
                          shmem_domain_t domain[]);
void shmemx_domain_destroy(int num_domain,
                           shmem_domain_t domain[]);
int shmemx_ctx_create(shmem_domain_t domain,
                      shmem_ctx_t *ctx);
void shmemx_ctx_destroy(shmem_ctx_t ctx);
void shmemx_ctx_fence(shmem_ctx_t ctx);
void shmemx_ctx_quiet(shmem_ctx_t ctx);
void shmemx_sync(int PE_start, int logPE_stride,
                 int PE_size, long *pSync);
void shmemx_sync_all(void);
```

Fig. 2. OpenSHMEM extensions for contexts-domains proposal

```
void shmemx_ctx_TYPE_p(TYPE *addr, TYPE value, int pe,
                       shmem_ctx_t ctx);
void shmemx_ctx_TYPE_get(TYPE *dest, const TYPE *source,
                         size_t nelems, int pe,
                         shmem_ctx_t ctx);
void shmemx_TYPE_inc(TYPE *dest, int pe, shmem_ctx_t ctx);
```

Fig. 3. OpenSHMEM extensions for context-based communications

Any thread can make use of a context object by using the context handle. Each of these contexts are not mapped to any particular thread. Based on the thread-level, any context can be accessed by any thread by referencing the context handle. For example, a group of contexts with thread-level SHMEM_THREAD_SINGLE forms a domain. But only one thread can access it at a time.

shmemx_ctx_fence and shmemx_ctx_quiet are context-based fence and quiet operations. A call to these by a thread only affects the context that was referenced by the context handle argument.

In addition to these routines, there are context versions of RMA and AMO routines that have an extra argument of shmem_ctx_t handle to specify the context on which the particular communication operation takes place. Figure 3, shows an example set of communication routines with a context handle argument.

2.4 Usage Details Using Thread-Safe and Contexts-Domains Extensions

Figure 4 shows the basic usage details of extensions associated with the two proposals.

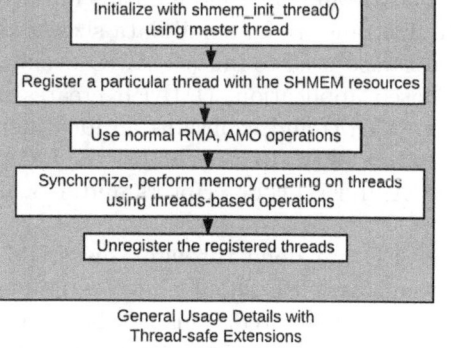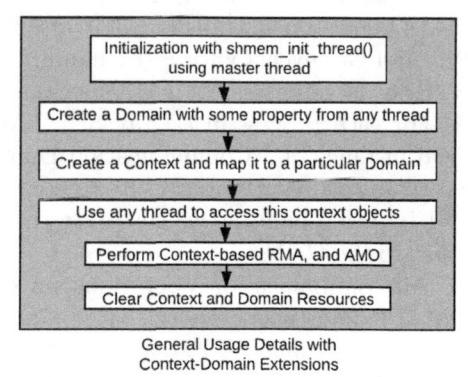

Fig. 4. Basic usage details of thread-safe and contexts-domains extensions

With the Thread-Safe feature, we register threads and then use normal RMA and AMO routines which are now thread-safe as a result of the combination `shmemx_init_thread` and `shmemx_thread_register`. Finally, we unregister the threads and exit after usage.

With the Contexts-Domains feature, any thread can create domain and context objects and make them visible to other threads. Any thread can pick these objects and use them for context-based communications. Threads involved in context and domain object creation or context-based communication operations need not be registered.

Thread-Safe APIs and Contexts-Domains APIs can be used in the same application, though not in the same SHMEM threaded region. Threads and contexts are two separate entities in an application. That said, even registered threads can make use of the context objects.

3   Implementation Details

In this Section, we provide basic implementation details of the Thread-Safe and Contexts-Domains extensions in Cray SHMEM.

3.1   DMAPP

The Cray DMAPP (Distributed Shared Memory Application) library is a low-level communication layer developed by Cray Inc. to provide support for logically shared, distributed memory programming models. It is designed to deliver the full hardware performance of the current Cray networks. DMAPP provides support for Remote Memory Access (RMA) between processes within a job in an one-sided manner. Cray's implementation of OpenSHMEM and Partitioned Global Address Space (PGAS) compilers, such as Coarray Fortran [14] and Unified Parallel C (UPC) [7], are implemented on top of DMAPP.

All PUT, GET, and AMO communication operations are called Events. There are two types of Remote Memory Access mechanisms: Fast Memory Access (FMA), and Block Transfer Engine (BTE). FMA and BTE mechanisms initiate Put and Get events with FMA handling data transfers for small data sizes and BTE for large data sizes. FMA mechanism is also used to initiate AMO events.

For each process in a Cray SHMEM based application, DMAPP creates a local instance of a Communication Domain (CDM) and it obtains an identifier called an `cdm_handle`, for future reference to this CDM. In order to use the FMA and BTE mechanisms we configure the FMA and BTE descriptors and attach them to the CDM.

All communication operations on that PE are done through this CDM. DMAPP does not support shared CDMs and each PE should have a unique CDM. The number of FMA descriptors per node is limited. This is a hardware limitation. For example, on Cray-developed Aries [2] RDMA interconnect the number of FMA descriptors per node is fixed to 120.

The event notification mechanism is through Completion Queues (CQ). The event notification mechanism is the process to track the progress of communication operations. Each CDM has its own CQ and all events on that particular CDM are tracked through this CQ. By DMAPP design, there is 1-to-1 relation between CDM and FMA descriptors, as well as with CDM and CQ.

3.2 Thread-Safe Implementation Details

As mentioned in Sect. 3, in a single threaded application, each PE has its own CDM and a corresponding CQ per CDM. In a multithreaded application, each registered thread gets its own CDM and a corresponding CQ. Only registerd threads can make OpenSHMEM calls.

If we over allocate the number of resources and register more threads than the number of CDMs per node, one or more threads are forced to share a CDM. For each thread, the cdm_handle that is uses to refer to its CDM is stored in Thread Local Storage (TLS). It is referenced during every communication operation from that thread.

The shmemx_thread_quiet routine for a particular thread waits for completion of all events in the associated CQ. In an over allocation scenario, if multiple threads share the same CQ, the shmemx_thread_quiet routine waits for completion of all events from all threads that share the CQ. This is because of the 1-to-1 relation between CDM and CQ.

Figure 5 shows the basic relation between threads and DMAPP network resources. In Fig. 5, we have three threads in PE and among them two are registered. These registered threads have their own CDMs with an allocated CQ. All events from these registered threads are tracked with their allocated CQs.

3.3 Context Implementation Details

In terms of Contexts-Domains implementation, in spite of nomenclature based similarities, context-based domains and DMAPP-based domains are two separate entities. In this paper, context-based domain is referred as domain and DMAPP-based resource domain is referred as CDM.

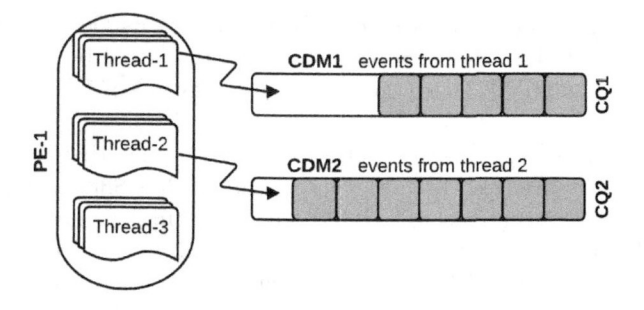

Fig. 5. Thread-safe design in cray SHMEM

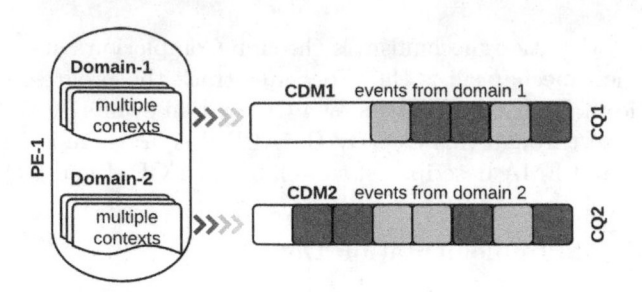

Fig. 6. Contexts-domains prototype: design-1 domain-based resource sharing

Domain and Context features are used to split up message injection resources from remote completion tracking. There are two different ways to track event completion. Based on remote completion tracking, we have designed two different Context prototypes.

– Design:1 Domain-based Resource Sharing; and
– Design:2 Context-based Resource Sharing

Design:1 Domain-Based Resource Sharing. Each domain has its own CDM, and all contexts from that particular CDM shares same CQ. Now, CQ tracks completion of all events on that particular domain, and this is of little use because all memory ordering operations are contexts-based. Hence, completion of all events from a context is tracked separately with a unique reference called sync_id. sync_id is generated for each context-based events. This sync_id is tracked separately in SHMEM library-level, rather than on the DMAPP-level. shmem_ctx_quiet operation on a particular context waits for completion of all sync_ids associated with that context.

Figure 6, shows basic design for domain-based resource sharing. In Fig. 6, we have two domains created for a particular PE, with multiple contexts per domain. Each domain has its registered CDM, with an allocated CQ. All events from contexts that shares the same domain is tracked by a single CQ. Different shades of the CQs represent events from multiple different contexts, and events tracked using their sync_id in the SHMEM library-level is not shown in Fig. 6.

Design:2 Context-Based Resource Sharing. In this Design, each context has its own CDM and all memory ordering operations will be tracked through CQ mapped to that CDM. Here, domain is just a group of CDMs with similar properties.

Figure 7, shows design for context-based resource sharing. There are two domains, each with different thread-levels. Domain-1 has SHMEM_THREAD_SINGLE as thread-level with 2 contexts associated with it. Domain-2 has thread-level as SHMEM_THREAD_MULTIPLE, with 2 contexts associated with it. There are only 3 CDMs available to share within that PE. Due to thread-levels, all contexts in Domain-1 gets a unique CDM, while Contexts in Domain-2 share a common CDM.

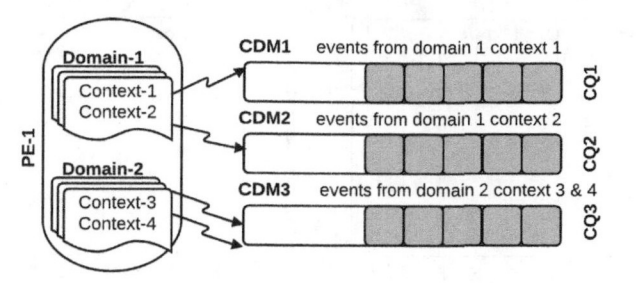

Fig. 7. Contexts-domains prototype: design-2 context-based resource sharing

4 Compare and Contrast Thread-Safe and Contexts-Domains Features

In this Section, we compare various features of thread-safe and context extensions. Features analyzed in subsections, may be generic or specific to a proposal. These features are analyzed in terms of the runtime and explains the reason behind the design decisions briefed in Sect. 3.

4.1 Experimental Setup

Features in Sect. 4, are experimented with Cray SHMEM version 7.4.0. Tests were run on a 52 node Cray XC system with 36 core Intel Broadwell processors per node with Cray-developed Aries interconnect architecture. In this paper, a node is a group of processors, memory, and network components that acts as network end points on system interconnection network. We also use Cray Programming Environment with Cray Compiler Environment (CCE) version 8.4 for tests. OpenMP [16] from CCE is used for all Microbenchmarks as hybrid design with OpenSHMEM.

4.2 Impact of Thread Local Storage (TLS)

As stated in the thread-safe extensions design in Sect. 3.2, each registered thread uses Thread Local Storage for storing cdm_handle. The performance impact of using TLS is analyzed in this Section. We modified the OSU Microbenchmarks and created a multithreaded version of the PUT benchmark with thread-level SHMEM_THREAD_MULTIPLE. The inter-node communication of a pair of PE making communication calls of different data sizes from 32 registered threads per PE to one another is analyzed.

In Fig. 8, cdm-handle-use-TLS represents the version of the modified OSU PUT Microbenchmark that uses TLS for storing cdm_handle. cdm-handle-no-TLS, uses a local variable instead of TLS. In the cdm-handle-no-TLS version, significant changes are made in Cray SHMEM implementation, to allow users to directly pass cdm_handle as an extra argument in the SHMEM communication calls. Though there are no performance difference on large data sizes,

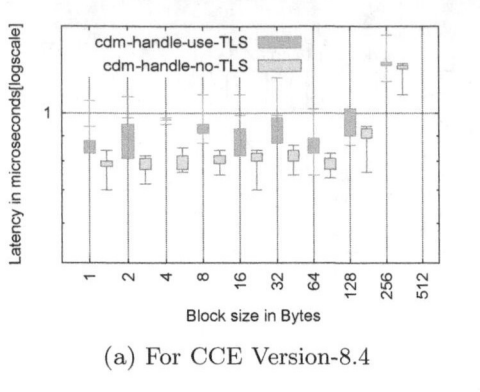 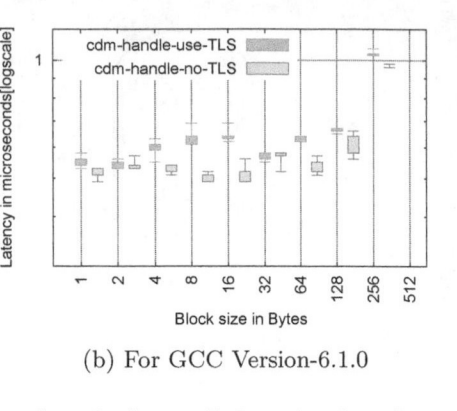

(a) For CCE Version-8.4   (b) For GCC Version-6.1.0

Fig. 8. Analysis of modified OSU put microbenchmarks for small data sizes less than 512 bytes with thread-level SHMEM_THREAD_MULTIPLE for cdm_handle stored in TLS and cdm_handle stored as Local variable

we see a variability on small data sizes less than 512 bytes. Figure 8 shows the performance variability for small data sizes less than 512 bytes. Comparing the median of multiple iterations, we see cdm-handle-no-TLS to perform 8% better than cdm-handle-use-TLS. Similar performances are observed on both GCC and CCE compiler.

4.3   Usage of Explicit and Implicit Non-blocking Operations

As mentioned in Sect. 3.3, in domain-based resource sharing design unique sync_id from each context-based events are tracked. Not all DMAPP events generate sync_ids. Only explicit non-blocking operations generate sync_ids and not the implicit non-blocking operations.

Figure 9(a) shows performance of modified OSU Microbenchmark with 2 PEs(32 threads per PE) on separate nodes that use 32 domains with 1 context per domain design. Each domain object is accessed by only one thread. Since, each domain has only one context, memory ordering can be tracked directly on CQs. In Fig. 9(a), explicit-events refers to benchmark version with all events as explicit operations, while implicit-events refers to version with all events as implicit operations.

We see for small message sizes less than 1M, using implicit operations shows 45% better latency when compared to using explicit operations. And for large data sizes, there is no obvious performance impact. This is because, for small data sizes there are optimizations performed over implicit operations in DMAPP to chain events together and generate a unique sync_id for a chain of non-blocking events rather than one sync_id per event.

This performance degradation can be avoided in context-based resource sharing design. While domain-based resource sharing requires conversion of all events into explicit operations to track sync_ids, context-based resource sharing does

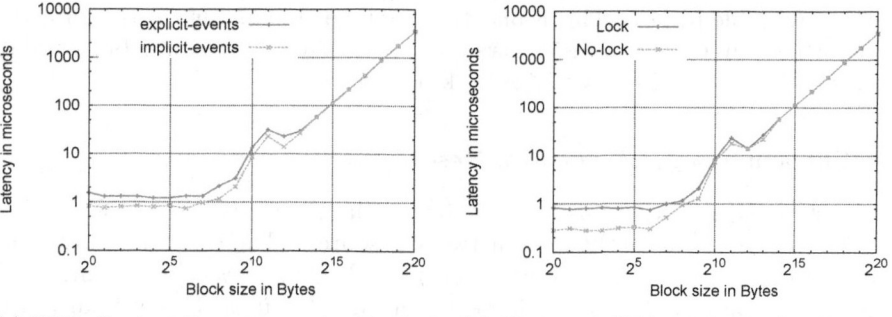

(a) With Context Prototype using Explicit vs. Implicit events for Communication

(b) With and Without Locks for Communication

Fig. 9. Analysis of `SHMEM_THREAD_MULTIPLE` implementation in modified OSU put microbenchmarks on 2 PEs from 2 separate nodes

not involve tracking of `sync_id`, as all events are tracked directly through CQs mapped to contexts.

4.4   Hierarchy of Threading Support

At present, Cray SHMEM supports two levels of threading: `SHMEM_THREAD_SINGLE`, and `SHMEM_THREAD_MULTIPLE`. This is also similar to thread-levels available in MPI [10]. The support for thread-levels similar to `MPI_THREAD_FUNNELED` and `MPI_THREAD_SERIAL` are not discussed for current proposals. The existing thread-levels are same in both the thread-safe and context features.

In thread-safe, `SHMEM_THREAD_SINGLE` allows registration of only one thread per process, while `SHMEM_THREAD_MULTIPLE` allows multiple thread registrations. This is a hint for implementations to provide thread-safety during communication, which in turn means introduction of locks to ensure thread-safety. The thread-safe proposal allows usage of one of the two thread-levels. Hence, if more than one thread gets involved in communication, locks are introduced by default in all CDMs. Locks are essential only in scenarios where number of registered threads being greater than number of CDMs. But, as determination of actual number of registered threads is not possible during initialization, all CDMs are locked by default.

Figure 9(b), shows performance difference between `SHMEM_THREAD_MULTIPLE` implementation with and without locks. We modified OSU PUT Microbenchmarks, to use multiple threads for simultaneous communication. We use 2 PEs with each PE on different nodes and with 32 threads registered per PE. We see `No-lock` based implementation is 4X times better than `lock` based implementation for small data sizes.

While `No-lock` design provides exceptional performance, this design cannot be used for thread-safe implementation, as it assumes ideal usage of threads. The ideal usage referred here is number of registered threads being equal to number of CDMs available per PE. This is one disadvantage of mapping threads directly to network resources. Section 4.5 shows how this is fixed with Contexts-Domains features and map resources with `No-lock` design.

4.5   Efficient Usage of Network Resources

This Section is an extension to Sect. 4.4, with more analysis on Contexts-Domains design to efficiently share network resources. There is a limitation on number of available network resources per node. Table 1 shows the growing need for network resource per node on different Cray architectures. This is a hardware limitation. Efficient usage of network resources is of an essence. In the DMAPP design, by network resources we refer to number of CDM's available per node. When applications subscribes for more than the actual available resources, then multiple threads or contexts (in context-based sharing) are forced to share a single CDM.

Though Contexts-Domains features cannot resolve this over allocation scenarios, it can help in providing sufficient hints to SHMEM runtime for efficient network resource mapping. The only possibility of providing such hints in thread-safe extensions is using `SHMEM_MAX_NUM_THREADS` environmental variable. It is used during initialization to refer the maximum number of possible thread registrations. But, this is not sufficient, and users do not have any control over the way network resources are shared by threads. There are multiple scenarios that `SHMEM_MAX_NUM_THREADS` fail to address. For example on over allocation;

- Even if threads are registered and over allocated only during a particular module of the application, locks are introduced on all CDMs starting from `shmem_init_thread` irrespective of the module where the over allocation occurs.
- Even if only the master thread is active at a time, though locks are not functional, check for locks is done during all communication events from master thread;

Table 1. Growing network resource demand (based on cray architectures)

Architecture	Threads/Node	Interconnect	CDMs/Node
Ivy Bridge	40+	Aries with Dragonfly	120
Haswell	56+	Aries with Dragonfly	120
Broadwell	70+	Aries with Dragonfly	120
Knights Landing	250+	Aries with Dragonfly	120

Context features helps to differentiate network resources from threads. While in thread-safe features the threads are mapped directly to a network resource, threads and context objects are two separate entities in Contexts-Domains. From

Sect. 2.3, we know contexts are mapped directly to network resources. The mapping is based on either domain-based resource sharing or context-based resource sharing design and threads as separate entities are not mapped to any particular contexts. If contexts handles are made visible to threads, any thread can make use of it.

Contexts with similar network features group together as a domain. In Fig. 10, `Context-1` belong to one particular domain, while `Context-2` and `Context-3` belong to a different domain. With this design, instead of locking all resources during `shmem_init_thread`, we can lock only particular resources based on the property of the contexts. Any thread can make use of this created contexts at any time, with usage is based on the

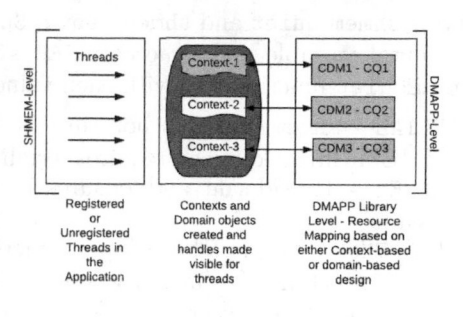

Fig. 10. Relation between threads and contexts

resource property of contexts. For example, if a particular context is created as a private context or with thread-level as `SHMEM_THREAD_SINGLE`, then only one thread should be allowed to access that particular context at a time. If a context is created as a shared context or with thread-level as `SHMEM_THREAD_MULTIPLE`, any number of threads can access that context simultaneously. Contexts created with thread-level as `SHMEM_THREAD_SINGLE` is similar to the `No-lock` design from Sect. 4.4 and provide better performance than the Contexts created with thread-level as `SHMEM_THREAD_MULTIPLE`.

If the above details explain the ways by which threads are separated from directly mapping against network resources, these same features also provides opportunities for fine-grain synchronization on a single thread by creating multiple communication streams per thread. For example, if the number of available network resources are more than actual threads being used. Then, a single thread can make use of multiple contexts, and each context with its own stream of communication provides better concurrency, and computation overlap. Dinan *et al.* [9], demonstrate this feature with experimental results from using context, and domain features on Mandelbrot Set Benchmark, and Integer Sort Benchmark.

4.6   Memory Ordering Extensions

One important property, that hinders the co-existence of both thread-safe and context features are memory ordering. Thread-safe features allows `shmem_quiet` and `shmem_fence` to perform memory ordering across all registered threads in a PE. Contexts-Domains avoids the property of `shmem_quiet` and `shmem_fence` to function across all created active contexts. This property in thread-safe extensions is expensive, and is fundamentally against the fine-grain synchronization principle of contexts.

A well-behaved, multithreaded application will not use `shmem_quiet` in a SHMEM threaded region and memory ordering is done with `shmem_thread_quiet` on a per thread basis. As part of thread-safe features, to support a well-behaved application we suggest to introduce an environmental variable to provide the users with an opportunity to decide the property of `shmem_quiet` and `shmem_fence`. `SHMEM_THREADED_QUIET` is the new environmental variable and it accepts `SERIAL`, `SHARED`, or `INDEPENDENT` as input. `shmem_quiet` functionality with each values are explained below:

- `SERIAL` - `shmem_quiet` is not thread-safe. Usage of `shmem_quiet` inside an SHMEM threaded region requires serialization and this is the default property;
- `SHARED` - thread-safe and ensures memory ordering across all registered threads; and
- `INDEPENDENT` - thread-safe, and functionality is similar to `shmem_thread_quiet`, which invokes memory ordering only on the current thread which initiated the `shmem_quiet` call.

Figure 11, shows the inter-node performance analysis of modified OSU Put multithreaded Microbenchmark on 2 PEs, with 16 registered threads per PE. We see the performance results across different data sizes, with different values for `SHMEM_THREADED_QUIET` environmental values.

Though there are no performance variations for large data sizes, for small data sizes we see `SHMEM_THREADED_QUIET` with value `SERIAL` to have better latency and message rate compared to `SHMEM_THREADED_QUIET` with value `SHARED`.

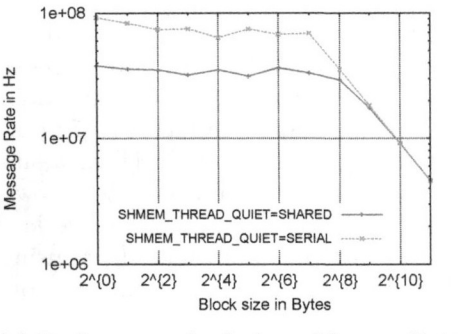
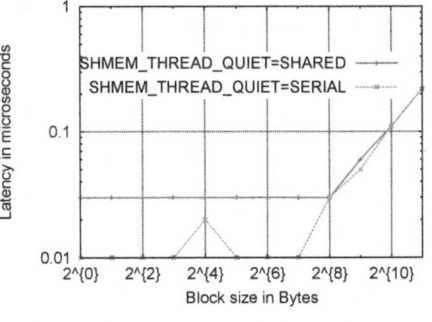

(a) Performance Analysis on Message Rate   (b) Performance Analysis on Latency

Fig. 11. Performance analysis on using different values for `SHMEM_THREADED_QUIET` environmental variable using OSU put microbenchmark

5   Experiments

The purpose of this experimentation is to analyze the impact of optimized network resource mapping. For this test, we implemented different versions of multithreaded all-to-all collective communication pattern.

We used a fixed data size of 4 MB per PE. Each PE uses 32 threads and latency is measured across different sets of PEs. As per the all-to-all collective communication pattern, based on number of PEs used, data is split equally among all PEs and sent to all other PEs. Further for multithreaded version of this communication pattern, on each PE this data is split further equally among its threads and threads are simultaneously used for communication.

There are three different versions of this benchmark. Figure 12(a) refers to the performance comparison between these versions. And, Fig. 12(b) to the usage details of 32 threads per PE.

- `Thread_safe_version`(TS), refers to the version implemented with thread-safe extensions. 32 threads per PE are registered, and each thread is used for communication.
- `Context_Design_1`(CTX1), refers to the version implemented with 1 domain (Domain-1) created using thread-level as SINGLE, and this domain has 32 contexts associated to it. For communication, 32 threads created in the application make use of 1 context object each.
- `Context_Design_2`(CTX2), refers to the version implemented with 2 domains. Domain-1 is created using thread-level as SINGLE and Domain-2 with thread-level as MULTIPLE. Each domain as 16 contexts. Then 32 threads in the application make use of 1 context object each.

This test is performed using 32 cores per node Broadwell machine with Aries interconnect. Since, Aries architecture has 120 CDMs, all registered thread in TS and all Contexts in CTX1, and CTX2 receive its own CDM. In TS, by design all its associated CDMs are locked. And as all contexts in CTX1 are created with thread-level as SINGLE, there are no locks in its associated CDMs. While, in CTX2 16 contexts which have the thread-level as MULTIPLE are locked, while the other 16 contexts with thread-level as SINGLE are not locked.

From the experimental evaluation, we see the performance of CTX1 to be 18% better than TS, and 7% better than CTX2.

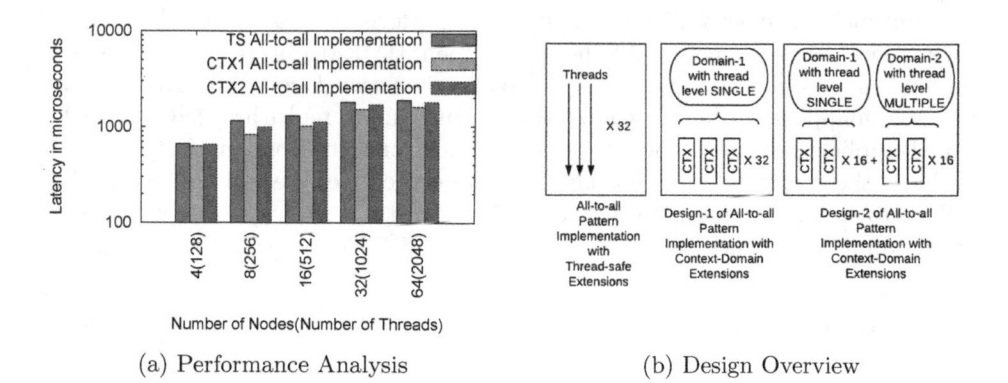

(a) Performance Analysis   (b) Design Overview

Fig. 12. Experimentation on different multi-threaded versions of all-to-all collective communication pattern

6 Related Work

6.1 PAMI

PAMI [12], Parallel Active Message Interface is a communication library for Blue Gene/Q Supercomputers. Contexts objects in PAMI are similar to the proposed Contexts-Domains extensions. In PAMI, progress of communication events on each context is independent and advance concurrently. However, the major difference is that all operations in PAMI contexts are not thread-safe. Hence, they can be considered as creating all contexts with thread-level property as SHMEM_THREAD_SINGLE.

6.2 MPI-3 RMA

In Cray-MPICH, MPI-3 RMA features are designed to provide contention-free multithreaded communication and message completion with high bandwidth and high message rate. This property of contention free communication, and message completion allows users to flush outstanding messages on one thread while other threads can continue to make uninterrupted progress driving further communication.

To detail further, MPI-3 RMA features allocate network resources to threads dynamically. This design scales upto any number of threads per rank. There will be contention for network resources, only if number of threads per rank that are simultaneously driving communication exceeds number of available network resource to threads on that rank, else this design is contention-free. This is true even when various threads are simultaneously making both communication and message completion calls, such as MPI_Win_flush.

7 Future Work

Experimentations and performance analysis in Sects. 4 and 5 were analyzed from the runtime's perspective. Those analysis are performed to understand the multithreaded features, that would allow the OpenSHMEM libraries to obtain the performance as close to the underlying communication layers through effecient resource mapping. In future work, we will study more multithreaded OpenSH-MEM applications using the Thread-Safe and Contexts-Domains features and evaluate these proposals more from a user's perspective. We will also study the different usage scenarios, with the suitability of features from particular proposal when compared to the other.

8 Conclusion

In this work, we presented an evaluation of two features that have been proposed as extensions to OpenSHMEM: "Thread-Safe" and "Contexts-Domains". The Thread-Safe feature has been implemented in Cray SHMEM and has been in released versions for some time. A prototype of the Contexts-Domains feature has been implemented in an unreleased version of Cray SHMEM.

Evaluation of different designs with various performance measurements allowed us to make more optimal design decisions. Limited network resources requires some interaction between user and library to make optimal use of these resources. The Thread-Safe feature provides a fairly simple way to increase concurrency of SHMEM operations in multithreaded SHMEM programs. The Contexts-Domains feature provides a different and somewhat more complicated way to increase concurrency of SHMEM operations in multithreaded SHMEM programs but with potential for greater concurrency than with thread-safe. Contexts-Domains feature exposes SHMEM users to a new layer of network properties and provide them with explicit control for resource allocation. A right level of abstraction is needed to avoid delegating the complete network resource allocation functionality to users.

These two features are not incompatible when used in threaded regions of a SHMEM application. Calls to Thread-Safe routines can be inserted in code regions that can benefit from it and calls to Contexts-Domains routines can be inserted in other code regions. In future work, we will study more on the interoperability of these two features.

Acknowledgments. The authors wish to acknowledge Cray Inc., employees who worked on design and implementation of thread-safe extensions to OpenSHMEM: Monika ten Bruggencate, Kim McMahon, and Steve Oyanagi. Special thanks to James Dinan (Intel) for all discussions on Context proposal. Any opinions, findings, and conclusions or recommendations expressed in this material are those of the authors and do not necessarily reflect the views of Cray Inc.

References

1. Cray - Message Passing Toolkit. http://goo.gl/Cts1uh
2. Cray-developed Aries Interconnect. http://goo.gl/Xf74rG
3. Cray Global Arrays. http://goo.gl/sRKRu5
4. OpenSHMEM specification version-1.3. http://goo.gl/YK2JKD
5. OSU Micro-benchmarks. http://goo.gl/LgMc8e
6. Almasi, G.: Encyclopedia of Parallel Computing. Ed. by Padua, D.A. (2011)
7. Carlson, W.W., Draper, J.M., Culler, D.E.: S-246, 187 Introduction to UPC and Language Specification
8. Chapman, B., Curtis, T., Pophale, S., Poole, S., Kuehn, J., Koelbel, C., Smith, L.: Introducing OpenSHMEM: SHMEM for the PGAS community. In: Proceedings of the Fourth Conference on Partitioned Global Address Space Programming Model, PGAS 2010 (2010)
9. Dinan, J., Flajslik, M.: Contexts: a mechanism for high throughput communication in OpenSHMEM. In: Proceedings of the 8th International Conference on Partitioned Global Address Space Programming Models, PGAS 2014, pp. 10:1–10:9 (2014)
10. The MPI Forum. MPI: A Message Passing Interface (1993)

11. Knaak, D., Namashivayam, N.: Proposing OpenSHMEM extensions towards a future for hybrid programming and heterogeneous computing. In: Gorentla Venkata, M., Shamis, P., Imam, N., Lopez, M.G. (eds.) OpenSHMEM 2014. LNCS, vol. 9397, pp. 53–68. Springer, Heidelberg (2015). doi:10.1007/978-3-319-26428-8_4

12. Kumar, S., Mamidala, A.R., Faraj, D.A., Smith, B., Blocksome, M., Cernohous, B., Miller, D., Parker, J., Ratterman, J., Heidelberger, P., Chen, D., Steinmacher-Burrow, B.: PAMI: A Parallel Active Message Interface for the Blue Gene/Q Supercomputer. In: IEEE 26th International Parallel Distributed Processing Symposium (IPDPS) 2012, pp. 763–773 (2012)

13. Lewis, B., Berg, D.J.: Multithreaded Programming with Pthreads (1998)

14. Numrich, R.W., Reid, J.: Co-array fortran for parallel programming. SIGPLAN Fortran Forum **17**(2) (1998)

15. OpenACC. OpenACC application program interface version 2.5, October 2015

16. OpenMP Architecture Review Board. OpenMP application program interface version 4.5, November 2015

17. ten Bruggencate, M., Roweth, D.: DMAPP: An API for One-Sided Programming Model on Baker Systems. Technical report, Cray Users Group (CUG), August 2010

18. ten Bruggencate, M., Roweth, D., Oyanagi, S.: Thread-safe SHMEM extensions. In: Poole, S., Hernandez, O., Shamis, P. (eds.) OpenSHMEM 2014. LNCS, vol. 8356, pp. 178–185. Springer, Heidelberg (2014). doi:10.1007/978-3-319-05215-1_13

OpenCL + OpenSHMEM Hybrid Programming Model for the Adapteva Epiphany Architecture

David A. Richie[1] and James A. Ross[2]([⊠])

[1] Brown Deer Technology, Forest Hill, MD 21050, USA
drichie@browndeertechnology.com
[2] U.S. Army Research Laboratory, Aberdeen Proving Ground,
Adelphi, MD 21005, USA
james.a.ross176.civ@mail.mil

Abstract. There is interest in exploring hybrid OpenSHMEM + X programming models to extend the applicability of the OpenSHMEM interface to more hardware architectures. We present a hybrid OpenCL + OpenSHMEM programming model for device-level programming for architectures like the Adapteva Epiphany many-core RISC array processor. The Epiphany architecture comprises a 2D array of low-power RISC cores with minimal uncore functionality connected by a 2D mesh Network-on-Chip (NoC). The Epiphany architecture offers high computational energy efficiency for integer and floating point calculations as well as parallel scalability. The Epiphany-III is available as a coprocessor in platforms that also utilize an ARM CPU host. OpenCL provides good functionality for supporting a co-design programming model in which the host CPU offloads parallel work to a coprocessor. However, the OpenCL memory model is inconsistent with the Epiphany memory architecture and lacks support for inter-core communication. We propose a hybrid programming model in which OpenSHMEM provides a better solution by replacing the non-standard OpenCL extensions introduced to achieve high performance with the Epiphany architecture. We demonstrate the proposed programming model for matrix-matrix multiplication based on Cannon's algorithm showing that the hybrid model addresses the deficiencies of using OpenCL alone to achieve good benchmark performance.

Keywords: OpenCL · OpenSHMEM · Hybrid programming model · Single-board computer · Network-on-Chip (NoC)

1 Introduction and Motivation

The emergence of a wide range of parallel processor architectures continues to present the challenge of identifying an effective programming model that provides access to the capabilities of the architecture while simultaneously providing the programmer with familiar, if not standardized, semantics and syntax. The programmer is often left with the choice of using a non-standard programming model specific to the architecture or a standardized programming model that

© Springer International Publishing AG 2016
M. Gorentla Venkata et al. (Eds.): OpenSHMEM 2016, LNCS 10007, pp. 181–192, 2016.
DOI: 10.1007/978-3-319-50995-2_12

yields poor control and performance. The parallel RISC processor investigated in this work has presented precisely this challenge as suitable programming models matched to the architecture have been explored.

The Adapteva Epiphany RISC array architecture [1] is a scalable 2D array of low-power RISC cores with minimal uncore functionality supported by an on-chip 2D mesh Network-on-Chip (NoC) for fast inter-core communication. The Epiphany architecture is scalable to 4,096 cores and represents an example of an architecture designed for power-efficiency at extreme on-chip core counts. Processors based on this architecture exhibit good performance/power metrics [2] and scalability via the 2D mesh network [3,4], but require a suitable programming model to fully exploit these capabilities. A 16-core Epiphany-III coprocessor [5] has been integrated into the Parallella mini-computer platform [6] where the RISC array is supported by a dual-core ARM CPU and asymmetric shared-memory access to off-chip global memory.

RISC array processors such as those based on the Epiphany architecture may offer significant computational power efficiency in the near future with requirements in increased floating point performance, including long-term plans for exascale platforms. The power efficiency of the Epiphany architecture has been specifically identified as both a guide and prospective architecture for such platforms [7]. The Epiphany-IV processor has a performance efficiency of 50 GFLOPS/W (single precision) [2] making it one of the most efficient fully divergent parallel processors based on general-purpose cores. This approaches the threshold for exascale computing requirements of a power budget of 20 MW [8]. This architecture has characteristics consistent with future processor predictions arguing hundreds [9] and thousands [10,11] of cores on a chip.

One aspect of the low-power design of the Epiphany architecture is the use of a cache-less distributed on-chip memory architecture that for the Epiphany-III provides 32 KB of local memory per core for both instructions and data. Utilizing this core local memory and managing inter-core communication is critical to achieving good performance and this is a central element in the design of the architecture. In previous work, these technical challenges were the primary factors in achieving good performance with threaded MPI and less favorable results using OpenCL. Here we revisit OpenCL with a hybrid model that uses OpenSHMEM to resolve the deficiencies of OpenCL in the context of this architecture. Our main contributions are the presentation of a hybrid OpenCL + OpenSHMEM programming model with benchmarks for the application to matrix-matrix multiplication.

An outline of the remainder of the paper is as follows. Section 2 describes the Epiphany architecture and previous work using OpenCL and OpenSHMEM as parallel programming models. Section 3 presents the proposed hybrid OpenCL + OpenSHMEM programming model for device-level programming. Section 4 discusses the application of the proposed programming model to Cannon's algorithm for matrix-matrix multiplication, including benchmark results. Section 5 discusses conclusions and future work.

2   Background

Interest in exploring hybrid OpenSHMEM + X programming models has been expressed recently within the OpenSHMEM community [12]. Just as the two-tier parallel hybrid OpenMP + MPI model handles both symmetric multiprocessing (SMP) execution within a node and distributed message passing for attached network nodes, it is assumed that similar hybrid models may benefit from mixing code with OpenSHMEM. In the specific case detailed within this paper, the hybrid OpenCL + OpenSHMEM model exists at the same parallelism tier and the combination of the programming models address the deficiencies of each within the context of the Parallella platform and Epiphany architecture. While OpenCL may do well addressing SMP architectures with hierarchical memory, it does not provide semantics for inter-processor communication between processing elements or multiprocessors. OpenSHMEM provides the semantics for non-uniform memory access (NUMA) across a partitioned global address space (PGAS) and may not be ideal for SMP architectures. The OpenSHMEM concept of memory exists virtually in a flat one-dimensional domain and lacks the semantics of the tiered memory hierarchy found in the SMP-based OpenCL programming model. Fundamentally, the Epiphany device-level architecture has characteristics of both SMP and PGAS platforms so it makes sense to address the architecture with a hybrid SMP and PGAS programming model.

2.1   Epiphany Architecture

The Adapteva Epiphany MIMD architecture is a scalable 2D array of RISC cores with minimal uncore functionality connected with a fast 2D mesh Network-on-Chip (NoC). Processors based on this architecture exhibit good energy efficiency and scalability via the 2D mesh network, but require a suitable programming model to fully exploit the architecture. The 16-core Epiphany-III coprocessor has been integrated into the Parallella minicomputer platform where the RISC array is supported by a dual-core ARM CPU and asymmetric shared-memory access to off-chip global memory. Figure 1 shows the high-level architectural features of the coprocessor. Each of the 16 Epiphany-III mesh nodes contains 32 KB of shared local memory (used for both program instructions and data), a mesh network interface, a dual-channel DMA engine, and a RISC CPU core. Each RISC CPU core contains a 64-word register file, sequencer, interrupt handler, arithmetic logic unit, and a floating point unit. Each processor tile is very small at $0.5\,mm^2$ on the 65 nm process and $0.128\,mm^2$ on the 28 nm process. Peak single-precision performance for the Epiphany-III is 19.2 GFLOPS with a 600 MHz clock. Fabricated on the 65 nm process, the Epiphany-III consumes 594 mW for an energy efficiency of 32.3 GFLOPS per watt [Olofsson, personal communication]. The 64-core Epiphany IV, fabricated on the 28 nm process, has demonstrated energy efficiency exceeding 50 GFLOPS per watt [2].

The raw performance of currently available Epiphany coprocessors is relatively low compared to modern high-performance CPUs and GPUs; however, the Epiphany architecture provides greater energy efficiency and is designed to

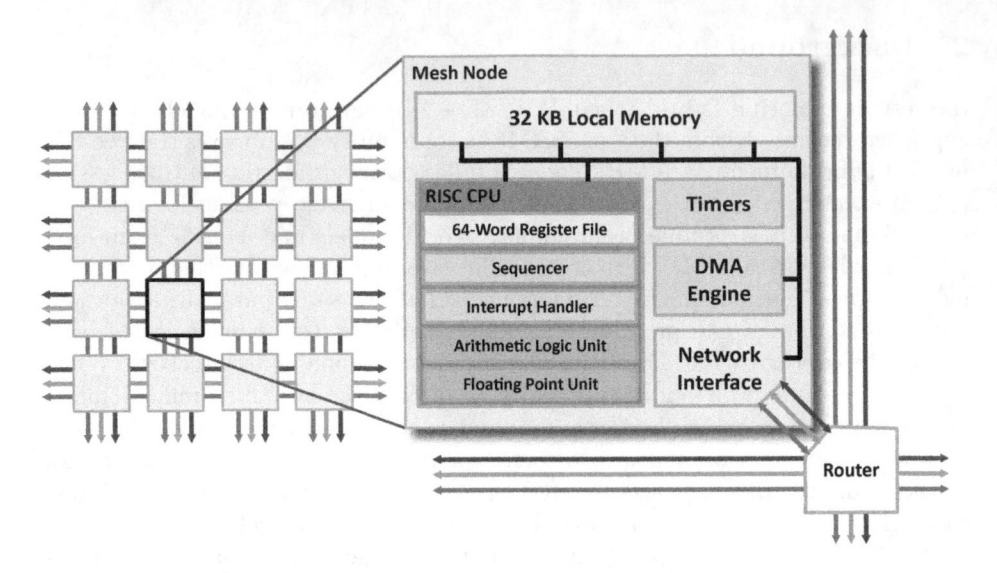

Fig. 1. Adapteva Epiphany-III architecture diagram

be highly scalable. The published architecture road map specifies a scale-out of the architecture to exceed 1,000 cores in the near future and, shortly thereafter, tens of thousands of cores with an energy efficiency approaching one TFLOPS per watt. Within this context of a highly scalable architecture with high energy efficiency, we view it as a competitive processor technology comparable to GPUs and other coprocessors.

While architecture energy efficiency is important, achievable performance with a compelling programming model is equally, if not more, important. Key to performance with the Epiphany architecture is data re-use, requiring precise control of inter-core communication since the architecture does not provide a hardware cache at any level. The cores can access off-chip mapped memory with a significant performance penalty in both latency and bandwidth relative to accessing on-chip core memory of any core.

2.2   OpenCL for Epiphany

OpenCL is an industry standard API for parallel programming accelerators or coprocessors on heterogeneous platforms [13]. Designed primarily for computing with general-purpose graphics processing units (GPUs), the API may be used to access the compute capability of other types of devices including multi-core CPUs and other accelerators. OpenCL support is provided for most mainstream high-performance computing accelerators including Nvidia and AMD GPUs, Intel and AMD multi-core CPUs, Intel Xeon Phi, and mobile CPU+GPU hybrid processors. In this context, there is merit in exploring the use of OpenCL for exposing the compute capability of the Epiphany coprocessor on the Parallella.

OpenCL consists of a kernel programming API used to program the coprocessor device and a run-time host API used to coordinate the execution of these kernels and perform other operations such as memory synchronization so that parallel computationally intensive work can be offloaded from the host platform. The OpenCL programming model is based on the parallel execution of a kernel over many threads to exploit SIMD or SIMT architectures. From the perspective of the host platform, parallel kernels are enqueued for execution on the coprocessor device. Each kernel is executed over a global n-dimensional range of work items logically partitioned into local workgroups. Threads of execution within a workgroup are allowed limited synchronization through the use of barriers, and no synchronization between workgroups is allowed.

OpenCL was the first standard parallel programming API implemented for the Epiphany architecture, and partial support for the OpenCL 1.1 standard was available as part of the COPRTHR-1.5 SDK for Epiphany [14]. The selection of OpenCL was supported by several factors. The Epiphany-III coprocessor was available as part of a heterogeneous mini-computer (Parallella) that included a dual-core ARM CPU host running Linux. As a result, the OpenCL co-design programming model premised on the host-directed offload of parallel work to a coprocessor was well suited to the platform.

The focus of the implementation of OpenCL for Epiphany was to leverage the API to support effective parallel programming and take advantage of the underlying architecture. As with other non-GPU architectures, limitations and constraints exist in the use of OpenCL for targeting the Epiphany architecture. OpenCL was designed for massively multithreaded architectures such as GPUs. However Epiphany has no hardware support for multithreading and early experiments with software supported multithreading were not successful due in part to resource constraints. As a result, implementation of the OpenCL device execution model for Epiphany must constrain the workgroup size to the number of physical cores on the device.

The most significant technical issue encountered in the implementation of OpenCL for Epiphany was reconciling the physical memory architecture of the Epiphany coprocessor with the logical memory model defined by the OpenCL standard, shown in Fig. 2. OpenCL address space qualifiers co-mingle the concepts of physical locality and visibility. For the Epiphany architecture, the physical memory co-located with each core executing a thread in an OpenCL workgroup is best described as symmetric distributed shared memory. This memory is physically local to the executing thread while also having shared visibility with all other threads since remote cores have non-uniform memory access to the local memory of any core. Managing the use and re-use of this symmetric distributed memory is critical to performance with the Epiphany architecture. An implementation treating this memory as OpenCL local may prove functionally correct and consistent within the standard, but the programmer will be left with poor performance without an interface to treat the memory correctly. Therefore, an interface for the symmetric distributed shared memory is needed to properly manage on-chip data movement.

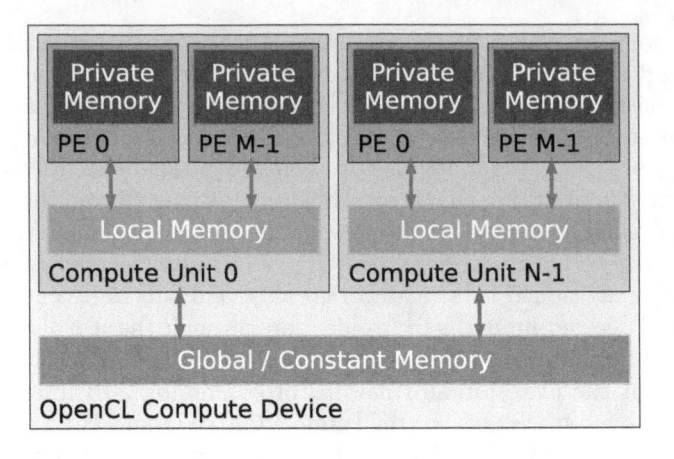

Fig. 2. OpenCL memory model

For this reason extensions were initially provided within the OpenCL implementation for Epiphany. A set of inter-thread memory copy routines were provided to allow for the direct copying of data between the local memory of one core to another. These routines resolved the problem with OpenCL in a nonstandard way that nevertheless enabled algorithms to be implemented with good performance. At the time of this development the OpenSHMEM standard was close to publication but not yet released. In hindsight, OpenSHMEM was precisely the interface that was needed to resolve this critical issue that arises from the use of OpenCL for Epiphany.

2.3   OpenSHMEM for Epiphany

An implementation of OpenSHMEM targeting the Epiphany architecture was recently developed [15]. The interface provides access the complete OpenSHMEM

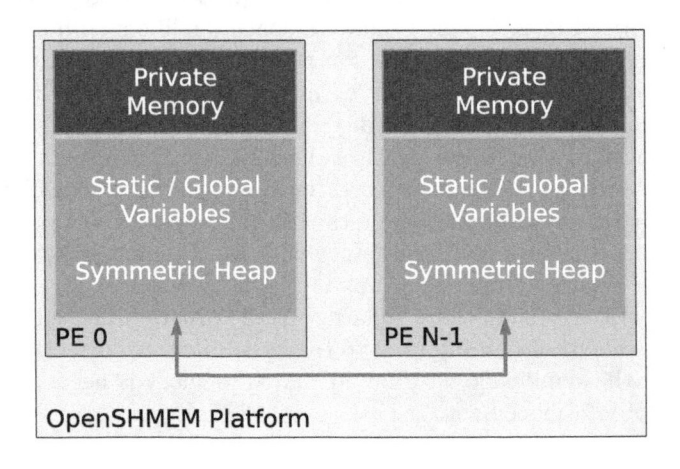

Fig. 3. OpenSHMEM memory model

1.3 standard for Epiphany device-level execution. It fills the void left by the lack of a standard programming model able to achieve good performance with on-chip memory distributed through the NoC. Conceptually, the physical memory of the Epiphany architecture maps directly to the OpenSHMEM and PGAS memory model (shown in Fig. 3). The OpenSHMEM interface for Epiphany does not address the concept of coprocessor offload or off-chip memory. For applications requiring these concepts, a hybrid programming model is required.

3   Hybrid OpenCL + OpenSHMEM Programming Model

Based on this prior work we propose a hybrid programming model that combines OpenCL with OpenSHMEM for device-level programming of parallel processors like those based on the Epiphany architecture. In the simplest terms, OpenSHMEM directly resolves the most critical technical issue encountered in the implementation of OpenCL for such architectures, and replaces the non-standard extensions that were originally introduced to support inter-core data re-use and achieve good performance when implementing algorithms for Epiphany. At the same time, OpenCL complements OpenSHMEM in that for hybrid platforms that employ a parallel coprocessor, OpenCL provides support for the offload of parallel work to the coprocessor while there is no equivalent operation defined within the OpenSHMEM standard.

OpenSHMEM for Epiphany provides the inter-core communication between the OpenCL concept of a processing element or multiprocessor. In the case of the Epiphany architecture, they are one in the same. There is a single processing element per multiprocessor in order to address the hierarchical memory concept of local memory within the OpenCL specification. The OpenCL interface defines the global or constant memory (shown in Fig. 4).

The hybrid OpenCL + OpenSHMEM programming model uses OpenCL for the development of host code that controls the overall application and directs the operations of the coprocessor through the offload of parallel computational kernels. The OpenCL kernel programming language, closely related to standard C, is used for the implementation of kernels. The distributed shared memory for which OpenCL provides no suitable API is then exposed using OpenSHMEM from within the OpenCL kernel. The OpenSHMEM programming model is nested within OpenCL and may be thought of as extending the latter. Developing applications with this hybrid programming model will follow closely the approach taken with OpenCL.

From an application development perspective, the OpenCL co-design model is still used with no change in the development of OpenCL host code. It is the OpenCL device programming API that is extended with OpenSHMEM. In this way each OpenCL kernel would contain within it a unique OpenSHMEM parallel job with a context inherited from the OpenCL kernel. All initialization and allocation requirements in support of the OpenSHMEM API are performed within the OpenCL kernel each time it is enqueued for execution. Whereas OpenCL kernels are permitted to communicate through global memory, no communication

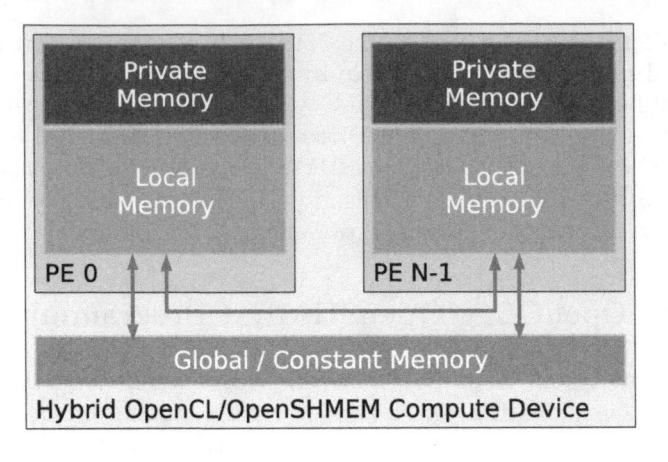

Fig. 4. Hybrid OpenCL + OpenSHMEM memory model

using the OpenSHMEM API is permitted between kernels or between OpenCL work groups. This follows from the OpenCL execution model that allows synchronization within a work group but disallows synchronization between work groups. The restriction upon synchronization between OpenCL work groups has limited significance since the nested parallelism of OpenCL mode in which work is distributed across multiple work groups containing multiple work items can be ignored if a single work group is used. This simplification is employed in the application of OpenCL to the Epiphany architecture. Since the OpenSHMEM API is contained within the OpenCL device kernel context, all OpenSHMEM memory allocation is only visible within a kernel and is not persistent across multiple kernel invocations. This aspect of the hybrid programming model could be revisited in the future but was unnecessary for the initial demonstrations reported here.

It is worth addressing the issue of portability in the context of the proposed hybrid programming model. As with the case of the use of non-standard extensions originally employed to achieve good performance for OpenCL development targeting Epiphany, the use of a hybrid OpenCL + OpenSHMEM programming model will not be compliant with the OpenCL standard and will not be portable to other architectures for which only a pure OpenCL implementation exists. This issue cuts directly to the relevance of standards in the development of high-performance code across differing architectures. The very concept of performance-portability is questionable and completely separate from that of portability in general. A code that is non-standard and utilizes architecture-specific features is no less useful than a code that is completely portable and compliant with a given programming standard but achieves poor performance. For this reason, we contend that the utility of programming standards such as OpenCL has less to do with portability and more to do with providing programmers familiar syntax and semantics for creating architecture-specific code.

Therefore the lack of general portability of our proposed programming model is not a significant concern for programmers developing high-performance code.

4   Application and Results

Multiplication of matrices is a central building block in many scientific applications. We apply the hybrid OpenCL + OpenSHMEM programming model to matrix-matrix multiplication using the Cannon algorithm [16]. Cannon's algorithm exemplifies the use of 2D parallel decomposition to effectively exploit this type of parallel architecture. The algorithm decomposes a square matrix-matrix multiplication problem ($C = A * B$) across an N-by-N collection of processing elements. Sub-matrices are shared between neighboring processing elements after each submatrix-submatrix multiplication. As illustrated in Fig. 5, the communication pattern begins by skewing the columns of matrix A left and the rows of B upward within the 2D mesh network topology.

For reference, a purely OpenCL implementation is benchmarked in which each thread per core must read in submatrices from global memory. This implementation lacks the data re-use that will lead to higher performance. Instead of communicating submatrices for A and B to the left and upward, respectively, equivalent bookkeeping is used to allow each thread to simply read in the submatrix that is needed from global memory. The performance using OpenCL alone

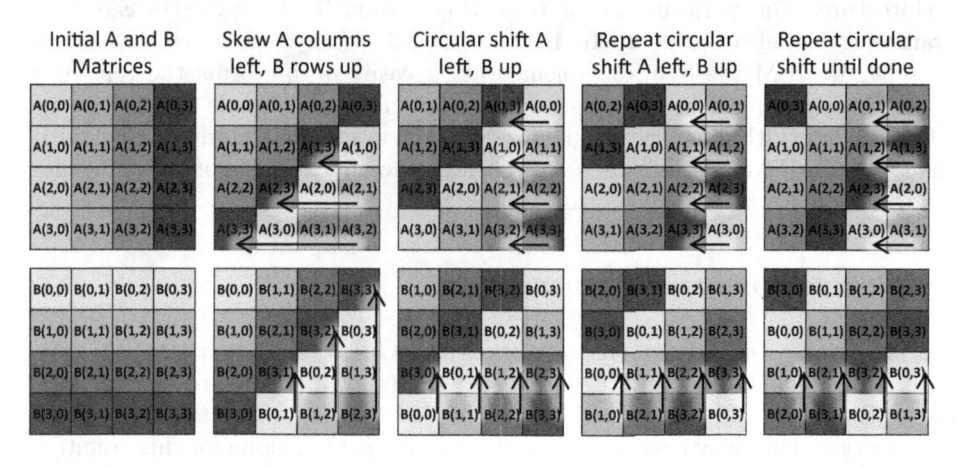

Fig. 5. The 2D mesh network topology communication patterns for submatrix skewing and shifting. A submatrix-submatrix multiplication occurs after each communication step. For the Epiphany-III processor, this figure represents the full inter-core communication pattern between the 16 cores on the device although the communication pattern can be applied generally to larger or smaller square arrays of cores. The initial skew communication may be unnecessary if the submatrices are read in pre-skewed. An additional communication step is needed to restore the shifted and skewed matrices if desired, but this is unnecessary since a copy of the A and B matrices remains within shared device memory.

Table 1. On-chip matrix-matrix multiplication performance with pure OpenCL and hybrid OpenCL + OpenSHMEM programming model

Matrix size	Programming model performance (MFLOPS)		Speedup
	OpenCL	OpenCL + OpenSHMEM	
32×32	218	504	2.3x
64×64	424	1000	2.4x
128×128	794	1817	2.3x

achieves up to 794 MFLOPS for a matrix sizes of 128×128. It is worth noting that the architecture is quite limited by the off-chip bandwidth, particularly when loading memory directly rather than by using the off-chip DMA engine (a feature not addressed by either OpenCL or OpenSHMEM standards).

The same OpenCL code is then modified with OpenSHMEM. No changes are required for the OpenCL host code. The OpenSHMEM header is included in the OpenCL kernel, and the core-local buffers for matrices A, B and C are allocated using OpenSHMEM semantics for symmetric shared memory. The OpenCL kernel is further modified to use an OpenSHMEM put call with appropriate barrier synchronization between threads to implement the shifting of submatrices. The result is that a submatrix is read once from global memory and then re-used. This is known to be necessary to achieve optimal performance on the Epiphany architecture. The performance of the hybrid OpenCL + OpenSHMEM programming model achieves up to 1812 MFLOPS. With data re-use supported by OpenSHMEM the hybrid implementation easily outperforms the reference OpenCL-only implementation. Performance for this application is still limited by off-chip bandwidth, however, the inclusion of the inter-core communication with the OpenSHMEM interface increases performance by a factor of 2.3x. Results for various matrix sizes are shown in Table 1.

5   Conclusions and Future Work

We have proposed and demonstrated a hybrid OpenCL + OpenSHMEM programming model for device-level parallel programming architectures like the low-power Epiphany RISC array processor. This hybrid model directly resolves the most critical deficiency encountered in the use of OpenCL alone for this architecture. The introduction of OpenSHMEM allows the proper management of the on-chip distributed symmetric shared memory, which is critical for obtaining high performance with this architecture. Benchmarks for matrix-matrix multiplication demonstrate that the hybrid programming model can achieve better performance for this architecture and substantially outperforms the use of OpenCL alone.

References

1. Adapteva Introduction. http://www.adapteva.com/introduction/. Accessed 24 May 2016
2. Olofsson, A., Nordstrm, T., Ul-Abdin, Z.: Kickstarting high-performance energy-efficient manycore architectures with epiphany. In: 2014 48th Asilomar Conference on Signals, Systems and Computers, pp. 1719–1726, November 2014
3. Wentzlaff, D., Griffin, P., Hoffmann, H., Bao, L., Edwards, B., Ramey, C., Mattina, M., Miao, C.-C., Brown III, J.F., Agarwal, A.: On-chip interconnection architecture of the tile processor. IEEE Micro **27**(5), 15–31 (2007)
4. Taylor, M.B., Kim, J., Miller, J., Wentzlaff, D., Ghodrat, F., Greenwald, B., Hoffman, H., Johnson, P., Lee, W., Saraf, A., Shnidman, N., Strumpen, V., Amarasinghe, S., Agarwal, A.: A 16-issue multiple-program-counter microprocessor with point-to-point scalar operand network. In: 2003 IEEE International Solid-State Circuits Conference, Digest of Technical Papers. ISSCC, vol. 1, pp. 170–171, February 2003
5. Adapteva: E16G301 Epiphany 16-Core Microprocessor Datasheet, March 2014. Rev. 14 Mar 2011
6. Adapteva: Parallella-1.x Reference Manual, September 2014. Rev. 09 Sep 2014
7. Varghese, A., Edwards, B., Mitra, G., Rendell, A.P.: Programming the adapteva epiphany 64-core network-on-chip coprocessor. In: Proceedings of the 2014 IEEE International Parallel & Distributed Processing Symposium Workshops, IPDPSW 2014, pp. 984–992. IEEE Computer Society, Washington, DC (2014)
8. Bergman, K., Borkar, S., Campbell, D., Carlson, W., Dally, W., Denneau, M., Franzon, P., Harrod, W., Hiller, J., Karp, S., Keckler, S., Klein, D., Lucas, R., Richards, M., Scarpelli, A., Scott, S., Snavely, A., Sterling, T., Williams, R.S., Yelick, K., Bergman, K., Borkar, S., Campbell, D., Carlson, W., Dally, W., Denneau, M., Franzon, P., Harrod, W., Hiller, J., Keckler, S., Klein, D., Kogge, P., Williams, R.S., Yelick, K.: ExaScale Computing Study: Technology Challenges in Achieving Exascale Systems Peter Kogge, Editor & Study Lead, September 2008
9. Adl-Tabatabai, A., Dubey, P., Dunning, D., Espig, M., Grochowski, E., Gonzalez, A., Hahn, S., Huggahalli, R., Jayasimha, J., Kumar, A., Kundu, P., Mattson, T., McAuley, D., Munoz, A., Narad, C., Newell, D., Ramanathan, R.M., Sawicki, T., Schoenberg, S., Schoinas, I., Shen, J., Sutton, J., Vara, M., Vij, M.: White paper : From a Few Cores to Many: A Tera-scale Computing Research Overview. Technical report, Intel
10. Asanovic, K., Bodik, R., Catanzaro, B.C., Gebis, J.J., Husbands, P., Keutzer, K., Patterson, D.A., Plishker, W.L., Shalf, J., Williams, S.W., Yelick, K.A.: The Landscape of Parallel Computing Research: A View from Berkeley. Technical report, UC Berkeley (2006)
11. Borkar, S., Chips, T.C.: A technology perspective. In: Proceedings of the 44th Annual Design Automation Conference, DAC 2007, pp. 746–749. ACM, New York (2007)
12. Baker, M., Pophale, S., Vasnier, J.-C., Jin, H., Hernandez, O.: Hybrid programming using OpenSHMEM and OpenACC. In: Poole, S., Hernandez, O., Shamis, P. (eds.) OpenSHMEM 2014. LNCS, vol. 8356, pp. 74–89. Springer International Publishing, Cham (2014). doi:10.1007/978-3-319-05215-1_6
13. Stone, J.E., Gohara, D., Shi, G.: OpenCL: a parallel programming standard for heterogeneous computing systems. IEEE Des. Test **12**(3), 66–73 (2010)

14. GitHub - The CO-PRocessing THReads (COPRTHR) SDK. https://github.com/browndeer/coprthr. Accessed 24 May 2016
15. Ross, J., Richie, D.: An OpenSHMEM implementation for the adapteva epiphany coprocessor. In: Venkata, M.G., Imam, N., Pophale, S., Mintz, T.M. (eds.) Open-SHMEM 2016. LNCS, vol. 10007, pp. 146–159. Springer, Cham (2016)
16. Cannon, L.E.: A Cellular Computer to Implement the Kalman Filter Algorithm. Ph.D. thesis, Bozeman, MT, USA (1969). AAI7010025

OpenSHMEM Implementation of HPCG Benchmark

Eduardo D'Azevedo[1(✉)], Sarah Powers[1], and Neena Imam[2]

[1] Computer Science and Mathematics Division,
Oak Ridge National Laboratory, Oak Ridge, TN 37831, USA
dazevedoef@ornl.gov
[2] Computing and Computational Sciences Directorate,
Oak Ridge National Laboratory, Oak Ridge, TN 37831, USA

Abstract. We describe the effort to implement the HPCG benchmark using OpenSHMEM and MPI one-sided communication. Unlike the High Performance LINPACK (HPL) benchmark that places emphasis on large dense matrix computations, the HPCG benchmark is dominated by sparse operations such as sparse matrix-vector product, sparse matrix triangular solve, and long vector operations. The MPI one-sided implementation is developed using the one-sided OpenSHMEM implementation. Preliminary results comparing the original MPI, OpenSHMEM, and MPI one-sided implementations on an SGI cluster, Cray XK7 and Cray XC30 are presented. The results suggest the MPI, OpenSHMEM, and MPI one-sided implementations all obtain similar overall performance but the MPI one-sided implementation seems to slightly increase the run time for multigrid preconditioning in HPCG on the Cray XK7 and Cray XC30.

1 Introduction

This OpenSHMEM implementation of the High Performance Conjugate Gradient Benchmark (HPCG) modifies version 3.0 of HPCG available at http://hpcg-benchmark.org/. Details of the original HPCG benchmark are also available at the web site.

The HPCG benchmark is aimed at providing more application-oriented measurements of system performance [3,4,6]. Unlike the High Performance LINPACK[1] (HPL) benchmark (which is used for ranking TOP 500 computers[2]) that

Notice: "This manuscript has been authored by UT-Battelle, LLC under Contract No. DE-AC05-00OR22725 with the U.S. Department of Energy. The United States Government retains and the publisher, by accepting the article for publication, acknowledges that the United States Government retains a non-exclusive, paid-up, irrevocable, world-wide license to publish or reproduce the published form of this manuscript, or allow others to do so, for United States Government purposes. The Department of Energy will provide public access to these results of federally sponsored research in accordance with the DOE Public Access Plan (http://energy.gov/downloads/doe-public-access-plan).

[1] http://www.netlib.org/benchmark/hpl/.
[2] http://www.top500.org.

© Springer International Publishing AG 2016
M. Gorentla Venkata et al. (Eds.): OpenSHMEM 2016, LNCS 10007, pp. 193–203, 2016.
DOI: 10.1007/978-3-319-50995-2_13

places emphasis on raw floating-point performance in the parallel solution of a large dense matrix by LU factorization, HPCG was designed to test performance of real-world applications in solving Partial Differential Equations (PDEs). The HPCG benchmark is dominated by sparse operations such as sparse matrix-vector product, sparse matrix triangular solve, and long vector operations. This stresses the memory subsystem and tests the communication system for neighborhood collectives for computing dot-products, and halo (domain boundary) exchanges. The HPCG benchmark shows the times for components and estimates the effective Giga Flops per second (Gflop/s) rate.

HPCG is a complete, stand-alone C++ code that measures the performance of basic operations in a unified code. HPCG uses a Preconditioned Conjugate Gradient (PCG) algorithm for solving the Laplace heat equation discretized on a 3D rectangular grid using a 27-point stencil. The Conjugate Gradient (CG) iteration includes a multi-grid preconditioner based on local Gauss-Seidel smoothing using sparse matrix triangular solves. HPCG measures the time for sparse matrix-vector multiplication in the iterative PCG solver where the sparse matrix is stored in compressed sparse row storage [11]. HPCG also measures the performance of vector update operations, and global reduction operations in computing global dot products and in determining convergence.

In this evaluation, the HPCG version 3.0, which uses two-sided MPI communication, was modified to use OpenSHMEM one-sided communication primitives for global reduction operations and in the boundary halo exchange kernel. A similar version using MPI-3 one-sided communication was obtained by converting the OpenSHMEM primitives to equivalent MPI one-sided operations.

Section 2 describes the approach taken to generate an OpenSHMEM version based on one-sided communication. Section 3 is a summary of results on the Cray XK7 Titan supercomputer in the Oak Ridge Leadership Computing Facility (OLCF) at the Oak Ridge National Laboratory. Section 4 summarizes the results on the Durmstrang SGI Turing cluster and Sect. 5 summarizes the results on the Cray XC30 Eos computer in OLCF. Finally, the summary analysis is in Sect. 6.

2   Implementation Details

The pure OpenSHMEM version [2,8–10] of HPCG was developed based on the C++ version 3.0 of the HPCG benchmark. The HPCG benchmark generates a synthetic problem for solving a three-dimensional second order elliptic partial differential equation with zero Dirichlet boundary conditions that is discretized on a rectangular grid using a 27-point stencil. The MPI tasks are arranged in a three-dimensional processor grid $(p_x \times p_y \times p_z)$ where each processor contains a $(n_x \times n_y \times n_z)$ local grid. The global domain is discretized as a $((n_x * p_x) \times (n_y * p_y) \times (n_z * p_z))$ grid. The local grid dimension and number of processors used are read from a text input data file `hpcg.dat`. The resulting sparse linear equation has 27 non-zeros per row for interior equations and 7 to 18 non-zero entries for vertices on the boundary. The sparse matrix is symmetric positive definite and is solved by the preconditioned conjugate gradient [11] method. The sparse matrix is stored in a compressed sparse row storage scheme [11]. The exact solution vector is specified with all entries equal to 1.0 and used to generate the right-hand side vector. An initial guess of all zeros is used. Although there is much regularity in the sparsity pattern (since it was generated from a rectangular grid of processors of a problem discretized on a rectangular grid), the benchmark does not try to take advantage of this structure but treats the problem as a general unstructured sparse system.

The benchmark prints out the times taken in several major components:

DDOT: Global reduction in computing vector dot products
SPMV: Sparse matrix-vector multiplication used in the iterative solver and includes communication times for halo boundary exchanges $(y(:) \leftarrow A * x(:))$
WAXPY: Vector operations $(W(:) \leftarrow a * X(:) + b * Y(:))$
MG: Multi-grid preconditioner including Gauss-Seidel smoothing operations (sparse triangular solve)

Most of the communication is performed in the halo exchange of data in the extended domain with immediate neighbors (in the routine `ExchangeHalo`) for performing matrix-vector multiplication. The original version of HPCG initiates

```
for(int i=0; i < num_neighbors; i++) {
  int pe = neighbors[i];
  shmem_int_inc(&nreceivers_ready, pe );
  }
shmem_fence();
shmem_quiet();

shmem_int_wait_until(&nreceivers_ready, _SHMEM_CMP_EQ, num_neighbors );
shmem_int_swap(&nreceivers_ready, 0, shmem_my_pe() );

for (int i = 0; i < num_neighbors; i++) {
  local_int_t n_send = sendLength[i];
  local_int_t offset = remoteOffset[i];
  int pe = neighbors[i];
  int nelem = n_send;
  double *src = sendBuffer;
  double *dest = &(recvBuffer[offset]);
  shmem_double_put( dest, src, nelem, pe );

  sendBuffer += n_send;
}
shmem_fence();

for(int i=0; i < num_neighbors; i++) {
  int pe = neighbors[i];
  shmem_int_inc(&nreceived, pe );
  };
shmem_fence();
shmem_quiet();

// wait for messages to arrive
shmem_int_wait_until(&nreceived ,_SHMEM_CMP_EQ, num_neighbors);
shmem_int_swap( &nreceived, 0, shmem_my_pe() );
```

Fig. 1. Code fragment to illustrate the use of SHMEM in `ExchangeHalo()`.

two-sided MPI communication using `MPI_Irecv()` into receive buffers, it then copies the data to be sent into send buffers for `MPI_Send()` and finally uses `MPI_Wait()` to wait for the arrival of data.

The SHMEM one-sided communication version uses `shmem_int_inc()` and `shmem_int_wait_until()` for synchronization to indicate that the neighbor processors are ready for the halo exchange. It uses the same send buffers but the receive buffer is allocated in the shared memory heap. Figure 1 shows the use of `shmem_double_put()` to perform remote data transfers. Again `shmem_int_inc()` and `shmem_int_wait_until()` are used to indicate the completion of data transfers (similar to `MPI_Wait()`).

In the MPI one-sided implementation, the MPI window is created and destroyed within each invocation of `ExchangeHalo()`. Figure 2 shows the straight-forward replacement of `MPI_Put` for `shmem_double_put()` in performing the one-sided data transfer. Note that `MPI_Win_fence()` is used to mark the beginning and end of the epoch. This use of `MPI_Win_fence()` and `MPI_Put` is similar to the example used in Chap. 3 of [5] to exchange ghost values in a mesh decomposition.

```
status = MPI_Win_fence(0, win);
assert(status == MPI_SUCCESS);

for (int i = 0; i < num_neighbors; i++) {
    local_int_t n_send = sendLength[i];
    local_int_t offset = remoteOffset[i];
    status = MPI_Put(sendBuffer, n_send, MPI_DOUBLE,
            neighbors[i], offset, n_send, MPI_DOUBLE, win);
    assert(status == MPI_SUCCESS);

    sendBuffer += n_send;
}

status = MPI_Win_fence(0, win);
assert(status == MPI_SUCCESS);
```

Fig. 2. Code fragment to illustrate the use of MPI one-sided communication in `ExchangeHalo()`.

3   Cray XK7 Titan

The Cray XK7 Titan machine in the Oak Ridge Leadership Computing Facility (OLCF) at ORNL consists of 18,688 compute nodes. Each compute node has 32 GBytes of memory, one 16-core AMD Opteron 6200 Interlagos processor and a NVidia Kepler Graphics Processing Unit (GPU) with 6 GBytes of device memory. Each Interlagos processor has eight 256-bit floating point compute units shared by 16 integer cores. Two compute nodes are connected to a Cray Gemini network device (NIC) that has over 160 GBytes/sec of routing capacity. The global network is arranged as a three-dimensional (3D) torus. The Random Ring benchmark in the HPC Challenge Benchmark Suite [7] achieves transfer rates of about 0.055 GBytes/sec per rank and the STREAMS benchmark for testing memory subsystem achieves about 72 GBytes/sec.

For this HPCG benchmark, only the CPU cores were used and the GPUs were untouched. The batch policy on Titan cannot guarantee allocation of contiguous nodes and this can lead to some variations in the communication performance. For example, two MPI tasks may be adjacent nodes on the 3D network in one batch run, but may require many hops across the network in another batch submission.

The native Cray SHMEM implementation (module cray-shmem version 7.2.5) was used to build the benchmark. A $104 \times 104 \times 104$ local grid and 15 MPI tasks were used in all cases. Figure 3 gives a summary of performance of the three versions of HPCG on Cray XK7 Titan. The time in DDOT is small compared to the overall time. The times for halo boundary exchanges are included in the SPMV time for sparse matrix vector multiplication. The MPI one-sided implementation is slower compared to the OpenSHMEM or original version and increases for higher number of processors. This might be due to the implicit synchronization in MPI_Win_fence(). The difference in SPMV is only about

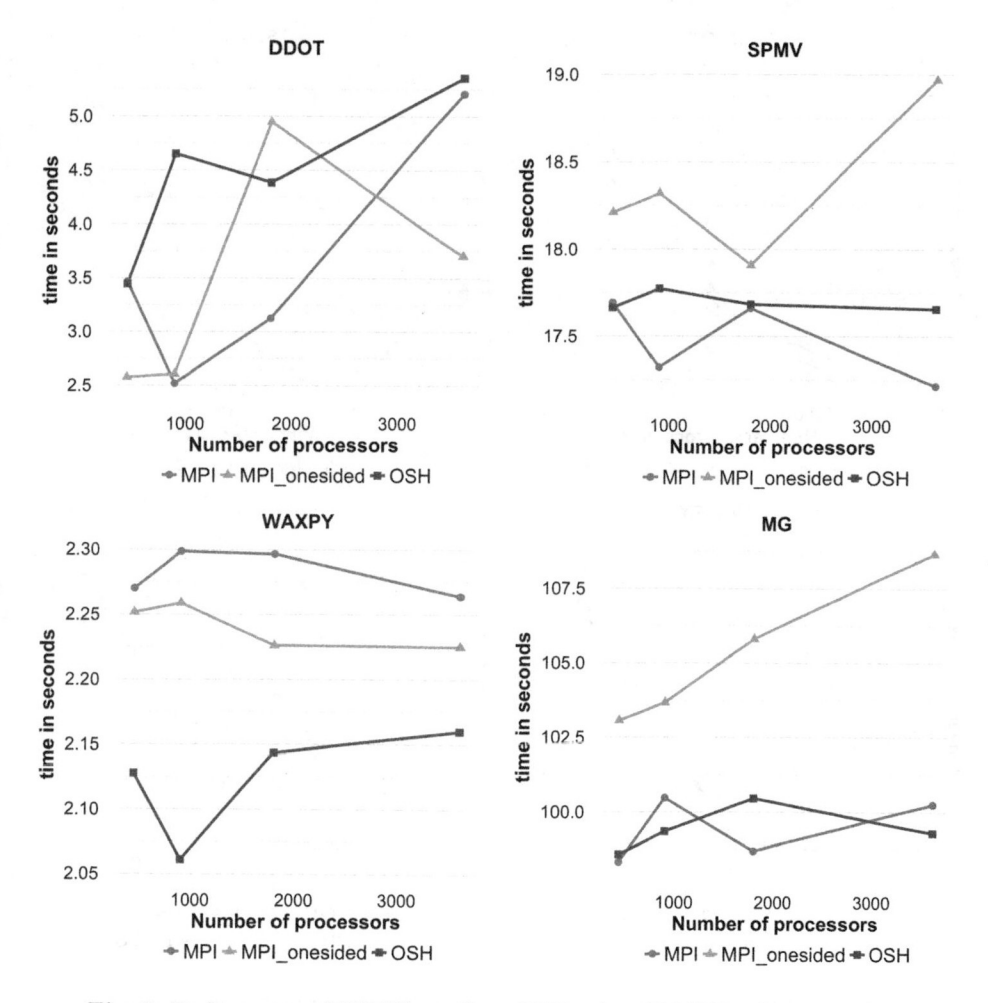

Fig. 3. Performance of HPCG on Cray XK7 using 15 MPI tasks per node.

1 s out of 18 s. The times for WAXPY for the three versions are similar. The times for MG seems to suggest that the MPI one-sided implementation has a slightly higher run time and that the difference is at most 10%. Since the MG computation is not communication intensive, one conjecture might be that an extra background progress thread is created for the MPI one-sided implementation and so incurs higher overhead or affects the affinity or mapping of threads to CPU cores.

4   SGI Turing Cluster

The SGI Turing Cluster consists of 16 compute nodes, each node has two Intel Xeon E5-2660 processors, each Xeon has 10 cores running at 2.6 GHz (105 Watts) for a total of 20 physical cores (or 40 virtual cores with Intel Hyper-Threading

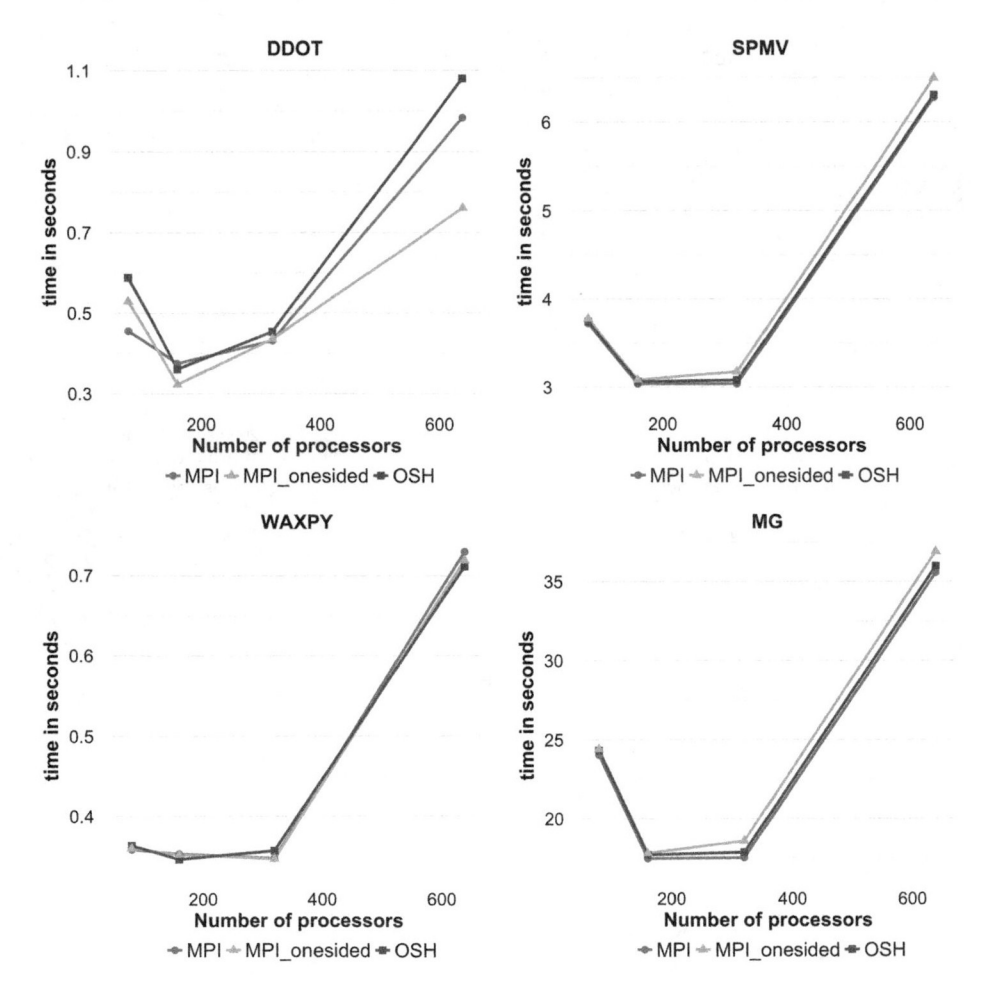

Fig. 4. Performance of HPCG on SGI turing cluster.

enabled). The node has eight 16 GBytes DDR4 memory cards for a total of 128 GBytes of memory. Each node also has a fast 1 TByte 10 K revolutions per minute (RPM) SATA hard disk with 6 Gbits/sec peak transfer rate, one Intel Xeon Phi 7120P PCIE accelerator and is connected with a Mellanox ConnectX-4 VPI adapter card, EDR IB (100 Gbits/sec) and 100 Gbits/s ethernet, single-port QSFP, PCIe3.0 × 16 network connector. The nodes are connected with a Mellanox InfiniBand Edge Switch with 36 QSFP ports with a non-blocking switching capacity of 7.2 Tbits/sec.

The native SGI MPT implementation of SHMEM (module mpt version 2.13) was used to build the benchmark. A 104 × 104 × 104 local grid and at most 40 MPI tasks were used on a node. For this HPCG benchmark only the CPUs were used and the Intel Xeon Phi accelerators were untouched.

Figure 4 gives a summary of the performance of the three versions of HPCG on the SGI Turing cluster. The global reduction operations in DDOT may have an implicit synchronization and so may include idle time or load imbalance. There may be higher overhead in the OpenSHMEM version when initializing the pSync and work arrays for global reduction operations. Note that the time in DDOT is small compared to the overall time. The times for halo boundary exchanges are included in the SPMV time for sparse matrix vector multiplication. The times for all versions are very similar. The times for WAXPY for the three versions are also very similar as well as the times for MG multi-grid computations.

5   Cray XC30 Eos

The Cray XC30 Eos machine in the OLCF at ORNL consists of 736 compute nodes. Each compute node has at least 64 GBytes of memory and two 8-core 2.6 GHz Intel Xeon E5-2670 for a total of 16 physical cores or 32 logical cores with Intel Hyper-Threading enabled. Thus in total, the Eos machine contains over 11776 physical cores (23552 logical cores with Intel Hyper-Threading enabled) and over 47 TBytes of memory. Every four compute nodes (or 64 physical cores) are connected to a single Aries interconnect and organized in the network topology called Dragonfly. According to Cray literature [1], the Aries/Dragonfly network provides a higher bandwidth and lower latency interconnect than the Gemini network on the Cray XK7 Titan. The Aries/Dragonfly network provides a three-fold increase (over the Gemini network) in peak injection bandwidth to about 10 GBytes/sec. The global bandwidth is about three times to twenty times higher (depending on configuration) than the Cray XK7. The hardware injection rate for small puts and gets for Aries is about 120 M/sec (or 1.875 M/sec per core), which is about three times higher than Gemini. Measured end-to-end latencies for user-space communication[3] on a quiet network are 0.8 μs for an 8-byte put, 1.6 μs for an 8-byte get and approximately 1.3 μs for an 8-byte MPI message. Note that a 1.6 μs get latency suggests an effective maximum rate of

---

[3] Latency measured on CPU core that is directly connected to the Aries NIC, other CPU cores may have higher latencies.

0.67 M requests per second if performed with no further concurrency. A nearest point-to-point communication benchmark shows latency that is less than 1.4 μs and with bandwidth of over 8.5 GBytes/sec. The Random Ring benchmark in the HPC Challenge Benchmark Suite achieves a transfer rate of 0.141 GBytes/sec per rank and the STREAMS benchmark for testing the memory system achieves about 78 GBytes/sec per node.

HPCG was built using the native Cray SHMEM library (module cray-shmem version 7.2.5). A $104 \times 104 \times 104$ local grid and at most 32 MPI tasks were used in all cases. Figure 5 gives a summary of performance of the three versions of HPCG using only 1 MPI task on each Cray XC30 Eos node. The performance in all cases was very similar. The DDOT time for OpenSHMEM seems to be slightly higher compared to MPI one-sided implementation. However, this difference is small (about 0.5 s) compared to the time in MG (about 35 s).

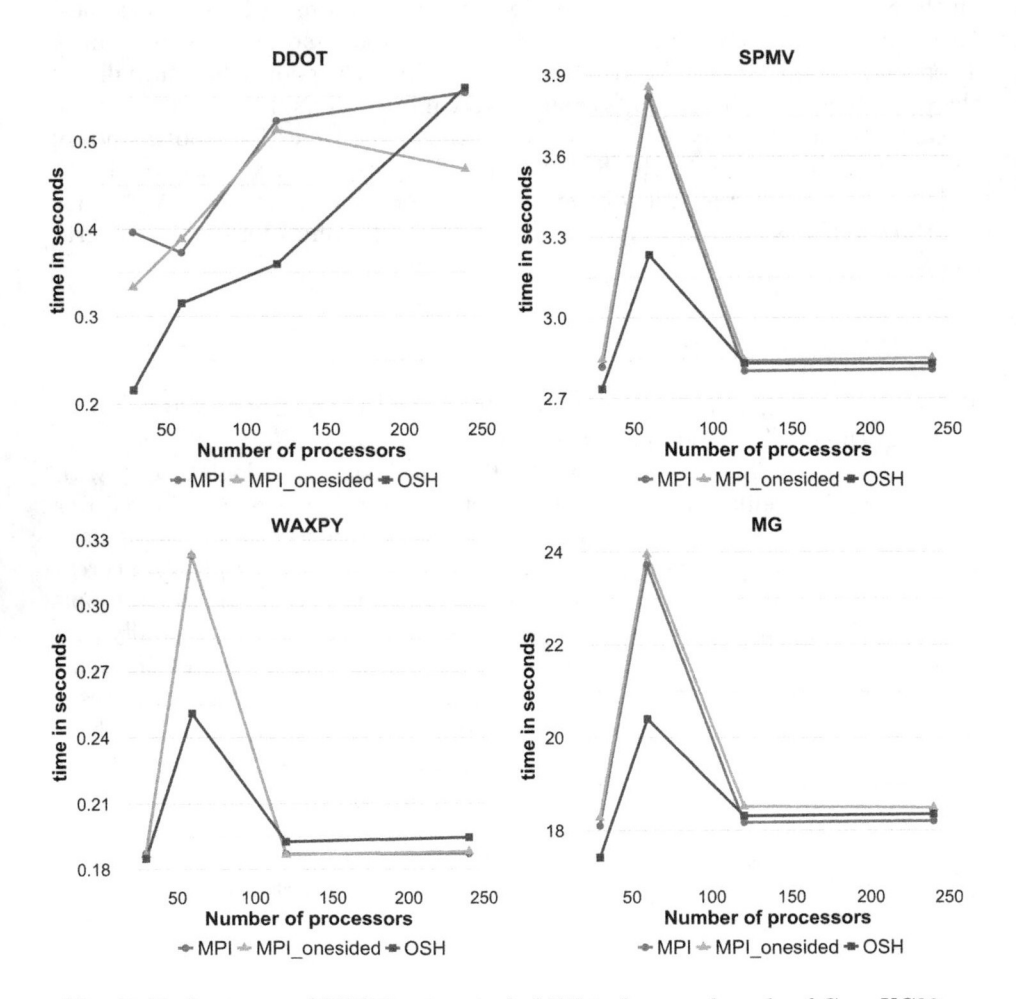

Fig. 5. Performance of HPCG using single MPI task on each node of Cray XC30.

Figure 6 gives a summary of performance of the three versions of HPCG using 32 MPI tasks (on 32 virtual cores with hyper threading) on each node of the Cray XC30 Eos. The time spent in SPMV in MPI one-sided implementation is slightly higher compared to the OpenSHMEM version and increases slightly for higher number of processors. This might be due to the implicit synchronization in `MPI_Win_fence()`. The performance in MG for MPI one-sided implementation is also about 10% higher compared to the MPI or OpenSHMEM versions. One conjecture is that the MPI one-sided implementation uses an extra background progress thread that may affect the affinity mapping of threads to CPU cores.

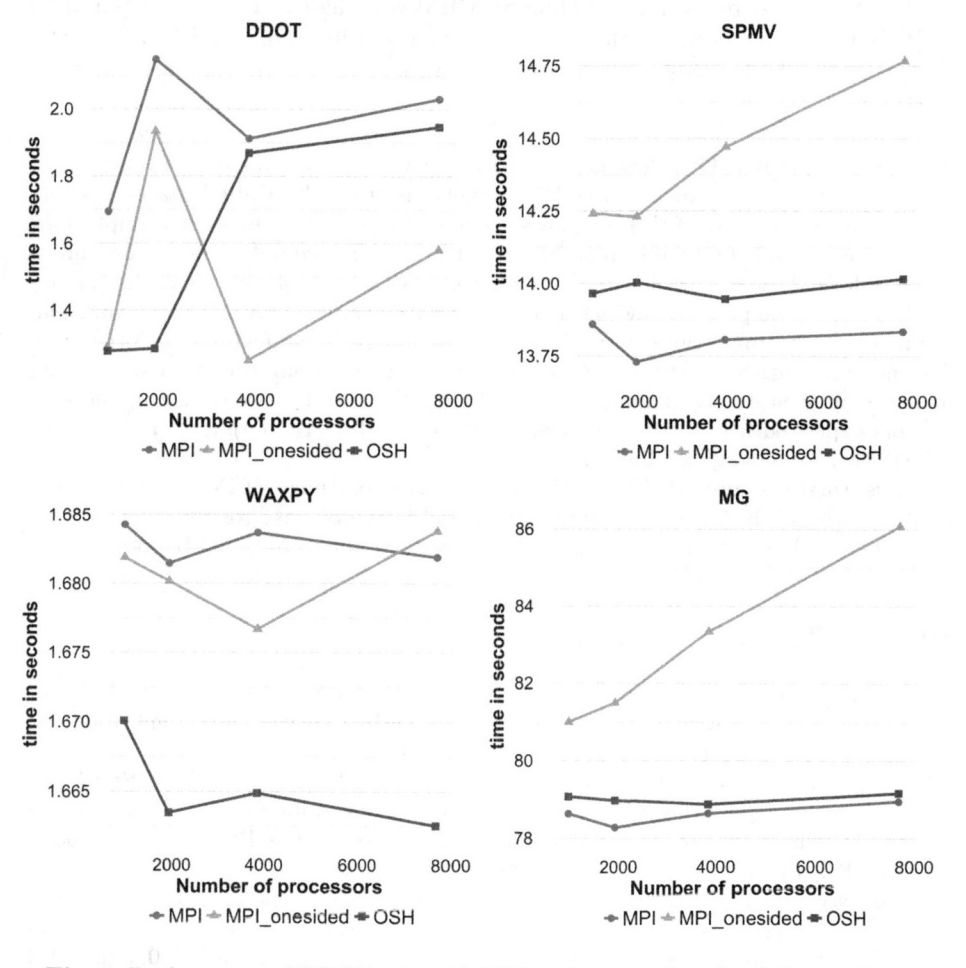

Fig. 6. Performance of HPCG using 32 MPI tasks on each node of Cray XC30.

6   Summary

The HPCG benchmark has been tested on high performance supercomputers with the state-of-the-art networks on the Cray XK7 Titan, and the Aries interconnect on the Cray XC30. The benchmark has also been tested on an SGI cluster using the SGI MPT version of SHMEM over Infiniband network. The HPCG benchmark that uses MPI one-sided implementation has also been developed based on the OpenSHMEM version for comparison with OpenSHMEM. The results for MPI, OpenSHMEM, and MPI-3 one-sided implementations are all very similar. The times for MG for MPI one-sided are about 10% higher on Cray XK7 Titan and Cray XC30 Eos on the largest scale. One conjecture might be that the MPI one-sided implementation uses an extra background progress thread and this affects the affinity mapping of threads to CPU cores. The times for DDOT global reduction for OpenSHMEM are slightly higher compared to MPI. This may be due to the need to initialize the pSync and Work arrays. However, this higher cost has insignificant impact on the overall solution time in HPCG.

Acknowledgment. This document was prepared as an account of work sponsored by an agency of the United States Government. Neither the United States nor any agency thereof, nor any of their employees, makes any warranty, express or implied, or assumes any legal liability or responsibility for the accuracy, completeness, or usefulness of any information, apparatus, product, or process disclosed, or represents that its use would not infringe privately owned rights. Reference herein to any specific commercial product, process, or service by trade name, trademark, manufacturer, or otherwise, does not necessarily constitute or imply its endorsement, recommendation, or favoring by the United States Government or any agency thereof. The views and opinions of authors expressed herein do not necessarily state or reflect those of the United States Government or any agency thereof.

This work was supported by the United States Department of Defense (DoD) and used resources of the Computational Research and Development Programs and the Oak Ridge Leadership Computing Facility (OLCF) at Oak Ridge National Laboratory.

References

1. Alverson, B., Froese, E., Kaplan, L., Roweth, D.: Cray XC series network. Technical report WP-Aries01-1112, Cray Inc. (2012). http://www.cray.com/Products/Computing/XC.aspx
2. Chapman, B., Curtis, T., Pophale, S., Poole, S., Kuehn, J., Koelbel, C., Smith, L.: Introducing OpenSHMEM: SHMEM for the PGAS community. In: Proceedings of the Fourth Conference on Partitioned Global Address Space Programming Model, PGAS 2010, New York, NY, USA (2010)
3. Dongarra, J., Heroux, M.A.: Toward a new metric for ranking high performance computing systems. Technical Report SAND2013-4744, Sandia National Laboratory, Albuquerque, New Mexico 87185 and Livermore, California 94550, June 2013
4. Dongarra, J., Heroux, M.A., Luszczek, P.: High-performance conjugate-gradient benchmark: a new metric for ranking high-performance computing systems. Int. J. High Perform. Comput. Appl. **30**(1), 3–10 (2016). https://github.com/hpcg-benchmark/hpcg
5. Gropp, W., Hoefler, T., Thakur, R., Lusk, E.: Using Advanced MPI. The MIT Press, Cambridge (2014)

6. Heroux, M.A., Dongarra, J., Luszczek, P.: HPCG technical specification. Technical Report SAND2013-8752, Sandia National Laboratory, Albuquerque, New Mexico 87185 and Livermore, California 94550, October 2013

7. Luszczek, P., Dongarra, J.J., Koester, D., Rabenseifner, R., Lucas, B., Kepner, J., Mccalpin, J., Bailey, D., Takahashi, D.: Introduction to the HPC challenge benchmark suite. Technical report (2005)

8. Poole, S.W., Hernandez, O., Kuehn, J.A., Shipman, G.M., Curtis, A., Feind, K.: OpenSHMEM - toward a unified RMA model. In: Padua, D. (ed.) Encyclopedia of Parallel Computing, pp. 1379–1391. Springer, Heidelberg (2011)

9. Pophale, S., Curtis, T., Chapman, B.: Improving performance of OpenSHMEM reference library by portable PE mapping techniques. In: Proceedings of the 27th International ACM Conference on supercomputing, pp. 485–486. ACM New York (2013)

10. Pophale, S.S.: SRC: OpenSHMEM library development. In: Proceedings of the International Conference on Supercomputing, NY, USA, p. 374. ACM, New York (2011)

11. Saad, Y.: Iterative Methods for Sparse Linear Systems. Society for Industrial and Applied Mathematics (2003). http://www-users.cs.umn.edu/saad/~IterMethBook_2ndEd.pdf

Using Hybrid Model OpenSHMEM + CUDA to Implement the SHOC Benchmark Suite

Megan Grodowitz[✉], Eduardo D'Azevedo, Sarah Powers, and Neena Imam

Oak Ridge National Lab, Oak Ridge, TN 37830, USA
{grodowitzml,dazevedoef,powersss,imamn}@ornl.gov

Abstract. This work describes the process of porting the Scalable HeterOgeneous Computing (SHOC) benchmark suite from the hybrid MPI + CUDA implementation to OpenSHMEM + CUDA. SHOC includes a wide variety of benchmark kernels used to measure accelerator performance in both single node and cluster configurations. The hybrid model implementation attempts to place all major computation on accelerator devices, and uses MPI to synchronize and aggregate results. In some cases, MPI Groups are used to gradually reduce the number of accelerators used for computation as the problem size drops. Porting this behavior to OpenSHMEM required implementing several synchronizing collective operations, and using SHMEM teams to replace MPI Group functionality. Benchmark results on a Cray XK7 system with one GPU per compute node show that SHMEM performance is equal to MPI performance in these hybrid tasks. These results and porting experience show that using OpenSHMEM for accelerator devices benefits from adding functionality for synchronization and teams, and would further benefit from adding support for communication within accelerator kernels. (Notice: This manuscript has been authored by UT-Battelle, LLC under Contract No. DE- AC05-00OR22725 with the U.S. Department of Energy. The United States Government retains and the publisher, by accepting the article for publication, acknowledges that the United States Government retains a non-exclusive, paid-up, irrevocable, world-wide license to publish or reproduce the published form of this manuscript, or allow others to do so, for United States Government purposes. The Department of Energy will provide public access to these results of federally sponsored research in accordance with the DOE Public Access Plan (http://energy.gov/downloads/doe-public-access-plan). This research used resources of the Center for Computational Sciences at Oak Ridge National Laboratory, which is supported by the Office of Science of the U.S. Department of Energy under Contract No. De-AC05-00OR22725.)

Keywords: Parallel computing · Programming models · CUDA · SHMEM

© Springer International Publishing AG 2016
M. Gorentla Venkata et al. (Eds.): OpenSHMEM 2016, LNCS 10007, pp. 204–216, 2016.
DOI: 10.1007/978-3-319-50995-2_14

1   Introduction: Programming Models for Hardware Accelerated Parallel Systems

In the past decade, many high performance parallel computing systems have included hardware accelerators, such as GPUs or Xeon Phi Coprocessors. These accelerators provide many more operations per watt than traditional multicore CMOS chips. Often, accelerators also offer significant speedup for application kernels.

Accelerator programming models are very efficient at targeting specific hardware devices, but have minimal support for controlling multiple devices on multiple distributed nodes. For example, the CUDA language is commonly used to program NVidia GPUs. To program a system that contains many GPUs on many nodes, programs typically combine CUDA with a distributed communication layer, such as MPI, into a hybrid programming model.

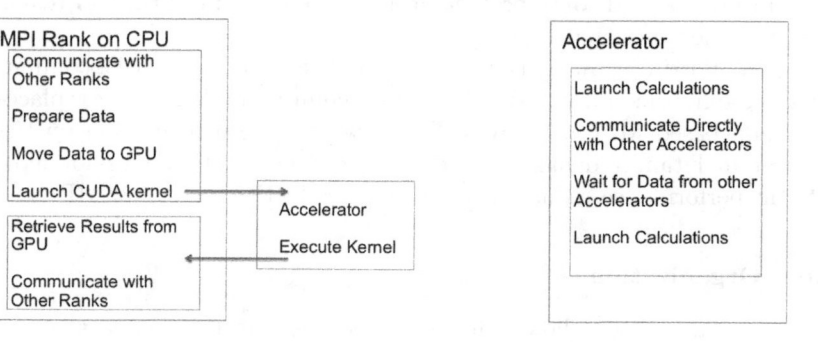

Fig. 1. Hybrid MPI + CUDA model   **Fig. 2.** Unified CUDA with communication

Figure 1 diagrams a hybrid model program. The programmer uses MPI ranks to individually control CUDA kernels on a per device basis. A traditional CPU core shuttles data to and from the accelerator and launches a CUDA kernels. Any inter-device communication occurs outside the CUDA kernel, under the control of the CPU. This is undesirable because it is inefficient to require CPU interaction for all communication. Accelerators have begun to add support for direct communication without CPU interaction [1, 12]. This direct communication will enable a change in programming model, with support for communication within the accelerator kernel, such as shown in Fig. 2.

1.1   OpenSHMEM as an Alternative to MPI

OpenSHMEM presents an alternative to message passing for inter-device communication in accelerated systems. Programs can combine OpenSHMEM with

CUDA or OpenCL in a hybrid model that uses one-sided memory access to communicate between devices. Future systems could add symmetric memory regions and one-sided access into accelerator kernels.

In this work, we pose a question: If a programmer uses SHMEM instead of MPI to write a hybrid program, what features do they require and how does the program perform? To answer this question, we ported the Scalable HeterOgeneous Computing (SHOC) benchmark suite [4] from MPI + CUDA to OpenSHMEM + CUDA.

The SHOC benchmark suite represents a range of applications that have been shown to benefit from hardware acceleration. Porting these benchmarks shows how SHMEM can be used for periodic synchronization and communication between accelerator kernels. SHOC requires an atypical use of SHMEM, where we do not attempt to engineer communication/computation overlap with one-sided accesses inside a computational core. So, we provide implementations of several MPI collectives using only SHMEM. We also find that these codes require the use of MPI groups, and so we provide an implementation of SHMEM teams to provide the same functionality.

The results of porting show that SHMEM is sufficient to replace MPI communication for these hybrid codes. Using SHMEM required implementing replacements for group based MPI collectives. We tested the implementation on the Cray XK7 system Titan, to demonstrate that the implementation does not show any significant performance reduction when using SHMEM instead of MPI.

1.2 Paper Organization

This paper is organized as follows. In Sect. 2 we describe the contents of the SHOC benchmark suite and the ways in which MPI and CUDA are mixed in that code. We then briefly describe other work using OpenSHMEM with accelerated parallel systems. Section 3 describes the implementation specifics of structures ported from MPI to OpenSHMEM in SHOC. Finally, Sect. 4 presents the performance results of the ported code on the Cray XK7 Titan system.

2 Background and Related Work

This section first provides an overview of the SHOC benchmark suite. This is followed by a brief description of the SHMEM libraries used as the target for porting.

2.1 SHOC Benchmark Suite

The Scalable HeterOgeneous Computing (SHOC) benchmark suite [4] was designed to benchmark systems employing one or more hardware accelerators. SHOC benchmarks devices that can be programmed with either OpenCL or CUDA, and has been used most extensively on GPU based systems.

SHOC is divided into three levels of benchmarks. Level 0 benchmarks are artificial microkernels that measure bandwidth over the device bus, max floating point operations, and kernel compile times. Level 1 benchmarks are common parallel algorithms such as matrix-matrix multiplication and breadth-first-search. Level 2 benchmarks are kernels extracted from real applications.

Most benchmarks are written in both OpenCL and CUDA. The exceptions are Level 0 benchmarks that test OpenCL compile time and OpenCL command queue overhead, which have no CUDA equivalent. For both OpenCL and CUDA variants, the benchmark suite can be run on one or more nodes with one or more devices per node. MPI is used for all inter-node communication.

Each benchmark is classified as S (Serial), EP (Embarrassingly Parallel), or TP (Truly Parallel). Serial (S) uses only a single accelerator device. All benchmarks can run as in S mode or EP mode. In EP mode, there is no communication between devices. All accelerators solve a local version of the problem only. A few benchmarks have a TP implementation, where results are computed across multiple nodes. For example, a prefix scan can be run as EP using N MPI ranks to give result of N different scan arrays, one on each rank. The same benchmark can be run as TP on N MPI ranks to give a result of a single scan array across all N ranks.

Benchmark Descriptions. This section describes all of the SHOC benchmarks by level. Benchmarks are labeled TP if they provide a truly parallel implementation. These are the only benchmarks where replacing MPI with SHMEM will have any impact on benchmark execution.

0. **Level 0** (No communication)
   0.1 **BusSpeedDownload** and
   0.2 **BusSpeedReadback** copy data to and from devices over the PCIe bus.
   0.3 **KernelCompile** and
   0.4 **QueueDelay** are OpenCL only kernels to measure compile times and command queue delay, respectively.
   0.5 **MaxFLOPS** reports maximum GigaFLOPS achieved on a set of hand-tuned microkernels, in both single and double precision mode.
   0.6 **DeviceMemory** measures the speed to access data stored in different memory regions of an accelerator.
1. **Level 1** (Some truly parallel, others embarrassingly parallel)
   1.1 (TP) **Reduction** performs a basic reduction operation on an array of single or double precision numbers.
   1.2 (TP) **Scan** performs a parallel prefix sum operation on an array of single or double precision numbers.
   1.3 (TP) **Stencil2D** performs a 9-point stencil operation on a 2D data set. This benchmark uses MPI topologies to arrange the 2D data in a grid to facilitate the halo exchanges between processes.
   1.4 (EP) **BFS** computes a breadth-first-search tree for a randomly generated graph. This benchmark uses atomic operations, and so can be used to test performance of the SHMEM atomics.

1.5 (EP) **FFT** computes a forward and reverse 1D Fast Fourier Transform

1.6 (EP) **GEMM** implements matrix-matrix multiplication

1.7 (EP) **MD** computes the Lennard-Jones potential from molecular dynamics

1.8 (EP) **MD5Hash** computes many small MD5 digests. The significance for benchmarking GPUs comes from the dependence on bitwise operations.

1.9 (EP) **NeuralNet**

1.10 (EP) **Sort** sorts an array of key-value pairs using a radix sort algorithm

1.11 (EP) **Spmv** implements sparse matrix-vector multiplication

1.12 (EP) **Triad** is a version of the STREAM Triad benchmark. The kernel fetches three values from memory, then multiplies one by a value and adds it to another. The significance for benchmarking is that this allows testing of fused multiply-add capabilities.

2. **Level 2** (Application inspired kernels)

2.1 (TP) **QTC** implements quality threshold clustering. This algorithm is used in data analysis to partition data points based on an a priori specification of a threshold distance between points in a cluster and minimum number of points per cluster. The algorithm was originally designed for gene classification.

2.2 (EP) **S3D** is an embarrassingly parallel computationally intensive kernel from the S3D turbulent combustion simulation.

2.2 Previous SHMEM Work with Teams, Collectives, and Hardware Accelerators

SHMEM Teams and Collectives. To overcome some difficulties experienced when using OpenSHMEM with Accelerators Knaak et al. [7] list a set of extensions along with microbenchmarks to test the extensions. For synchronization, we used put followed by wait many times in these collectives, so a put with signal, as proposed here, would be very useful.

As mentioned the Cray Message Passing Toolkit recently added flexible process group team operations [3] which is very similar to the API described in [7] and the one which we implement for this work. Hanebutte et al. [5] further propose federations as a way to extend teams with topologies that group pes within a team. Our work does not explore processor topologies.

Regarding collectives, some work has been done to optimize existing OpenSHMEM collectives by mapping them to MPI [6]. There is not other work that we are aware of that addresses implementing MPI collectives using SHMEM teams.

SHMEM with Hardware Accelerators and Hybrid Programming Models. Baker et al. [2] ported an MPI + OpenMP application to SHMEM + OpenACC. Since they started with an application that does not use hardware acceleration, most of the focus on optimizing the OpenACC for the NVidia hardware on the Cray XK7. For the SHMEM portion, they note the same patterns as we saw in SHOC, that accelerator code is limited by the need to have all communication outside of the accelerator kernels and that synchronization is required between kernel launches.

To address the problem of overheads in moving data between main memory and GPU, NVidia GPU direct technologies [8,9,11] allow data movement between nodes, but still require CPU involvement. The proposed model of NVSHMEM [10] moves SHMEM communication directly into the CUDA kernel and uses the GPU-GPU communication to move data between devices without requiring the program to split up communication and kernel code. This model will be explored in the next phase of SHOC benchmark porting.

3   Porting MPI Communication Structures in SHOC

There were two main tasks required to support the communication requirements of the SHOC benchmarks in OpenSHMEM: MPI-style synchronization collectives and process teams. These were required by the four truly parallel (TP) benchmarks that used inter-device communication and synchronization. Table 1 summarizes the requirements that were implemented for each of the TP benchmarks.

Table 1. SHOC benchmark requirements

Benchmark	Requirements
QTC	Team Split, Team Barrier, Team Broadcast, Team AllReduce Sum
Scan	Parallel Prefix Scan
Reduction	AllReduce Sum
Stencil2D	Reduce Sum, AllReduce Sum
Parallel Results DB[a]	AllGather

[a]Parallel results database is used in all EP and TP benchmarks.

3.1   Process Teams for Gradual Reduction of Devices

The QTC benchmark iteratively clusters elements into groups. At each iteration, the number of elements to be clustered shrinks, meaning that eventually there may be too few elements to use all of the GPU devices in the systems. This pattern is representative of many iterative clustering algorithms, and could be used in various data mining applications.

At a very high level, QTC executes the following:

1: **procedure** QTC Main Loop
2:    Calculate total number of ranks needed for current work
3:    **if** my rank is needed to do work **then**

```
 4:          color ← 1
 5:     else
 6:          color ← 0
 7:     end if
 8:     mygroup ← result of split mygroup by color
 9:     if color == 0 then
10:          Exit Main Loop
11:     end if
12:     Move Data to CUDA device
13:     Find local results using CUDA device
14:     Use mygroup communicator to find global results using collectives
15:     Use global results to create work for next iteration
16:     goto top of main loop
17: end procedure
```

To support this pattern, we ported the code in two stages. In the first stage, we used the Cray Message Passing Toolkit implementation of SHMEM, which provides several team based operations. We used the following:

```
void shmem_team_split(shmem_team_t parent_team, int color,
int key, shmem_team_t *newteam)

int shmem_team_translate_pe(shmem_team_t team1, int team1_pe,
shmem_team_t team2)

void shmem_team_barrier(shmem_team_t myteam, long *pSync)

void shmem_team_free(shmem_team_t *newteam)

int shmem_team_npes(shmem_team_t newteam)

int shmem_team_mype(shmem_team_t newteam)
```

The first three functions are collectives that must be called by all team members. The second three can be called by any pe in the team. These functions provided two of the four requirements for QTC listed in Table 1. We implemented team based broadcast and reduction sum-to-all using these along with shmem_get, shmem_put, shmem_wait functions.

In the second phase of porting, we implemented a shmem_team_t type and the listed Cray SHMEM team function prototypes and on top of the OpenSHMEM API. The only difference in function prototype between our OpenSHMEM team functions and the Cray SHMEM functions was that our team split operation had the following prototype:

```
void shmem_team_split(shmem_team_t parent_team, int color,
int key, shmem_team_t *newteam, long *pSyncBar)
```

We had to add the synchronization barrier symmetric array because our team split operation was built on top of a team based gather collective that required a barrier.

3.2   Synchronization Collectives

To provide replacement SHMEM collectives for the MPI collectives in Table 1, we implemented the following functions. We used C++ templates to provide a friendlier API

```
template<class T>
void gather(vector<T>& gvec, T *val, int root,
shmem_team_t tm, long *pSyncBar);

template<class T>
void all_gather(vector<T>& gvec, T *val, shmem_team_t tm,
long *pSyncBar);

template<class T>
T reduction_sum(T val, int root, shmem_team_t tm,
long *pSyncBar);

template<class T>
T reduction_sum_all(T val, shmem_team_t tm,
long *pSyncBar);

template<class T>
T prefix_scan(T val, shmem_team_t tm, long *pSyncBar);

template<class T>
T ex_prefix_scan(T val, shmem_team_t tm, long *pSyncBar);

template<class T>
void bcast(T *buf, int count, int root, shmem_team_t tm,
          long *pSyncBar);
```

In cases where shmem_team_t was equal to SHMEM_TEAM_WORLD, global collective functions were used.

Gather Implementation. Generally, shmem_put is preferred over get, since it returns more quickly. However, doing a gather operation based on put would require each PE in the team to have a specific location on the root PE in which to shmem_put its value. But this would mean the root PE would need to have a symmetric space in which to put that value. That symmetric space would be the resulting gathered array, which cannot be shmalloc'd in a team based way. Instead, using a non-blocking shmem_get into a local, non-symmetric vector, the problem is avoided altogether.

Since we use only the global get, put, and wait operations, these all rely on translating all team based pe numbers into global pe numbers with shmem_translate_pe. Having a fast version of this function is imported to all of the team collective implementations.

Reduction Implementation. For a reduction sum operation, a tree based reduction was used. As with gather, the amount of symmetric space required per PE was constant, no matter the total team size, to avoid any need for dynamic memory allocation.

Processors were arranged into a k-ary tree, where k was specified at compile time. Results were summed up the tree, with each pe accumulating values from k children. Each PE blocked using the `shmem_int_wait` function on a counter atomically incremented by each child until the counter reached k. The final result eventually accumulates at the root of the tree.

We tested various values of k, and eventually decided on a binary tree that avoided the use of atomic increment, as this was faster than any of the values of k tested. We also tested the choice of using tree based value broadcast versus a single rank putting values to all PEs. The tree based broadcast became faster at 16 nodes, whereas the barrier was faster at lower node counts.

Broadcast Implementation. Team broadcast uses the same algorithm as the final stage of reduction. Values are passed down a binary tree from root to leaves.

Prefix Scan Implementation. Prefix scan is implemented using conventional upsweep and downsweep phases. The synchronization is mostly point-to-point, though several barriers are required to ensure that flag values are properly reset to 0. To support non power-of-two sized teams, the scan uses teams internally to split the scan into sub-scans that are all power-of-two sized. The results of the sub-scans are then scanned, and the results broadcast back to the sub-teams.

4   Performance Demonstration

This section provides the performance results of our team and collective implementations. Then, performance results from the SHOC benchmarks are presented.

4.1   Hardware Platform: Cray XK7

These benchmarks were run on the Cray XK7 Titan system at Oak Ridge National Labs. The most relevant feature of using this system was the availability of the above mentioned team functions in the Cray Message Passing Toolkit.

4.2   Scaling of Collectives

Figures 3, 4 and 5 compare the performance of these collectives implemented on top of SHMEM vs the native MPI implementations. As expected, the native, highly optimized MPI collectives are much faster for reduction and allgather. However, the SHMEM gather implementation is significantly faster than the

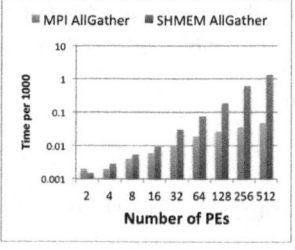
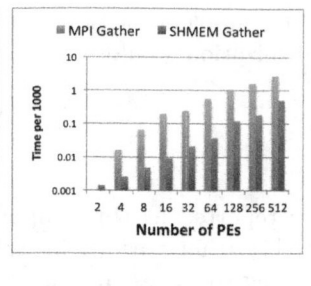
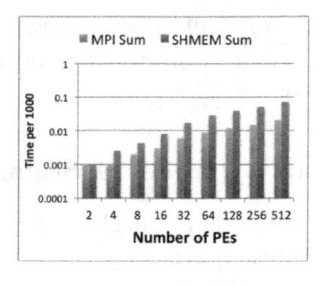

Fig. 3. AllGather   **Fig. 4.** Gather   **Fig. 5.** Sum

MPI implementation. This was a surprise, since we were not able to overlap any of this gather operation with other computation. As mentioned above, the gather operation simply issued non-blocking one-sided get operations to all processes, then performed a barrier to prevent overwriting symmetric data too early.

4.3   Portable Teams Implementation

To port this code to other systems, a non-Cray SHMEM implementation was needed. We tested the portable teams API layer using the OpenMPI 1.8.2 compiler on a commodity Linux cluster. The cluster has similar attributes to Titan, with 16 cores per node. Still, total runtime is less important than scaling trends, since different hardware was used. Figures 6, 7 and 8 show the scaling results. The Cray team barrier operation shows a major slowdown at 32 cores (2 nodes), then speeds up again. By contrast, the tree based barrier does fine up to 16 nodes, then scales poorly.

The split implementation on Cray SHMEM is also clearly different. It is slower at low core count, but scales up much better. The OpenSHMEM based split uses an AllGather collective underneath, so it will tend to scale poorly to higher core counts.

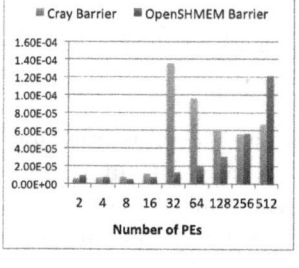
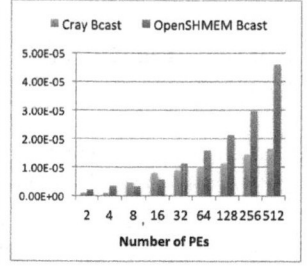
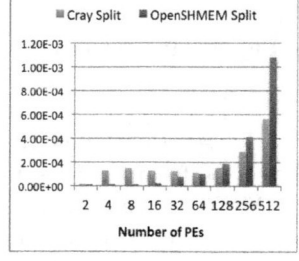

Fig. 6. Team barrier   **Fig. 7.** Team broadcast   **Fig. 8.** Team split

Overall, the portable teams implementation is usable at moderate core counts. More testing and optimization would be needed to scale to large core counts.

4.4 Benchmark Scaling

SHOC benchmark results are reported as throughput rates, rather than runtimes. Throughput is reported so that various benchmarks can be compared against each other, despite having runtimes that are not comparable.

The only SHMEM communication in the embarrassingly parallel (EP) benchmarks was in the results aggregation in the parallel database. This communication time is not included in any benchmark results, so all EP benchmarks ran, as expected, exactly the same with either MPI or SHMEM. Their results are not reported here, but may become relevant later, as a baseline, for future work in porting SHOC CUDA kernels.

The four TP benchmarks use SHOC for communication outside of the CUDA kernels. So, we were interested to see if there was any significant change in runtime between MPI and OpenSHMEM implementations at varying node counts. When running the benchmarks on up to 32 nodes, we did not observe any change in runtime when using OpenSHMEM, as shown in Figs. 9 and 10.

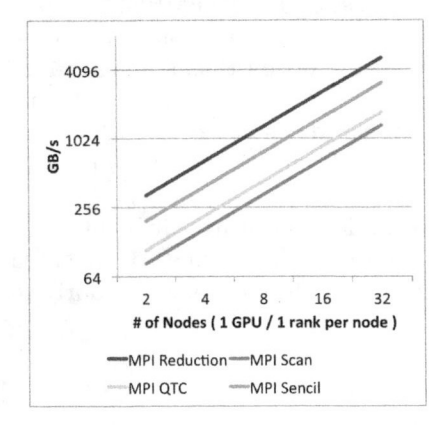 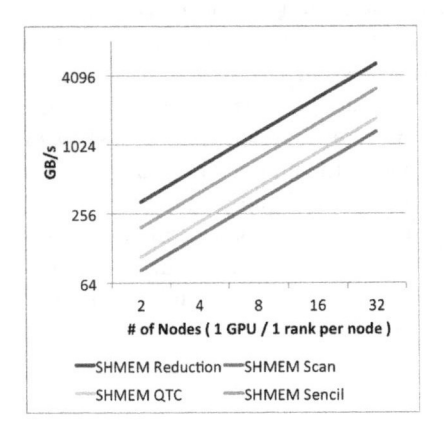

Fig. 9. TP benchmarks with MPI   **Fig. 10.** TP benchmarks with SHMEM

These results show that SHMEM can be effectively used as a communication layer, performing the same functions as MPI. However, migrating from MPI to SHMEM for hybrid programs is most natural when synchronizing collectives are available. The implementations here perform decently well on moderate core counts, but more testing and optimization would be needed to scale very large.

5   Conclusion and Future Work

Porting the SHOC benchmarks to OpenSHMEM has demonstrated that teams and collective operations are beneficial to supporting hybrid programming with OpenSHMEM. To successfully port these codes to OpenSHMEM, we implemented team data types, team split, free, barrier, and translate pe. In addition, we implemented C++ template functions for team based gather, reduction sum, prefix scan, and broadcast.

The performance of our implementation layer was good enough for low core counts. More scalable implementations with lower level optimizations will be required for larger job sizes.

The next phase of porting these benchmarks will be to look at moving the SHMEM communication into the CUDA kernels using NVSHMEM.

References

1. Nvidia nvlink high-speed interconnect. http://www.nvidia.com/object/nvlink.html
2. Baker, M., Pophale, S., Vasnier, J.-C., Jin, H., Hernandez, O.: Hybrid programming using OpenSHMEM and OpenACC. In: Poole, S., Hernandez, O., Shamis, P. (eds.) OpenSHMEM 2014. LNCS, vol. 8356, pp. 74–89. Springer, Heidelberg (2014). doi:10.1007/978-3-319-05215-1_6
3. ten Bruggencate, M.: Cray SHMEM update. In: OpenSHMEM Workshop, March 2014. http://www.csm.ornl.gov/workshops/openshmem2013/documents/presentations_and_tutorials/tenBruggencate_Cray_SHMEM_Update.pdf
4. Danalis, A., Marin, G., McCurdy, C., Meredith, J.S., Roth, P.C., Spafford, K., Tipparaju, V., Vetter, J.S.: The scalable heterogeneous computing (shoc) benchmark suite. In: Proceedings of the 3rd Workshop on General-Purpose Computation on Graphics Processing Units, pp. 63–74. ACM (2010)
5. Hanebutte, U.R., Dinan, J., Robichaux, J.: Toward an openshmem teams extension to enable topology-aware parallel programming. In: OpenSHMEM and Related Technologies. Experiences, Implementations, and Technologies: Second Workshop, OpenSHMEM 2015, Annapolis, MD, USA, 4–6 August 2015, vol. 9397, p. 195. Springer, Heidelberg (2015). Revised Selected Papers
6. Jose, J., Kandalla, K., Zhang, J., Potluri, S., Panda, D.: Optimizing collective communication in openshmem. In: 7th International Conference on PGAS Programming Models, p. 185
7. Knaak, D., Namashivayam, N.: Proposing OpenSHMEM extensions towards a future for hybrid programming and heterogeneous computing. In: Gorentla Venkata, M., Shamis, P., Imam, N., Lopez, M.G. (eds.) OpenSHMEM 2014. LNCS, vol. 9397, pp. 53–68. Springer, Heidelberg (2015). doi:10.1007/978-3-319-26428-8_4
8. NVIDIA: GPUdirect (2015). https://developer.nvidia.com/gpudirect
9. NVIDIA: GPUdirect RDMA (2015). http://docs.nvidia.com/cuda/gpudirect-rdma
10. Potluri, S., Rossetti, D., Becker, D., Poole, D., Gorentla Venkata, M., Hernandez, O., Shamis, P., Lopez, M.G., Baker, M., Poole, W.: Exploring OpenSHMEM model to program GPU-based extreme-scale systems. In: Gorentla Venkata, M., Shamis, P., Imam, N., Lopez, M.G. (eds.) OpenSHMEM 2014. LNCS, vol. 9397, pp. 18–35. Springer International Publishing, Cham (2015). doi:10.1007/978-3-319-26428-8_2

11. Rossetti, D.: GPUDirect: integrating the GPU with a network interface. In: GPU Technology Conference (2015)
12. Sodani, A., Gramunt, R., Corbal, J., Kim, H.S., Vinod, K., Chinthamani, S., Hutsell, S., Agarwal, R., Liu, Y.C.: Knights landing: second-generation Intel Xeon Phi product. IEEE Micro. **36**(2), 34–46 (2016)

OpenSHMEM Tools

Profiling Production OpenSHMEM Applications

John C. Linford[1]([✉]), Samuel Khuvis[1], Sameer Shende[1], Allen Malony[1],
Neena Imam[2], and Manjunath Gorentla Venkata[2]

[1] ParaTools, Inc., 2836 Kincaid St., Eugene, OR 97405, USA
{jlinford,skhuvis,sameer,malony}@paratools.com
http://www.paratools.com/
[2] Oak Ridge National Laboratory, 1 Bethel Valley Road, Oak Ridge, TN 37831, USA
{imamn,manjugv}@ornl.gov
http://ut-battelle.org/

Abstract. Developing high performance OpenSHMEM applications routinely involves gaining a deeper understanding of software execution, yet there are numerous hurdles to gathering performance metrics in a production environment. Most OpenSHMEM performance profilers rely on the PSHMEM interface but PSHMEM is an optional and often unavailable feature. We present a tool that generates direct measurement performance profiles of OpenSHMEM applications even when PSHMEM is unavailable. The tool operates on dynamically linked and statically linked application binaries, does not require debugging symbols, and functions regardless of compiler optimization level. Integrated in the TAU Performance System, the tool uses automatically-generated wrapper libraries that intercept OpenSHMEM API calls to gather performance metrics with minimal overhead. Dynamically linked applications may use the tool without modifying the application binary in any way.

Keywords: Profiling · Tracing · Performance analysis · The TAU Performance System · Code generation · Library wrapping

1 Introduction

OpenSHMEM application performance can be characterized via profiling and tracing tools built on the PSHMEM interface. For every routine in the OpenSHMEM standard, PSHMEM provides an analogous routine with a slightly different name. This allows profiling tools to intercept and measure OpenSHMEM calls made by a user's application by defining routines with the same function signatures as OpenSHMEM routines – *wrapper functions* – which call the appropriate PSHMEM routines. For example, the TAU Performance System® [7] provides an OpenSHMEM wrapper library which can be linked to any OpenSHMEM application to acquire runtime measurements of OpenSHMEM routines. The library can be used with statically or dynamically linked applications with runtime overhead between 1.5% and 4% [4]. Regardless of which events are recorded, TAU's overhead is approximately O(1) in the number of application processes, i.e. as the

© Springer International Publishing AG 2016
M. Gorentla Venkata et al. (Eds.): OpenSHMEM 2016, LNCS 10007, pp. 219–224, 2016.
DOI: 10.1007/978-3-319-50995-2_15

number of SHMEM processing elements (PEs) increases the overhead incurred by TAU remains relatively constant. This makes TAU an appropriate choice for profiling large-scale OpenSHMEM applications when PSHMEM is available.

For reasons of practicality, applications are typically developed on small-scale representative systems before being deployed on large-scale production systems. Yet it is often the case that performance bugs – software faults that affect the application's performance but not correctness – present themselves only at scale. Metrics such as time spent in code regions, compute intensity, message size, and communication volume are especially difficult to discern in production environments or at large scale. A production system may use highly optimized runtime libraries where performance tool interfaces (i.e. PSHMEM) have been disabled, rendering profiling and tracing tools like TAU ineffective. Tools that do not rely on PSHMEM but instead periodically sample the application (e.g. HPC-Toolkit [1,5]) cannot resolve this problem due to their inability to capture atomic events (e.g. the size, sender, and receiver of a message or the size of a memory allocation) and their reliance on debugging symbols, which are often stripped from production binaries. In short, OpenSHMEM developers would like to characterize the performance of production applications operating at large scales without modifying the application or relying on debugging symbols or special tools interfaces like PSHMEM.

This work-in-progress paper presents a tool that generates direct measurement (i.e. not sampled) performance profiles and traces of OpenSHMEM applications when PSHMEM is unavailable. The tool extends the existing OpenSHMEM profiling capabilities in TAU and therefore has similar runtime overhead (less than 4%). By building on TAU, we receive the full benefit of TAU's measurement layer so there are no restrictions to the types of performance data that can be gathered, i.e. PAPI can be used to gather hardware performance counters without any caveats. As detailed in Sect. 2, the tool parses the OpenSHMEM header files and automatically generates source code for wrapper libraries that intercept OpenSHMEM API calls at link-time or at run-time so that both dynamically and statically linked applications can be profiled. Since the tool uses source code parsing and code generation, it does not require debugging symbols and functions regardless of compiler optimization level.

2   Approach

Our goal is to provide performance data without relying on any special features of a particular OpenSHMEM implementation, i.e. PSHMEM. At a high level this involves two steps: constructing functionality similar to what is provided by the PSHMEM interface and making it available to the application.

2.1   Symbol Wrapping

For every routine in the OpenSHMEM standard, PSHMEM provides an analogous routine with a slightly different name. We use *symbol wrapping* via the

program linker to do the same. Nearly all program linkers support a `-wrap`
`foosym` command line option to enable wrapping of the symbol `foosym`. Any
undefined reference to `foosym` will be resolved to `__wrap_foosym` and any undefined reference to `__real_foosym` will be resolved to `foosym`. In this case, we use
symbol wrapping to provide a unique wrapper function for each API function
defined in an OpenSHMEM implementation's header files. When the application's object files are linked to form the executable file, a `-wrap` flag for every
OpenSHMEM API call is passed to the linker via the special `@argfile` syntax
supported by most linkers.

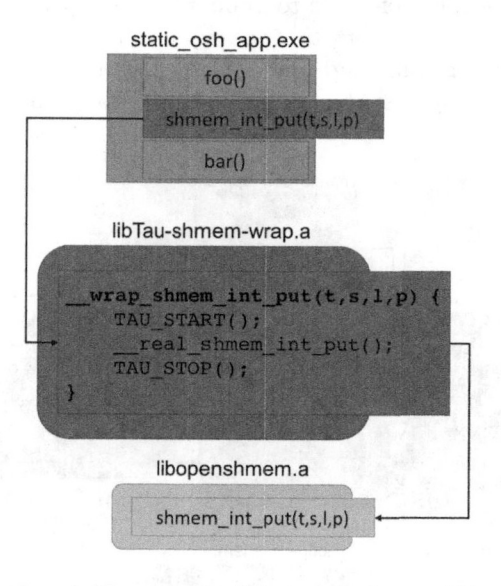

Fig. 1. Symbol wrapping via the program linker replacing a call to `shmem_int_put` with
a wrapper function at link time. The wrapper function uses TAU to record performance
data and invokes the original `shmem_int_put`.

Figure 1 demonstrates symbol wrapping with an OpenSHMEM application that is statically linked against the OpenSHMEM implementation library
`libopenshmem.a`. At link time, the call to `shmem_int_put` in the application
is replaced with a call to `__wrap_shmem_int_put`, which is implemented in the
`libTau-shmem-wrap.a` wrapper library. The wrapper function uses TAU to
record performance data and invokes `__real_shmem_int_put`, which the linker
replaces with a call to the original `shmem_int_put` as defined in `libopenshmem.a`.

Symbol wrapping works equally well for statically linked applications
and dynamically linked applications that statically link against the OpenSH-
MEM implementation. However, applications that link dynamically against
`libopenshmem.so` should use library preloading instead of symbol wrapping
because symbol wrapping will only intercept SHMEM calls made from the application itself.

2.2   Library Preloading

Symbol wrapping is a powerful, low overhead way to wrap the OpenSHMEM API, but it requires the user to re-link their application against a special library of wrapper functions. This is not always possible in a production environment, so we use *library preloading* to achieve dynamically what the linker does statically. The LD_PRELOAD environment variable specifies a list of additional shared libraries to be loaded before all others, selectively overriding functions in other shared libraries. We use the LD_PRELOAD environment variable to insert a *dynamic symbol wrapper* at the front of the search list. The dynamic symbol wrapper will resolve any undefined reference to foosym to __wrap_foosym and any undefined reference to __real_foosym to foosym, just as the linker does statically when passed the -wrap command line option. This requires the application to be dynamically linked against the OpenSHMEM implementation library.

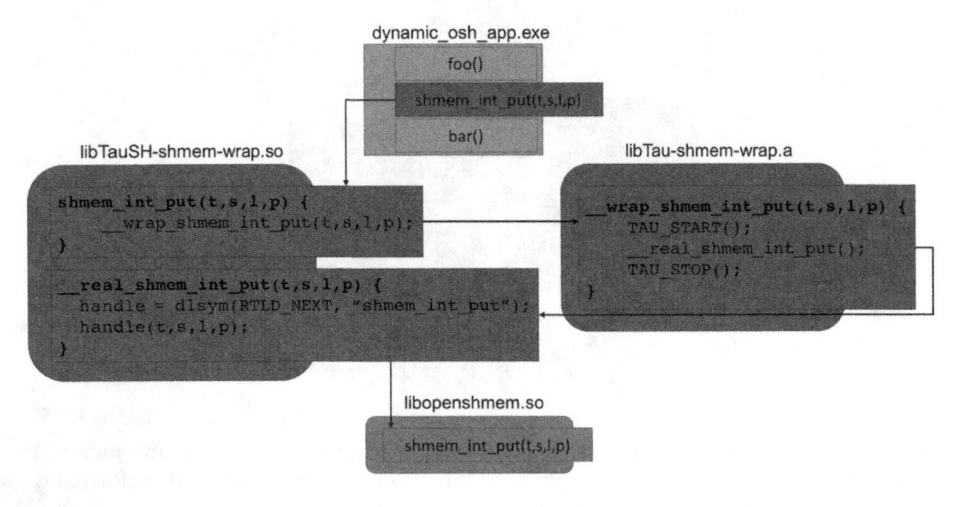

Fig. 2. Using a dynamic symbol wrapper to dynamically resolve undefined references to shmem_int_put to __wrap_shmem_int_put and undefined references to __real_shmem_int_put to shmem_int_put.

Figure 2 shows how the dynamic symbol wrapper library achieves symbol wrapping at runtime when libTauSH-shmem-wrap.so is prepended to the LD_PRELOAD environment variable. Because the dynamic symbol wrapper is the first library on the search list, the call to shmem_int_put in the application resolves to the definition of shmem_int_put provided by the dynamic symbol wrapper. This implementation simply passes control to the __wrap_shmem_int_put function defined in our wrapper library. When the wrapper library invokes __real_shmem_int_put, that symbol resolves dynamically to the implementation provided in libTauSH-shmem-wrap.so. The dynamic linker's programing interface is then used to discover the address of the original implementation of shmem_int_put as defined in libopenshmem.so.

2.3 Automatic Wrapper Library Generation

In order to construct a tools interface for an arbitrary SHMEM implementation, we use the Program Database Toolkit (PDT) [3,6] to parse the implementation's header files (e.g. `shmem.h` and `shmemx.h`) and discover the available API. For each API function parsed, a wrapper function is automatically generated that tracks the performance characteristics of that routine, e.g. wall clock time. If the routine also sends or receives data (e.g. `shmem_int_put`) then the wrapper also tracks the message size, target PE, and source PE. The wrapper functions can also measure hardware performance counters via PAPI [2] to track cache misses, operation counts, etc. For example, the application profile will show if a call to `shmem_barrier` used busy-wait.

3 Conclusions and Future Work

We present a tool that generates direct measurement performance profiles of OpenSHMEM applications even when PSHMEM is unavailable. The tool operates on dynamically linked and statically linked application binaries, does not require debugging symbols, and functions regardless of compiler optimization level. This work completely removes the need for a PSHMEM interface with no significant disadvantage to the user, however PSHMEM is still valuable to tools other than TAU which cannot automatically generate wrapper libraries.

Many OpenSHMEM implementations – most notably OpenSHMEM reference implementation 1.2 – do not provide the implementation library in both static and dynamic forms by default. Only the static library, `libopenshmem.a`, is built by default. Performance tools that use this approach would benefit from having both the static and dynamic libraries available by default as it would fully enable the library wrapping features we have described. Without a dynamic library, only link-time wrapping is possible.

TAU could also benefit from an interface which exposes synchronization of the symmetric heap. At present, TAU intercepts the underlying system allocation and deallocation calls and OpenSHMEM library calls to mark operations on the symmetric heap. However, it is difficult to observe in a trace when an update to the symmetric heap becomes visible to other PEs. TAU could make use of a mechanism for notifying a performance measurement system of symmetric heap updates when they occur to improve the quality of the performance data.

Acknowledgments. This work was supported by the United States Department of Defense (DoD) and used resources of the Computational Research and Development Programs and the Oak Ridge Leadership Computing Facility (OLCF) at Oak Ridge National Laboratory.

References

1. Adhianto, L., Banerjee, S., Fagan, M., Krentel, M., Marin, G., Mellor-Crummey, J., Tallent, N.R.: HPCToolkit: tools for performance analysis of optimized parallel programs. Concurrency Comput. Pract. Exp. **22**(6), 685–701 (2010)

2. Browne, S., Dongarra, J., Garner, N., Ho, G., Mucci, P.: A portable programming interface for performance evaluation on modern processors. Int. J. High Perform. Comput. Appl. **3**(14), 189–204 (2000)
3. Lindlan, K., Cuny, J., Malony, A., Shende, S., Mohr, B., Rivenburgh, R.: A tool framework for static and dynamic analysis of object oriented software with templates. In: SC 2000: High Performance Networking and Computing Conference (2000). http://www.cs.uoregon.edu/research/pdt
4. Linford, J., Simon, T.A., Shende, S., Malony, A.D.: Profiling non-numeric OpenSH-MEM applications with the TAU performance system. In: Poole, S., Hernandez, O., Shamis, P. (eds.) OpenSHMEM 2014. LNCS, vol. 8356, pp. 105–119. Springer, Heidelberg (2014). doi:10.1007/978-3-319-05215-1_8
5. Malony, A., Mellor-Crummey, J., Shende, S.: Methods and strategies for parallel performance measurement and analysis: experiences with TAU and HPCToolkit. In: Bailey, D., Lucas, R., Williams, S. (eds.) Performance Tuning of Scientific Applications. CRC Press, New York (2010)
6. Quinlan, D.: ROSE: compiler support for object-oriented frameworks. In: Proceedings of Conference on Parallel Compilers (CPC 2000), Aussois, France, January 2000
7. Shende, S., Malony, A.: The TAU parallel performance system. Int. J. High Perform. Comput. Appl. **20**(2), 287–311 (2006)

Short Papers

SHMEM-MT: A Benchmark Suite for Assessing Multi-threaded SHMEM Performance

Hans Weeks[1(✉)], Matthew G.F. Dosanjh[2],
Patrick G. Bridges[1], and Ryan E. Grant[2]

[1] Department of Computer Science, University of New Mexico, Albuquerque, USA
{hansel,bridges}@cs.unm.edu
[2] Center for Computing Research, Sandia National Laboratories, Albuquerque, USA
{mdosanj,regrant}@sandia.gov

1 Introduction

OpenSHMEM is a popular one-sided communication library for high-performance computing systems developed around 2010 at the University of Houston [2]. It is becoming an increasingly popular programming model for next-generation HPC applications and systems because of its simple, intuitive interface and the proliferation of one-sided communication devices such as Infiniband [1]. Despite its increasing popularity, there are few benchmarks or mini-applications for evaluating and optimizing OpenSHMEM system software and hardware performance. This is particularly true for emerging multi-core and many-core systems on which OpenSHMEM is particularly important.

In this paper, we present the first set of OpenSHMEM benchmarks of which we are aware for systematically evaluating OpenSHMEM communication performance. A key element of these benchmarks is their support for multi-threading, based on the OpenSHMEM thread API proposed by Cray [9]. These benchmarks are based on one-sided benchmarks and mini-applications previously developed for MPI [4]. The initial version described in this paper focuses on simple messaging micro-benchmarks and HPC mini-applications, in both cases with simple synchronization strategies; support for additional benchmarks, mini-applications, and synchronization methods is planned.

2 SHMEM-MT Benchmarking Approach

To develop a set of OpenSHMEM benchmarks for driving communication system design and optimization, we have thus far focused on porting the MPI RMA-MT benchmarks [4]. This work primarily focused on identifying the proper way to port MPI RMA one-sided calls to OpenSHMEM, how the benchmarks were

Sandia National Laboratories is a multiprogram laboratory managed and operated by Sandia Corporation, a wholly owned subsidiary of Lockheed Martin Corporation, for the United States Department of Energy's National Nuclear Security Administration under contract DE-AC04-94AL85000.

M. Gorentla Venkata et al. (Eds.): OpenSHMEM 2016, LNCS 10007, pp. 227–231, 2016.
DOI: 10.1007/978-3-319-50995-2_16

converted from MPI RMA to OpenSHMEM, and how threading was supported when appropriate in the current version of these benchmarks.

The RMA-MT benchmark suite [4] was designed to provide a robust set of tests to verify the functionality and measure the performance of MPI's one-sided communication implementation in a multi-threaded environment. These benchmarks are based on previous benchmarks, including Thakur and Gropp's multi-threaded latency and bandwidth tests [10], the Sandia Microbenchmarks (SMBs) [3], and a subset of the Mantevo Mini-Applications [5]. RMA-MT generally focuses on the most commonly-used subset of MPI one-sided calls. We used the RMA-MT benchmark suite as the basis for the OpenSHMEM benchmarks we present here.

Benchmark Conversion. When replacing synchronization methods in our benchmarks, we used the synchronization methods that best matched the communication pattern used by the benchmark. In latency and bandwidth benchmarks, we used `shmem_quiet` because only one processing element need be involved in the communication (passive target). For message-rate and mini-app benchmarks, we used `barrier_all` because the underlying applications already relied on barriers to synchronize the activities of multiple processes. Importantly, we have not yet attempted to port the lock-based versions of the RMA-MT benchmarks for SHMEM-MT because of the significant semantic differences between these communications (active target).

In contrast to the synchronization calls, converting the MPI window management and RMA calls was straightforward. In particular, we replaced the calls to `malloc` and `MPI_win_create` with appropriate `shmem_malloc` calls and replaced MPI_get/put with shmem_get/put. In addition, because command line arguments given to the benchmarks are global variables that are stored in symmetric memory, we were able to remove calls to broadcast these parameters that were present in the original RMA-MT benchmarks.

It is important to note that the mini-applications still use a hybrid MPI/-OpenSHMEM approach in some cases. As with the RMA-MT benchmarks, we focused on converting the main halo exchange of each application to OpenSH-MEM to test the performance-critical communications at scale in an application setting. Other communications such as set-up and tear-down, as well as a handful (one or two) `MPI_Allreduce` calls per iteration in each mini-application, are still performed using MPI. This approach is similar to that taken by other researchers [6,7]. We hope to convert the remaining MPI communication operations in these mini-applications to OpenSHMEM in the near future, but have not prioritized this effort as these calls are not generally performance critical at the scale at which we currently execute.

Threading Support. Because MPI works on a per-process basis, the RMA-MT messaging benchmarks rely on per-process synchronization and use threads only for RMA data movement operations. In particular, these benchmarks multi-thread operations between synchronization calls using a fork-join threading model. The benchmarks use this structure primarily because of the lack of fine-grained thread-level synchronization operations in current versions of MPI, as threads are not separate entities recognized by MPI, unlike in the OpenSHMEM thread extensions provided by Cray.

Our initial port of the RMA-MT benchmarks to OpenSHMEM preserves the basic fork-join threading structure of these benchmarks that results from the lack of thread-level synchronization primitives in MPI RMA calls. In particular, we preserved synchronization methods at the processing element granularity by calling `shmem_quiet` or `shmem_barrier_all` after `pthread_join` at the end of each test iteration, rather than relying on thread-level synchronization. Converting these benchmarks to use the thread-level synchronization primitives proposed for use in OpenSHMEM, for example `shmem_thread_quiet` and `shmem_thread_fence` is an important direction for future work.

3 Initial Results

In this section we present initial results using this benchmark suite on a Cray XC30 cluster. Each node has two Xeon Ivy Bridge 2.4 GHz 12-core processor with hyper-threading enabled, 32 GB of memory per node, and a Cray Aries network interface. SHMEM-MT benchmarks were compiled using the Cray compiler suite and Cray shmem version 7.3.2. Each data point in this section is an average of 10 runs with each run performing 10,000 iterations, in the case of the messaging benchmarks. Each point is plotted with error bars showing the standard deviation of the 10 runs; in a large number of cases, the standard deviation of the ten runs was small enough not to show up on the plots.

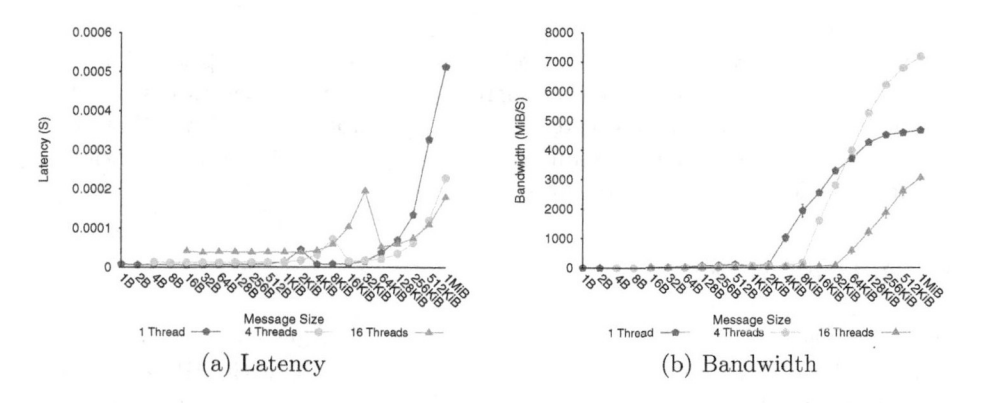

(a) Latency   (b) Bandwidth

Fig. 1. SHMEM-MT latency and bandwidth performance

Figure 1 shows the latency and bandwidth tests respectively. Both tests are setup similarly; as the number of threads increase each message is split into smaller equal pieces for each thread. We can see that for small messages, less than 32 KiB, Cray SHMEM achieves best performance when using a single thread.

After 32 KiB, 4 threads sending portions of the message appear to outperform the 1 thread case. For the message sizes used in this test, 16 threads performs worse in bandwidth than the other cases, likely due to insufficient hardware-level concurrency to amortize the increased synchronization overheads.

Figure 2 shows the runtime of the HPCCG and MiniFE mini-applications when run with 24 ranks per node on up to 32 nodes using a weak scaling problem size. In particular, HPCCG was set to 100^3 elements per PE while the MiniFE problem size was set at $(330 * nodes^{1/3})^3$. Note that, these mini-applications do not yet include full threading support. In this case, messaging concurrency is provided at the thread level, however we run a PE per core to maintain computational concurrency.

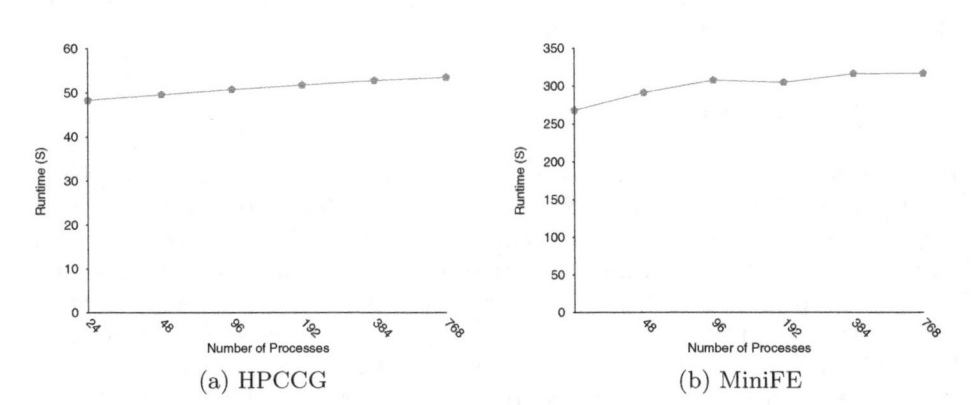

(a) HPCCG   (b) MiniFE

Fig. 2. SHMEM-MT mini-application weak-scaling runtime

In both cases, performance is largely constant as expected, particularly for MiniFE. HPCCG runtimes begin to increase slightly with increased scale, but to a level that is generally expected for this mini-application. Note that both mini-applications also include solution verifications provided from the original Mantevo versions that complete successfully.

4   Related Work

The most relevant related work to the work presented here is work by Luecke et al. [8] where they compared the performance of SHMEM with MPI-2 RMA on an SGI Origin 2000 and Cray T3E system. Unlike this work, they used a single threaded approach and the MPI-2 RMA interface was the only one available. Since that time, significant improvements have been made to the MPI RMA interfaces for MPI-3, and OpenSHMEM [2] has emerged as a standard, with matching implementations.

5 Conclusions and Future Work

Overall, our work provides a first set of benchmarks for evaluating OpenSH-MEM implementations and optimizations, particularly in the presence of multiple threads. Our initial results show OpenSHMEM performance that is generally comparable to other modern messaging systems; due to time and space limitations, we defer a complete performance comparison across MPI, OpenSHMEM, and similar messaging system implementations on different platforms for future work. In addition, the relative ease with which we converted MPI RMA benchmarks to OpenSHMEM demonstrates a path for developing further benchmarks and mini-applications.

References

1. I.T. Association. InfiniBand Architecture Specification: Release 1.0. In InfiniBand Trade Association (2000)
2. Chapman, B., Curtis, T., Pophale, S., Poole, S., Kuehn, J., Koelbel, C., Smith, L.: Introducing OpenSHMEM: SHMEM for the PGAS community. In: Proceedings of the Fourth Conference on Partitioned Global Address Space Programming Model, p. 2. ACM (2010)
3. Doefler, D., Barrett, B.W.: Sandia MPI microbenchmark suite (SMB). Technical report, Sandia National Laboratories (2009)
4. Dosanjh, M.G., Groves, T., Grant, R.E., Brightwell, R., Bridges, P.G.: RMA-MT: a benchmark suite for assessing MPI multi-threaded RMA performance. In: IEEE/ACM International Symposium on Cluster, Cloud and Grid Computing (IEEE/ACM CCGrid 2016) (2016)
5. Heroux, M.A., Doerfler, D.W., Crozier, P.S., Willenbring, J.M., Edwards, H.C., Williams, A., Rajan, M., Keiter, E.R., Thornquist, H.K., Numrich, R.W.: Improving performance via mini-applications. Sandia National Laboratories, Technical Report (2009)
6. Jose, J., Potluri, S., Tomko, K., Panda, D.K.: Designing scalable graph500 benchmark with hybrid MPI+OpenSHMEM programming models. In: Kunkel, J.M., Ludwig, T., Meuer, H.W. (eds.) ISC 2013. LNCS, vol. 7905, pp. 109–124. Springer, Heidelberg (2013). doi:10.1007/978-3-642-38750-0_9
7. Li, M., Lin, J., Lu, X., Hamidouche, K., Tomko, K., Panda, D.K.: Scalable MiniMD design with hybrid MPI and OpenSHMEM. In: Proceedings of the 8th International Conference on Partitioned Global Address Space Programming Models, p. 24. ACM (2014)
8. Luecke, G.R., Spanoyannis, S., Kraeva, M.: The performance and scalability of SHMEM and MPI-2 one-sided routines on a SGI Origin 2000 and a Cray T3E-600. Concurrency Comput. Pract. Exp. 16(10), 1037–1060 (2004)
9. ten Bruggencate, M., Roweth, D., Oyanagi, S.: Thread-Safe SHMEM extensions. In: Poole, S., Hernandez, O., Shamis, P. (eds.) OpenSHMEM 2014. LNCS, vol. 8356, pp. 178–185. Springer, Heidelberg (2014). doi:10.1007/978-3-319-05215-1_13
10. Thakur, R., Gropp, W.: Test suite for evaluating performance of MPI implementations that support **MPI_THREAD_MULTIPLE**. In: Cappello, F., Herault, T., Dongarra, J. (eds.) EuroPVM/MPI 2007. LNCS, vol. 4757, pp. 46–55. Springer, Heidelberg (2007). doi:10.1007/978-3-540-75416-9_13

Investigating Data Motion Power Trends to Enable Power-Efficient OpenSHMEM Implementations

Tiffany M. Mintz$^{(\boxtimes)}$, Eduardo D'Azevedo, Manjunath Gorentla Venkata,
and Chung-Hsing Hsu

Oak Ridge National Laboratory, Oak Ridge, TN, USA
mintztm@ornl.gov

Abstract. As we continue to develop extreme-scale systems, it is becoming increasingly important to be mindful and more in control of power consumed by these systems. With high performance requirements being more constrained by power and data movement quickly becoming the critical concern for both power and performance, now is an opportune time for OpenSHMEM implementations to address the need for more power-efficient data movement. In order to enable power efficient OpenSHMEM implementations, we have formulated power trend studies that emphasize power consumption for one-sided communications and the disparities in power consumption across multiple implementations. In this paper, we present power trend analysis, generate targeted hypotheses for increasing power efficiency with OpenSHMEM, and discuss prospective research for power efficient OpenSHMEM implementations.

1 Introduction

The OpenSHMEM community has spent nearly a decade developing a standard API for the Partitioned Global Address Space (PGAS) programming model. Alongside the development of a standard API has been a reference implementation of OpenSHMEM [4]. This implementation and other OpenSHMEM implementations [1–3,5] have been developed to be portable with comparable performance across multiple platforms. As with most message-passing implementations, the goal of developers has primarily been to optimize performance. But as high performance computing (HPC) reaches extreme scales of hundreds of

This manuscript has been authored by UT-Battelle, LLC under Contract No. DE-AC05-00OR22725 with the U.S. Department of Energy. The United States Government retains and the publisher, by accepting the article for publication, acknowledges that the United States Government retains a non-exclusive, paid-up, irrevocable, worldwide license to publish or reproduce the published form of this manuscript, or allow others to do so, for United States Government purposes. The Department of Energy will provide public access to these results of federally sponsored research in accordance with the DOE Public Access Plan (http://energy.gov/downloads/doe-public-access-plan).

© Springer International Publishing AG 2016
M. Gorentla Venkata et al. (Eds.): OpenSHMEM 2016, LNCS 10007, pp. 232–238, 2016.
DOI: 10.1007/978-3-319-50995-2_17

petaflops to exaflops with the potential of moving petabytes of data in a single application, computer hardware architects, software developers and computational scientists have all realized that power efficiency is proportionately important. As we continue to develop extreme-scale systems, it is becoming increasingly necessary to be mindful and more in control of power consumed by these systems. While much of what we can accomplish in power-efficient computing is dependent on system architecture, there is a significant portion of power-efficiency that can be exploited through 'intelligent' system software development.

In order to make intelligent decisions when developing OpenSHMEM software, we must first understand the correlations between software implementations of the OpenSHMEM API and the impact of the software design choices on power consumption. We develop this understanding by profiling the power consumption of a system under various configurations while executing benchmarks and applications of interests. There are many options for profiling power consumption, and we have chosen PowerInsight [7] to monitor and collect power profiles for OpenSHMEM benchmarks and applications.

The benchmarks that we have chosen to profile are put and get benchmarks from the OSU Micro-Benchmark Suite [8], as well as an OpenSHMEM implementation of the High Performance Conjugate Gradients (HPCG) Benchmark [6]. These profiles enable us to perform power trend analysis across the various implementations of OpenSHMEM and OpenMPI one-sided communications that is presented in Sect. 2. In Sect. 3, we generate hypotheses and discover insights into which OpenSHMEM implementation is more power-efficient and which operations would benefit most from re-engineering the software for power-efficiency without negatively impacting performance.

2   OpenSHMEM Power Trend Analysis

We performed power studies on a PowerInsight instrumented cluster with Dual Intel Xeon E5-2650v2 i7, 8 cores, 16 threads, a base frequency of 2.6 GHz, 64 GB DDR3-1600 SDRAM, and Infiniband ConnectX 3. We used two nodes to perform point-to-point studies with the OSU Micro-Benchmark Suite. For the purposes of this study, we selected the point-to-point OpenSHMEM and one-sided MPI latency benchmarks. For each of theses benchmarks, latency tests are performed for put and get operations for both the OpenSHMEM and MPI standards. For OpenSHMEM, tests are performed for heap memory allocation, and the MPI tests are performed for passive and active synchronization. In each experiment, rank 0 is the process actively executing the put or get operation.

To obtain power profiles that model more closely memory access and communication patterns found in scientific applications, we selected the HPCG Benchmark. For HPCG, we performed experiments on a single node, and executed weak and strong scaling experiments from 4 to 32 processes. For both HPCG and the OSU Benchmarks, the nodes were configured so that turbo boost was disabled to provide more consistent profiles across multiple executions of the same input configurations. We collect power consumption measures for three consecutive executions of the same input data size; the average of these measurements are taken to generate a single power profile.

2.1 OSU Micro-Benchmarks Power Analysis

The first set of power profiles compares the power consumed by put operations in the OpenSHMEM Reference implementation, the OpenMPI-OpenSHMEM implementation, and one-sided OpenMPI. Figure 1 shows the CPU and memory power profiles of ranks 0 and 1 for OpenSHMEM compared to OpenMPI with active and passive synchronization. In these profiles, we observe that the active process (rank 0) in the OpenSHMEM Reference implementation has a consistently higher profile than the other two implementations for both memory and CPU power. For CPU power, the reference implementation on average consumes approximately 11 W to 16 W more power and approximately 33 J to 63 J more energy. For memory on average, this implementation consumes approximately 2 W more power and 3 J to 14 J more energy. On the passive process (rank 1), the OpenSHMEM Reference implementation on average consumes about 12 W more CPU power and 22 J more energy on the CPU than the OpenMPI-OpenSHMEM implementation, as well as approximately 2 W more power and 3 J energy for memory accesses.

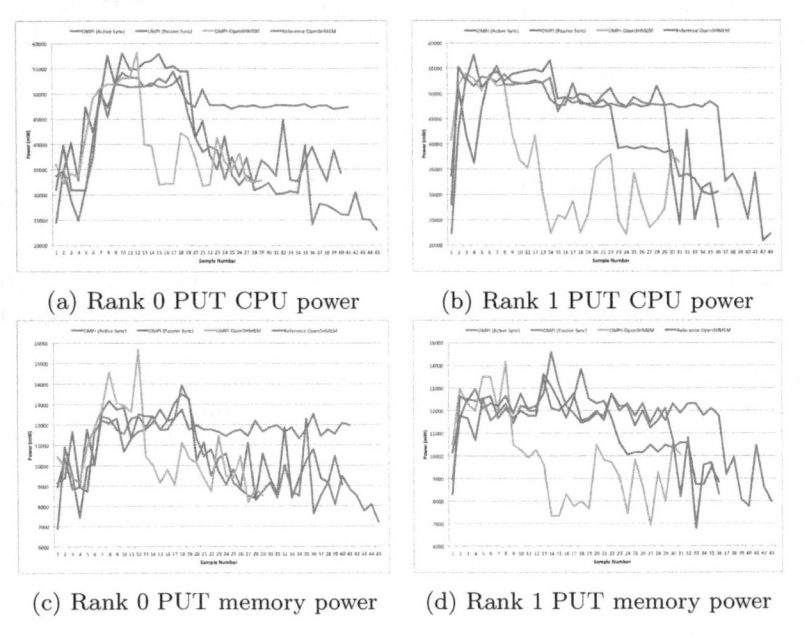

(a) Rank 0 PUT CPU power   (b) Rank 1 PUT CPU power

(c) Rank 0 PUT memory power   (d) Rank 1 PUT memory power

Fig. 1. PUT operations CPU and Memory power profiles

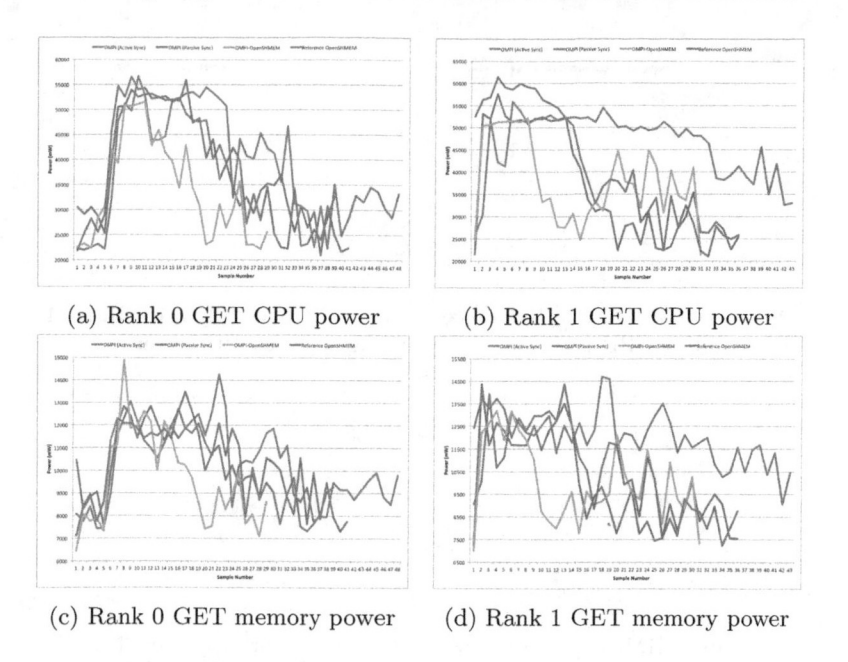

(a) Rank 0 GET CPU power   (b) Rank 1 GET CPU power

(c) Rank 0 GET memory power   (d) Rank 1 GET memory power

Fig. 2. GET operations CPU and Memory power profiles

The last set of profiles of the OSU Micro-Benchmark Suite is a comparison of get operation power consumption for the OpenSHMEM Reference implementation, the OpenMPI-OpenSHMEM implementation, one-sided OpenMPI. Figure 2 shows the CPU and memory power profile of ranks 0 and 1 for OpenSHMEM compared to OpenMPI. For the get operation power consumption, we observe that the OpenMPI-OpenSHMEM implementation, on average, consumes less power on the active process than the other two implementations, approximately 5 W to 9 W less CPU power and 63 J to 125J less energy on the CPU. For memory on average, the OpenMPI-OpenSHMEM implementation consumes less than 2 W less power and approximately 16 J to 31 J less energy.

2.2 HPCG Benchmark Power Analysis

Profiling the HPCG benchmark gives us a better understanding of how power consumption varies across OpenSHMEM implementations in a full communication pattern. The profiles for HPCG were collected for the OpenSHMEM Reference implementation and the OpenMPI-OpenSHMEM implementation. These studies focus primarily on power consumption scales with the number of processes as we redistribute the workload (strong scaling) and as the workload remains consistent across processes (weak scaling).

In the first set of HPCG power profiles, we study how CPU and memory power consumption scales as we increase the number of processes and redistribute the workload. In this set of experiments, we maintain a global matrix size of

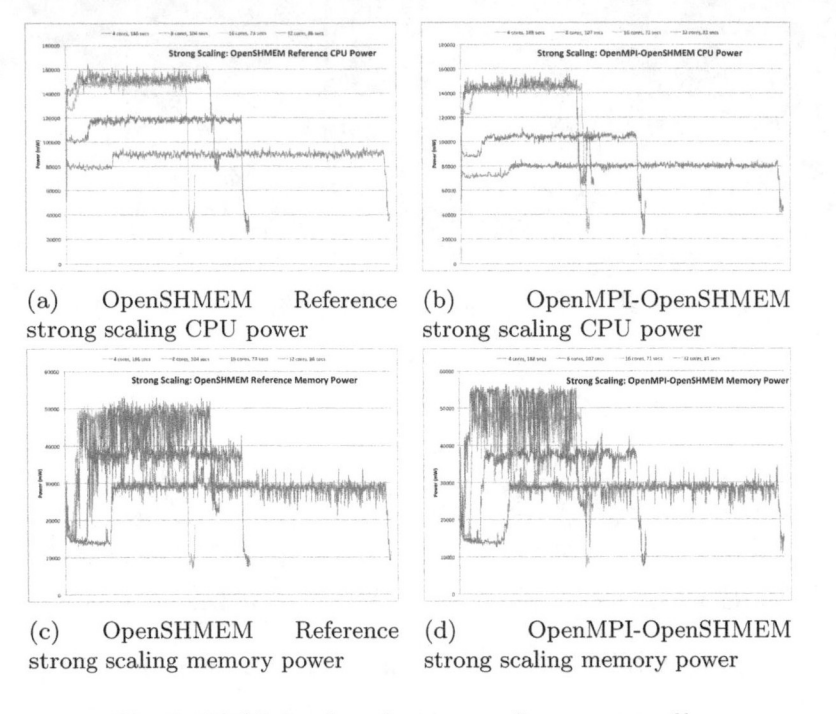

(a)   OpenSHMEM   Reference strong scaling CPU power

(b)   OpenMPI-OpenSHMEM strong scaling CPU power

(c)   OpenSHMEM   Reference strong scaling memory power

(d)   OpenMPI-OpenSHMEM strong scaling memory power

Fig. 3. HPCG Benchmark strong scaling power profiles

$256 \times 256 \times 128$ elements and scale the number of processes from 4 to 32 on a single node. In the case of 32 processes, the architecture is hyper-threaded with 16 physical cores and 2 threads per core. In Fig. 3, we compare the CPU and memory power profiles for the OpenSHMEM Reference and OpenMPI-OpenSHMEM implementations. The CPU profiles show strong scaling for power consumption as we scale the number of physical cores, but as hyper-threading is enabled for experiments with 32 processes, power no longer increases linearly with the number of the processes. We also observe that on average, the OpenSHMEM Reference implementation has a peak power profile of about 9 W more than the OpenMPI-OpenSHMEM implementation and consumes on average approximately 1200 J more energy. The most significant deviation in the power profiles of the two implementations for the strong scaling experiments is observed for memory power consumption for hyper-threaded executions. While the OpenMPI-OpenSHMEM implementation's peak power profile has a nearly 10 W increase from 16 to 32 processes, the OpenSHMEM Reference implementation memory power profile is nearly identical from 16 to 32 processes.

The next set of HPCG power profiles show how CPU and memory power consumption scales as the number of processes are increased from 4 to 32 and the workload remains constant on each process. In these experiments, each process maintains a local matrix size of $104 \times 104 \times 104$ elements. With these weak scaling studies, we make the same observations as with the strong scaling experiments. Figure 4 shows the CPU and memory power profiles for these experiments.

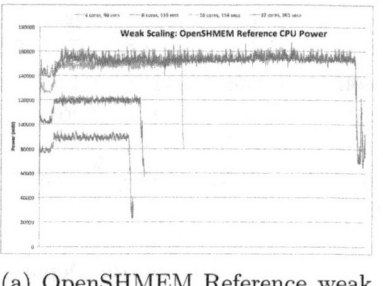

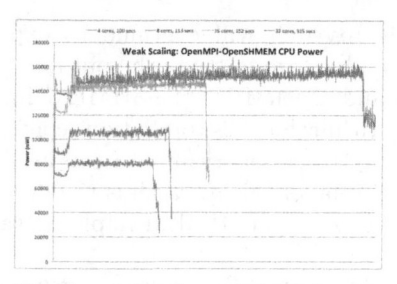

(a) OpenSHMEM Reference weak scaling CPU power

(b) OpenMPI-OpenSHMEM weak scaling CPU power

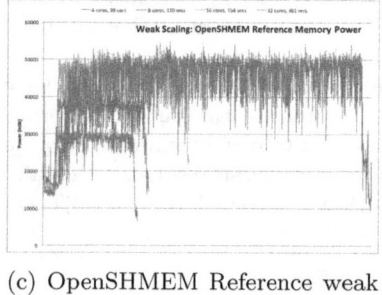

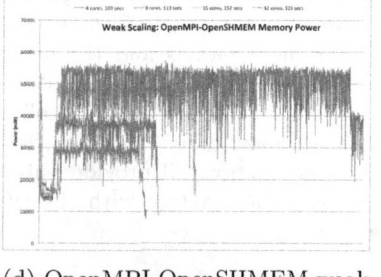

(c) OpenSHMEM Reference weak scaling memory power

(d) OpenMPI-OpenSHMEM weak scaling memory power

Fig. 4. HPCG Benchmark weak scaling power profiles

3   Insights and Prospective Research

Conducting power trend experiments for OpenSHMEM and one-side MPI implementations gives us some key insights into the potential for power efficiency with OpenSHMEM. This initial phase of research has been conducted to generate targeted hypotheses and help direct the development of power efficient OpenSHMEM implementations. Some hypotheses we deduce from our power profile analysis is that there is not a one-to-one mapping of performance to power consumption in message passing implementations, particularly OpenSHMEM. We have shown in our studies that power profiles of different OpenSHMEM implementations with similar performance measurements have dissimilar peak power costs. This leads to an additional hypothesis that there is a threshold for performance optimizations correlating with energy optimizations (i.e. there is a limit to performance optimizations that automatically realize energy optimizations). Another hypothesis we deduce from this study is that a less power efficient implementation may be optimized for power without degrading performance. Since the gap in performance between each implementation is minimal compared to the gap in power consumption, we can theoretically decrease the gap in power consumption by implementing some of the algorithms of the more power efficient implementation without adversely affecting performance.

This research will continue to explore these hypotheses. Our immediate research plans are to study the put and get operations in the OpenSHMEM Reference and OpenMPI-OpenSHMEM implementations, discover which parts of the algorithms for these operations contribute to minimizing power consumption, and apply these algorithms to the implementation that is less power efficient. The potential of this research is to develop power efficient software development standards for OpenSHMEM implementations.

Acknowledgment. This work was supported by the United States Department of Defense and used resources of the Extreme Scale Systems Center at Oak Ridge National Laboratory. This manuscript has been authored by UT-Battelle, LLC under Contract No.DE-AC05-00OR22725 with the U.S. Department of Energy. The United States Government retains and the publisher, by accepting the article for publication, acknowledges that the United States Government retains a non-exclusive, paidup, irrevocable, world-wide license to publish or reproduce the published form of this manuscript, or allow others to do so, for United States Government purposes. The Department of Energy will provide public access to these results of federally sponsored research in accordance with the DOE Public Access Plan (http://energy.gov/downloads/doe-public-access-plan).

References

1. Mellanox openshmem. http://www.mellanox.com/
2. Mvapich2-x. http://mvapich.cse.ohio-state.edu/overview/mvapich2x/
3. Openshmem in openmpi. https://www.open-mpi.org
4. Openshmem reference implementation. https://github.com/openshmem-org/openshmem
5. Sandia openshmem. https://github.com/Sandia-OpenSHMEM
6. Dongarra, J., Heroux, M.A., Luszczek, P.: HPCG benchmark: a new metric for ranking high performance computing systems. Technical Report UT-EECS-15-736, Electrical Engineering and Computer Science Department, University of Tennessee, November 2015
7. Laros, J.H., Pokorny, P., DeBonis, D.: Powerinsight - a commodity power measurement capability. In: 2013 International Green Computing Conference (IGCC), pp. 1–6, June 2013
8. Liu, J., Chandrasekaran, B., Yu, W., Wu, J., Buntinas, D., Kini, S., Panda, D.K., Wyckoff, P.: Microbenchmark performance comparison of high-speed cluster interconnects. IEEE Micro **24**(1), 42–51 (2004)

Author Index

Printed in the United States
By Bookmasters

Author Index